A Tour of Duty in the Pacific Northwest

My Cabin in the SPARROWHAWK from March 1865, to August 1868.

(original watercolor size: 14 x 9.75 in./35.5 x 24.5 cm)

A Tour of Duty in the Pacific Northwest

E. A. Porcher
and
H.M.S. *Sparrowhawk*, 1865-1868

Edited and annotated by
Dwight L. Smith

University of Alaska Press
Fairbanks, Alaska

Library of Congress Cataloging-in-Publication Data

Porcher, E. A. (Edmund Augustus)
A tour of duty in the Pacific Northwest : E.A. Porcher and H.M.S. Sparrowhawk, 1865–1868 / edited and annotated by Dwight L. Smith.
p. cm.
Includes bibliographical references (p.) and index.
ISBN 1-889963-06-2 (cloth : alk. paper)
1. Pacific Coast (B.C.)--Description and travel. 2. British Columbia--Description and travel. 3. Vancouver Island (B.C.)--Description and travel. 4. Porcher, E. A. (Edmund Augustus)--Diaries. 5. Sparrowhawk (Ship) 6. Ship captains--Great Britain--Diaries. 7. Great Britain. Royal Navy--Officers--Diaries. I. Smith, Dwight La Vern, 1918- II. Title.

F1089.P2 P67 2000
910'.0916'33--dc21

00-037709

International Standard Book Number: 1-889963-06-2
Library of Congress Catalog Number: 00-037709

Printed in Hong Kong by C & C Offset

This publication was printed on acid-free paper that meets the minimum requirements for the American National Standard for Information Science—Permanence of Paper for Printed Library Materials ANSA Z39.48-1984

Publication coordination, design, and production by Deborah González, University of Alaska Press.

Cover design by Dixon J. Jones, Academic Media Services, University of Alaska Fairbanks.

Front cover illustration: Fort Simpson, on the North extreme of British Columbia, June 13, 1867.
Back cover illustration: H.M.S. Sparrowhawk in the Fraser. July 7, 1866.

The original watercolor illustrations by Edmund Augustus Porcher are located in the Yale Collection of Western Americana, Beinecke Rare Book and Manuscript Library, Yale University Library, New Haven, Connecticut.

To Jane, Greg, Becki, and Anna Marie

Contents

Illustrations...xi

Preface...xv

Introduction...1

Chapter One The Atlantic Transit
9 March–3 July 1865

[Introduction]...13, Preparations for departure...14, Plymouth to Rio de Janeiro...15, Rio sojourn...15, Falkland Islands in winter...18, Strait of Magellan...20

Chapter Two The Pacific Transit
4 July–28 October 1865

[Introduction]...25, Smyth Channel passage...26, Anchorages in the Strait of Magellan and Smyth Channel...28, Valparaiso/Santiago visit...28, Valparaiso to Callao...31, Callao to Honolulu...34, Honolulu stopover...35, North Pacific navigation...36, Abstract of Passages...38, Distances run, England to Vancouver Island...38

Chapter Three Routine and a Northern Tour
6 November 1865–30 May 1866

[Introduction]...39, Policing Euclataw Indians...40, Cowichan Bay visit...41, Checking Euclataw compliance...42, Anchors and cables...43, San Francisco and return...43, Witness and prisoners...44, Paying the marines...46, Pursuing deserters...46, Escorting the governor...48, Northern assignment...49, Northward passage...50, Indians, repairs, Indians...52, Queen Charlotte Islands visit...55, Return to Esquimalt...56, Distances run, northern cruise...57

Chapter Four FENIANS, SAN FRANCISCO, AND WINTER ACTIVITIES
9 June 1866–6 January 1867

[Introduction]...59, Precautions against Fenians...60, San Francisco assignment...62, Coal consumption... 64, San Francisco mail call...65, Lime and coal...66, Puget Sound excursion...66, Duties and pleasures...68

Chapter Five ON DUTY AND OFF DUTY POTPOURRI
9 January–6 June 1867

[Introduction]...71, Rescue mission...72, *Mauna Kea* saga...76, Merchant ship beached...77, Drowned seamen...78 , Unsuccessful duck hunting...78, Altercation and drowning...80, Cowichan bay visit...81, San Francisco mail call...82, Lighthouse inspections...84, Churches and fishes...84, Boston Bar visit...85, Return to Esquimalt...87, Repairing the *Beaver*...88

Chapter Six A NORTHERN CRUISE AND AN INLAND JOURNEY
7 June–17 August 1867

[Introduction]...89, To northern settlements...90, Metlakatla settlement...92, Fort Simpson settlement...96, Russian America...98, Return to Esquimalt...101, Distances run, northern cruise...102, Pursuit of thieves...102, Cowichan cemetery consecration...103, San Juan inspection...103, Dispensing justice...104, Into the interior...104, Cariboo mining frontier...108, Downriver journey...109, Distances traveled...110, Return journey from Cariboo...112

Chapter Seven ACTIVITIES OF CIRCUMSTANCES AND OFFICIAL RESPONSIBILITIES
14 September 1867–18 May 1868

[Introduction]...113, Sooke harbor launching...114, New Westminster visit...114, Fraser River entrance...115, New Westminster interlude...116, Repairing the ship...117, Esquimalt winter...117, Secret dispatch delivery...118, Fenian alert...119, Court martial...119, Ceremonial appearance...119, Return of spring...120, Puget Sound tour...120, Distances to Puget Sound, San Juan, and return...123, Deadman's Island visit...123, San Juan errand...123, Gold Stream picnic...123, Routine activities...124, Move to Victoria...124

Chapter Eight THREE FINAL CRUISES
28 May–1 August 1868

[Introduction]...127, Northern inspection cruise...128, Metlakatla-Fort Simpson country...134, Return to Esquimalt...138, Distances run, northern cruise...140, *Sparrowhawk* recommissioning...140, Indian troubles and rescue mission...141, Distances to Shadwell Passage and return...143, Last northern cruise...143, Fort Simpson area duties...144, Return to Equimalt...146, Distances run, the last northern cruise...148

Chapter Nine RETURN TO ENGLAND
1 August–14 October 1868

[Introduction]...149, Preparations and farewells...150, Esquimalt to Panama...151, Crossing the Isthmus...153, Panama to Southampton...154, Distances, Vancouver Island to England...155, Expenses, Vancouver Island to England...155

BIBLIOGRAPHY...157

INDEX...165

Illustrations

Frontispiece

My Cabin in the Sparrowhawk from March 1865, to August 1868.

Page xvii

Map of the Pacific coast waters plied by Porcher and the H.M.S. *Sparrowhawk.*

Facing Page 14

Madeira. The Town of Funchal, and the Loo rock, looking to the Westward. April 11th 1865.

The Corcovado, Sugar Loaf, and the entrance of Rio de Janeiro, from the Praia Grande. May 17, 1865.

Rio de Janeiro. The Botanical Gardens, with the Corcovado, and Sugar Loaf. May 16, 1865.

Bennett's Hotel at Tejuca, 10 miles from Rio de Janeiro. May 19, 1865.

Falkland Islands. The Settlement of Stanley, from the Government House. June 19th 1865.

Patagonia. The Chilian settlement at Sandy Point, in the Straits of Magellan. June 29, 1865.

Port Famine, in the Straits of Magellan, looking towards Mount Tarn. June 30, 1865.

Port Famine, looking towards Mount St. Felipe, & the head of the Bay. July 1, 1865.

Facing Page 30

The hill of Santa Lucia, from the Cañada at Santiago. July 31, 1865.

Chili. The "Quebrada de Molinas," a ravine to the Eastward of Valparaiso. August 3, 1865.

Peru. The city of Lima, overlooking the river Rimac (he who speaks). August 16, 1865.

Peruvian Fruit. Chirimoya, Granandilla, Bananas, Orange, & an Apple. August 21, 1865.

Sandwich Islands. The Royal Palace of Kamehameha V, at Honolulu. September 28th 1865.

My Residence at Honolulu. September 29th 1865.

Sandwich Islands. The Eastern part of Honolulu, with the Hawaiian Church, and Diamond Hill in the distance. September 26th 1865.

Facing Page 48

An Indian Grave on Shell Island, looking towards Fort Rupert. May 8, 1866.

Indian Graves on Shell Island, at Fort Rupert. July 19, 1868.

The Coal mining settlement at Skidegate, Queen Charlotte's Island. May 24, 1866.

McKenzie's Farm, near Esquimalt. June 4, 1866.

Facing Page 64

The Government House at New Westminster, B.C. June 19, 1866.

Esquimalt. V.I. from the Hospital grounds. June 6, 1866.

H.M.S. Sparrowhawk in the Fraser. July 7, 1866.

The Navy yard, and sectional Dock at Mare Island, California. August 13, 1866.

The Coaling station of Nanaimo. Sept. 3, 1866.

Bridge over the Dead-man's river, near Esquimalt. Sept. 10, 1866.

Hudson Bay Company's Post at Nisqually, in Puget Sound. Oct. 5, 1866.

The Church at Esquimalt. June 28, 1867.

FACING PAGE 84

YALE, the head of navigation of the FRASER, & 125 miles from its mouth. May 16, 1867.

INDIAN Graves at CHAPMAN's Bar, 12 miles above YALE. May 18, 1867.

FACING PAGE 104

The Hudson Bay Company's stern wheeler ALEXANDRA in VICTORIA harbour. July 5, 1867.

FORT SIMPSON, on the North extreme of BRITISH COLUMBIA, June 13, 1867.

Indian CRESTS at FORT SIMPSON. June 13, 1867.

The QUAMICHAN Rancherie, on the COWITCHEN river. July 6, 1867.

The 150 mile house (from Lillooet & the same distance from CARIBOO). August 12, 1867.

CLINTON, the junction of the Lytton & Lillooet routes to CARIBOO, & 135 miles above YALE. August 13, 1867.

FACING PAGE 120

ESQUIMALT harbour, with the Fisguard and Race light-houses. Sept. 27, 1867.

Old H.B. Co's Fort at NANAIMO, now used as a Prison. May 4, 1866.

The SPARROWHAWK's boat establishment at ESQUIMALT. June 29, 1867.

Dog tombs at Gold stream, 12 miles from VICTORIA. May 9, 1868.

The English Camp on the island of SAN JUAN. May 12, 1868.

VANCOUVER ISLAND. VICTORIA, from Rock Bay. July 2, 1867.

FACING PAGE 140

The SAW MILLS at NANAIMO. May 29, 1866.

The 4th LAKE or Pike's, 7 miles from VICTORIA. June 19, 1868.

The NAHRITTI village on Hope Island, ½ mile from the rocks where the U.S. Steamer SUWANEE was lost on July 9, 1868.

Waterfall near CARTER's Bay, about 120 feet in height. July 21, 1868.

The Missionary station of KINCOLITH, at the mouth of the NASS river. July 26, 1868.

The deserted village of the Cheslakees, at the mouth of the Nimpkish river. July 30, 1868.

The Karmutsen Lake, 12 miles long, with the Nimpkish river flowing out of it. July 30, 1868.

Facing Page 150

The Cathedral at Victoria, destroyed by fire in 1869. August 29, 1868.

Central America. The Railway Station at Panama. Sept. 21, 1868.

The Statue of Tomas Herrera, in the Plaza at Panama. Sept. 22, 1868.

West Indies. The Harbour of St. Thomas, the scene of the severe hurricane, and tidal wave in October 1867. Sketched September 28th 1868.

PREFACE

THE BOUNDS AND GENERAL OUTLINES of Western Canadian history and history of the Pacific Rim have been well defined. In recent years the focus on particular topics has fleshed out these outlines. One intriguing consequence of the unfolding story is how its different aspects may be intimately related. Several years ago, I described a topic I was interested in to Archibald Hanna, curator of the Western Americana Collection, The Beinecke Rare Book and Manuscript Library, Yale University Library. It concerned the coincidence and relationship of the gold rushes in the interior of British Columbia, the statehood movement in Minnesota, and Minnesota sentiment for the annexation of western Canada. Minnesotans who caught the British Columbia gold fever, however viewed on either side of the Forty-ninth Parallel, illustrated these connections.

This gave Hanna an opening which he immediately exploited. Ever tempting scholars with the treasures of the Beinecke Library, he suggested another facet of the general subject. The American response to the news of gold in British Columbia was another cause of apprehension about how far the American idea of manifest destiny would change the political map of North America. Was the settlement of the Oregon question merely a temporary arrangement? For this and factors involving other countries, Britain had established its naval headquarters at Esquimalt on Vancouver Island.

The Beinecke Library had acquired the journal of Edmund Augustus Porcher, the captain of a Royal Navy vessel while he served an Esquimalt-based tour of duty. Porcher was a watercolor artist who made sketches of his tour of duty, from his departure from England in 1865 to his return home in 1868. Here was firsthand documentation and illustrations by one participant in the ongoing British presence that helped secure Canada's Pacific coast. This material also provides insight into what other functions or influence a war vessel and a navy commander might have beside a military or defensive role, the ostensible primary mission.

At my first opportunity, I surveyed the Porcher acquisition, and determined that it was both substantial and important. George Miles, Hanna's successor as Beinecke curator, shared my enthusiasm and promised to support my idea of publishing the document and watercolor collection.

I owe much to several persons and institutions that have extended me courtesies and help in my research. For many and varied reasons, too numerous to catalog here, I wish to acknowledge my indebtedness to the following people in England: the staff of the Public Record Office, Chancery Lane, London; librarians in the Official Publications Library, Map Library, and Main Reading Room of the British Library, London; the University of London Library; the staff of the Department of Printed Books and Manuscripts, National Maritime Museum, Greenwich; J. David Brown, Head, Naval Historical Branch, Ministry of Defence, London.

I have been given ready access to crucial research materials in Canada by: Captain A. K. Cameron, Curator Emeritus, and Bryan Klasse, Registrar in the Maritime Museum of British Columbia, Victoria; Brent McBride and Linda Webster in the Provincial Archives of British Columbia, Victoria; Doreen Stephens, Archivist, Anglican Provincial Synod of British Columbia, Vancouver; the staff of the map division in the Ministry of Environment, Province of British Columbia, Victoria; Mary Wyard, Microfilm Section, Canadian Library Association, Ottawa; Roger Sarty, Directorate of History, National Defence Headquarters, Ottawa.

Three persons have been helpful, particularly in answering my where-to-turn research queries: Bernard F. Cavalcante, Acting Head, Operational Archives Branch, Naval Historical Center, Department of the Navy, Washington, D.C.; Adam M. Mecinski, Reference Librarian, The Nimitz Library, United States Naval Academy, Annapolis, Maryland; R. Thomas Crew, Jr., Archivist, The Mariners' Museum, Newport News, Virginia.

Funds from the Faculty Research Committee, Miami University, made it possible for me to travel to several repositories critical to this project. Appointment as a Fellow of the Huntington Library, San Marino, California, enabled me to work in its substantial collections. Reference and staff members Virginia J. Renner, Martin Ridge, Leona Schonfeld, Mary Alice Shumate, Elsa Lee Sink, and Mary Wright generously contributed to that effort.

Special mention goes to Sarah Barr, Karen Clift, and Scott Van Dam, the Interlibrary Loan staff, Miami University Libraries, whose diligence and persistence secured important items for my scrutiny and study.

I am particularly grateful to Elizabeth Smith, Department of History, Miami University, whose typing and computer skills transformed my manuscript into a form and format presentable to the publisher. Charlotte Newman Goldy, Jeri Schaner, and Allan Winkler of the Department of History extended many courtesies that eased the research and progress of the manuscript.

The constant and unfailing support of my wife, Jane D. Smith, has sustained me in the years it has taken to bring this project to completion. Her meticulous alertness in the drudgery of proofreading has caught many of the errors that seem to bedevil all galley and page proofs.

Finally, on a more personal note, sailing the coastal waters of southern South America through the Strait of Magellan and plying the waters of the Pacific Northwest from Seattle to Seward has given me, albeit to a somewhat modified degree, a vicarious feeling for and appreciation of Porcher's skill in fulfilling his mission with H.M.S. *Sparrowhawk.*

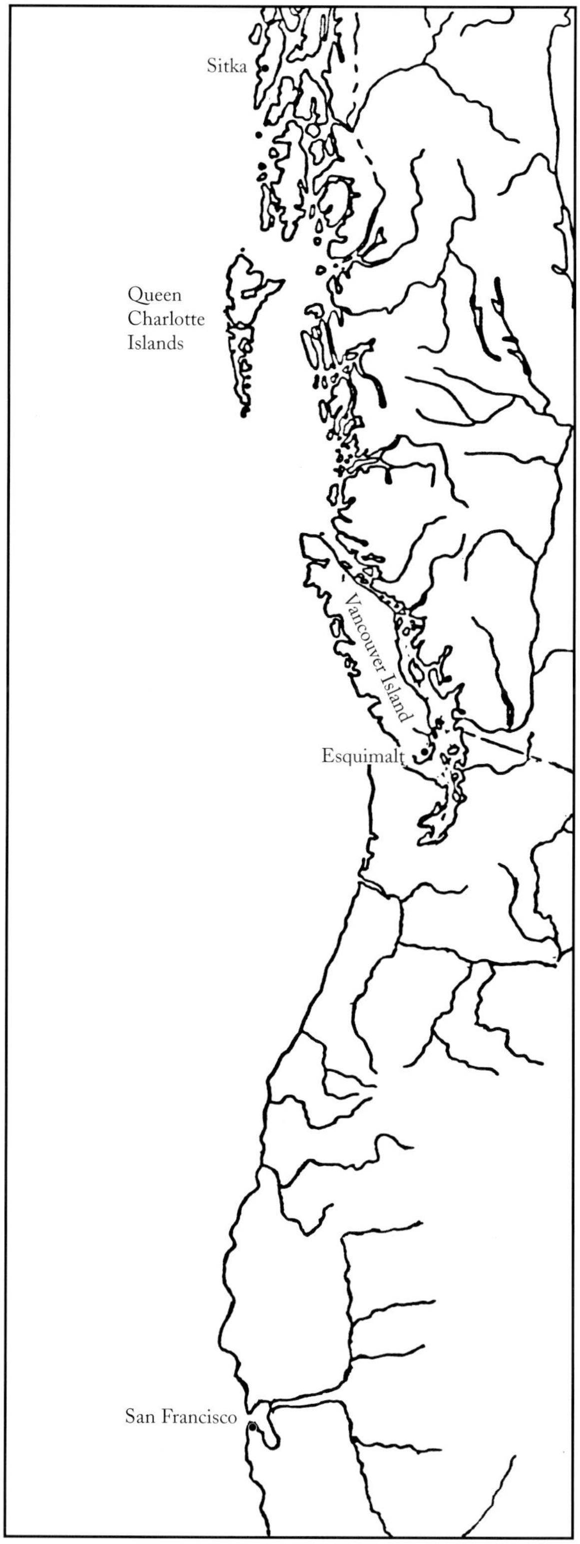

Based at Esquimalt, Vancouver Island, 1865–1868, H.M.S. *Sparrowhawk*, commanded by Edmund Augustus Porcher, plied the Pacific Coast waters on numerous assignments from New Archangel (Sitka), capital of Russian Alaska, to San Francisco.

Introduction

H.M.S. *Sparrowhawk*, commanded by Edmund Augustus Porcher, was assigned duty based at Esquimalt, Vancouver Island, 1865–1868.

From the sixteenth century onward, British strategy sought to counter and thwart Spanish geopolitical planning and activities in the Western Hemisphere and Pacific waters. The Royal Navy became a key factor in establishing and maintaining the British presence in the Pacific Northwest, particularly in what was to become British Columbia.

As the burgeoning British Empire challenged Spain's assertion of preeminence in the New World and the Pacific Ocean, the discovery and control of a mythical water passageway across North America from the Atlantic Ocean to the Pacific was paramount. Fur trader Samuel Hearne's extended exploration for the Hudson's Bay Company in search of copper ore in the Canadian Arctic confirmed that there was no such passage by way of Hudson Bay. This and a Russian map published in London shifted the search northward for a navigable east-west passage.

In the summer of 1778, while expeditions were probing for the Atlantic entrance, James Cook of the Royal Navy was trying to find the Pacific entrance. His instructions were to explore north of 65° north latitude. En route he spent a month at Nootka Sound, Vancouver Island, refueling and repairing, and then continued northward along the Alaska coast and briefly through Bering Strait into the Arctic Ocean.

Although Cook had been preceded there by Spanish and Russian explorers, it was the publication of accounts of his voyage that notified the world of the dramatic scenery and natives of the Pacific Northwest. Readers were told that the Nootka Indians had sea otter pelts that could be bartered for beads and inexpensive trade items, information that would have dire consequences. The pelts would fetch a handsome return in China. Soon, merchant ships from several nations were exploiting the rich potential of trans-Pacific trade.

Anglo-Spanish rivalry in the North Pacific came to a head in the early 1790s. In July 1789, the commandant of the small Spanish settlement at Nootka, had seized three fur trading ships that belonged to John Meares, a retired officer of the Royal Navy, and sent them to a Spanish base on the coast of Mexico. This occurred as the

London government was preparing a naval expedition to establish a whaling and trading depot on the Pacific Northwest coast. London and Madrid both prepared for war. Unable to persuade France to help, and faced with near three-to-one naval disadvantage against the Royal Navy, Spain agreed to the Nootka Convention and withdrew. The Spanish presence and influence in the North Pacific receded rapidly.

George Vancouver of the Royal Navy, who had been with Cook at Nootka and during his search for the Northwest Passage, was instructed to make a definitive determination about the fabled waterway. He was sent to receive the transfer of Nootka and to survey the mainland coastline. From 1791 to 1794 he established the insularity of Vancouver Island and "set aside every opinion of a *north-west passage*, or any water communication navigable for shipping" from Mexico to Cook Inlet, Alaska.

In the 1790s, as Britain became involved in wars with France, Americans increasingly dominated the Pacific Northwest sea otter trade. At the same time, they were extending their mainland trade westward. In 1811 John Jacob Astor's Pacific Fur Company established Astoria at the mouth of the Columbia River as its outlet for trans-Pacific trade. Meanwhile, the Montreal-based North West Company was pushing across the continent with a similar goal, and to counter the American thrust. The American post sold out to a company of Nor'westers before a company trading vessel with a Royal Navy escort could reach Astoria. With the arrival of a British frigate, the territory was proclaimed British. The Royal Navy blockade of the American Atlantic seaboard in the War of 1812 decided Astoria's fate.

When the North West Company and Hudson's Bay Company merged in 1821, the latter became the dominant force in the mainland Pacific Northwest. In 1824, given a twenty-one year monopoly in the Oregon country, as the region was generally known, the Hudson's Bay Company established Fort Vancouver some distance up the Columbia River. Russian agreements with the United States in 1824 and with Great Britain in 1825 limited her thrust in Alaska southward to 54°40', giving further sanction to the boundaries and status of the Oregon country.

Although the British had relinquished Astoria at the end of the War of 1812, the Oregon country was still open to exploitation by British and Americans alike. The Hudson's Bay Company continued to dominate the fur trade until it was no longer profitable. While the Monroe Doctrine, 1823, can be regarded as an American policy statement concerning the Western Hemisphere and did influence Russian ambitions in the Pacific Northwest, British and Americans agreed to a "free and open" status for the area. What came to be called Manifest Destiny posed an immediate and more serious threat to the British presence in the Pacific Northwest. American missionaries and settlers were moving into the Oregon country with expectations that the flag would follow them. By the mid-1840s, some Americans were demanding the entire territory.

For their part, the British made a military reconnaissance of the Oregon country, enlarged the Pacific squadron, extended Royal Navy protection to the Hudson's Bay Company, and held a considerable fleet in readiness for sea duty. The crisis was averted in 1846 when both powers agreed to extend the forty-ninth parallel boundary on the mainland westward from the Rocky Mountains. And Vancouver Island was British. Where the dividing line ran among the islands and in the channel separating Vancouver Island from the North American mainland was not precisely defined. Later, this would lead to tensions that were finally resolved by international arbitration.

In the nineteenth century, the Royal Navy became the means of implementing commercial and political policies of the British Empire's developing interests in the Pacific Ocean. In the early years, admiralty ships were sent to the western coasts of South and North America to protect whalers and traders. The Royal Navy was also attentive to the safety of British mercantile activities and investments in Pacific Latin America during the revolutions of liberation. It carried merchant and other moneys from the Pacific ports, and it served as "amphibious diplomatic agents."

For administrative purposes, Royal Navy service areas were organized by geographic zones or commands called stations. Reflecting reality, the Pacific Station was established in 1837. It extended to 170° west longitude in the mid-Pacific. Although the Pacific Station encompassed the vast area from the Bering Sea to the Antarctic, its principal concern was the southeast Pacific Ocean, particularly South American waters.

The ports of revolution-prone Latin American countries, however, did not provide ample security for Pacific squadron headquarters. As alternative possibilities were investigated, Esquimalt, Vancouver Island, became increasingly attractive and more regularly used. Britain faced intensifying colonial and mercantile competition from Russian, French, and American interests. As the Anglo-American dispute over the Oregon country unfolded in the mid-1840s, and with the 1849 founding of the Crown Colony of Vancouver Island to forestall further American advance northward into the Pacific Northwest, the Royal Navy extended its operations into the North Pacific.

A northern base for the navy would be useful and Esquimalt generally was thought the best location, although it was far from British south trans-Pacific trade routes; overland contact with Canada was at best sporadic and uncertain; and defense against American Manifest Destiny was problematical. Vancouver Island's isolation in the age of far-ranging sailing vessels hardly lessened with the introduction of steam-powered ships with cruising ranges only limited by coal capacity. Esquimalt was, however, a good natural and sheltered harbor, and was favored with a moderate climate; it remained the only British-owned base for naval operations in the North Pacific.

Nothing beyond the lobbying of the colonial governor and discussion by admiralty officials happened, however, until early in the Crimean War. An Anglo-French squadron sustained heavy casualties in an assault on a Russian base on Siberia's Kamchatka Peninsula. The wounded suffered unduly because there was no haven in the North Pacific where they could be given necessary attention ashore. Another attack on the Russian base was planned for the next year, 1855. The commander of the Pacific Station requested that the governor of the Crown Colony provide hospital accommodations for anticipated casualties. Three wooden hospital buildings were constructed and equipped. This was the beginning of the use of Esquimalt harbor as a naval base. A decade later, by an Order in Council of June 1865, it was designated as the Royal Naval Establishment of Esquimalt. It had thus become the headquarters for the North Pacific Squadron.

Depending on problems and needs in the 1850s and 1860s, the squadron had fourteen to sixteen ships—gunboats, a coastal survey vessel, a flagship, and steam-assisted frigates, corvettes, and sloops. The services they performed were varied, dictated more by situational needs than by precise instructions from the London government. Naval superiority over the American fleet helped secure British interests in the San Juan Island controversy. British commanders became "amphibious magistrates" in Indian-Indian and Indian-white relations. Gunboats symbolized British technological superiority and political authority over the area. In these and other situations, such as the mainland and island gold rushes, the Esquimalt-based Royal Navy vessels and commanders became the operational and symbolic muscle for implementing and enforcing colonial policies.

British warships supported the colonial administration and were the guardians of imperial interests; in short, they were "the tools of statecraft." "Gunboat diplomacy," a frequent characterization of their function, covers a variety and multitude of their activities, but not all. By the very presence of Royal Navy vessels and their personnel—by their involvement and their acceptance—they were an integral part of the young colony. This becomes quite clear, for example, by reading the attention accorded the Royal Navy in the press. It is well illustrated by the account of Edmund Porcher of his command of H.M.S. *Sparrowhawk* while he was stationed at Esquimalt.[1]

Edmund Augustus Porcher made little reference to his own past and his biographical data is fragmentary at best. He was born the second son of the Rev. George Porcher of Maiden Erlegh, Berks. A paternal uncle and his paternal grandfather had served in Parliament. His paternal grandmother was the daughter of an admiral who also held a baronage. His mother, Amelia Chamier, was the sister of a Royal Navy officer.[2]

According to one source, Porcher entered the navy in 1837. One tour of duty on the sloop *Fly*, 1842–1846, took him to the East Indies.[3] He passed the Royal Navy officer's examination in June 1844 and received his commission as lieutenant 9 November 1846.[4] On 18 November he entered his first assignment with duty on the steam frigate *Sidon* out of Portsmouth, along the coast of Portugal but principally in the Mediterranean Sea.[5] In April 1849 he joined *Cleopatra* out of Chatham for four and a half years in the East Indies. It was probably on this tour that he made extensive examination of the Coral Sea reefs off Australia and other islands. His keen scientific observations served him well on the lecture platform years later.[6] For several months in 1854 he was assigned to the screw steam ship *Majestic* out of

Sheerness on duty in the Baltic Sea, followed by sixteen months on the *Esk* out of Portsmouth, also on Baltic duty. The record is not very precise, but Porcher was serving on the steam gunboat *Cockchafer* in the early months of 1856, no station listed.[7]

He was assigned in February 1857 to the admiral's flagship, the screw steam ship *Hibernia*, stationed at Malta. Three months later, with no explanation, he was listed with those officers who were "entitled to wear medals."[8] During this tour, which extended into 1861, Porcher went on two special assignments that utilized skills not within the ordinarily expected capabilities of an officer in the Royal Navy. He was sent on a government-sponsored archeological expedition to Carthage. Whatever his specific duties, he was responsible for at least some, probably most, of the numerous professionally executed illustrations that appeared as engravings in the published account of the expedition. None are signed, but his services are acknowledged in the volume's preface.[9]

In mid-November 1860, Porcher joined Robert Murdoch Smith, a captain in the Royal Engineers, in an eleven-month expedition to explore the remains of Cyrene, the capital of the ancient Greek colony of Cyrenaica, on the Mediterranean coast of modern Libya. Under government auspices the project reaped sculptures for the British Museum. Smith and Porcher recounted the details of the mission in a published volume. The text is lavishly illustrated with dozens of meticulously detailed sketches and plans, in black, white, and color, of tombs, temples, maps, and other illustrations. Fifty-four were signed by Porcher. Others, although unsigned, appear to be his work. These evidence his skills with pen and brush and his knowledge of classical history and its archeology.[10]

Back from detached service, Porcher was now listed for "additional" duty on the *Hibernia*. Three times while assigned to this vessel, he had been given momentary additional duty on the *Bustler* and the *Redpole*, both Gibraltar-based paddle wheel steam tug vessels that were tenders to the *Hibernia*.[11] He was no longer on the roster of the *Hibernia* after 20 September 1861. Of officers entitled to wear medals, Porcher was now classified with those in the Transport Service Agents Afloat, as opposed to Residents Agents. On 27 December 1861 he was appointed to the rank of Commander.[12] He continued to be listed for the next three years, but with no assignment indicated. It seems unlikely, however, that he was on inactive status for the whole time until he received his own command on 4 March 1865.[13]

Porcher became captain of H.M.S. *Sparrowhawk* in Portsmouth for duty in the Pacific, based at Esquimalt, Vancouver Island. He retained this command until August 1868, after which he returned to England.

Some measure of the man becomes quite evident during the Esquimalt years, not only as a commanding naval officer, but also as a citizen of the community. In his own account he mentions several occasions, official and social, in which he participated. His lecture before the Mechanics' Institute, for example, was favorably received and reconfirmed to the public his wide experience and scientific knowledge. When he was invited by the governor to join an investigation into a contentious property dispute affair in the interior, the press complimented the governor on the choice.

Porcher was praised as a "gentleman...of the experience of...commanding large bodies of men,...who will be impartial in any judgment or conclusion he may come to."[14] His name is memorialized in Porcher Island, which lies in Chatham Sound, off the mouth of the Skeena River.[15]

He was promoted to the rank of Captain, 16 October 1868, but was given no further assignment.[16] He retired from the service 28 May 1872. His death was reported in the official roster June 1878. According to another source, he died in Germany.[17]

THE KEEL FOR H.M.S. *Sparrowhawk* was laid down 6 August 1855, by Magnay, Young & Co. at Limehouse. The vessel was launched 9 February 1856, and was completed March 1856, at a cost of £18,271 for the hull and £12,253 for the engines.

She was constructed as a sloop of the Wanderer Class, "vessels of modest size and light draft for operations in coastal waters" in the Crimean War. She was first employed, however, in 1857, after some initial structural problems were corrected, in the East Indies and China Station of the Royal Navy. Used primarily in the southern and western parts of that station, she apparently served only in a minor capacity in the later part of the Second Opium War.

Returned to her home port of Portsmouth in the spring of 1861 on reserve status, the *Sparrowhawk* was converted from a sloop or single-masted vessel to a barque of three masts. In March 1865 she was commissioned at Portsmouth by Edmund Augustus Porcher for the Pacific Station. She was recommissioned at the Esquimalt base by Henry W. Mist on 17 August 1868 and continued there in service. Early in 1872 her assignment was changed to "Ordered Home" and in midsummer "To be paid off and sold at Esquimalt."[18]

A Portland, Oregon, firm bought the vessel for $20,000 and sold the engines for $5,000 to a Moodyville (now North Vancouver) lumber mill, where they were used until 1909. The ship itself, now a sailing vessel, took two or three cargoes of lumber to China before she was lost in a typhoon.[19]

The *Sparrowhawk* has been variously described as a Gun Vessel, Screw Gun Vessel, Screw Despatch Vessel, or a Screw Despatch Gun Vessel, and was one hundred and ninety-nine feet, four inches long from figurehead to the taffrail. She carried a complement of ninety officers, engineers, seamen, carpenters, servants, boys, stokers, and marines. The three-masted ship was equipped for steam- or sail-powered navigation and carried five guns.[20]

EDMUND PORCHER DEPARTED ENGLAND ON 1 April 1865. He commanded the gun vessel H.M.S. *Sparrowhawk* on assignment to the Royal Navy's Pacific Station headquarters at Esquimalt, Vancouver Island, off the coast of British North America. His tour of duty would keep him out of England for three years and a half, while the *Sparrowhawk* would remain on further Esquimalt-based service.

Under sail or steam and sometimes both, the *Sparrowhawk's* course from Plymouth followed the well-established trans-Atlantic route to Rio de Janeiro, with stops at Madeira, the Canaries, and the Cape Verde Islands. Ever the inquisitive and observant tourist, Porcher took full advantage of days in port, visiting churches, museums, hospitals, natural features, and whatever other attractions the city and its environs held. Whenever possible, he talked to managers, curators, and engineers, to elicit information about their charges. He made courtesy calls on British Consuls and other officials, and he fraternized with captains of English and other ships. As leisure and inclination coincided, he recorded some of the scenic highlights in watercolors.

Porcher's comments on Rio, where he had visited previously in 1849, are a sixteen-year progress report. After refueling, replenishing supplies, and other chores, the *Sparrowhawk* set course for the Falkland Islands. As late May was "the commencement of the winter season," the *Sparrowhawk* took "the average time" of over three weeks to reach Port Stanley. Aside from the necessity of coaling here, this port of call had little to commend itself, offering the greatest possible contrast to Rio. The passage through the Strait of Magellan challenged the navigation skills of Porcher and his crew; but they met the test successfully and sailed northward along the west coast of South America.

More like Rio in their attractions were Valparaiso, the southern headquarters of the Royal Navy's Pacific Station, and Santiago, the capital city of Chile, a six-hour train ride inland. In his commentary, Porcher conveys word and watercolor pictures of these cities in the 1860s, as well as the anchorage at Callao and at Lima, the capital city of Peru. The *Sparrowhawk* joined naval vessels of a half dozen countries, including a Spanish squadron, already at anchor in the harbor of Callao. At both Callao and Lima, Porcher marveled at the ubiquitous vultures and the reasonably efficient garbage disposal system they provided.

After five weeks away from Callao, with no sight of land or any other ship, the *Sparrowhawk* made landfall at the Sandwich Islands. While his ship was coaling and taking on supplies, Porcher enjoyed Honolulu and its environs. They reached Esquimalt, their new home port, at the end of October, seven months out of Plymouth, England.

For the next two years and nine months, Porcher was occupied with responsibilities, assignments, opportunities, and pleasures. Routine and ceremonial duties and activities included calling on, and entertaining, civilians and military officials; courts martial, gunnery practice, lighthouse inspections, ships maintenance and repairs; escorting officials and attending recreational and social affairs.

On several occasions, the *Sparrowhawk* was sent to San Francisco to carry mail and dispatches. She went to the rescue of the crews of a wrecked American naval vessel and of a Hawaiian barque. She was put on alert to help frustrate a Fenian threat to the young colony. She escorted the bishop, the governor, and the admiral on various official missions to the islands and coastal locations. Porcher served in policing and dispensing justice to the Indians. And he escorted the governor on a mission to Russian America shortly before its transfer to the United States. He also went on official excursions into the interior of the mainland.

After H.M.S. *Sparrowhawk* was recommissioned, Porcher prepared to leave British Columbia. He was a well received and respected citizen of the community.

The numerous persons to whom he paid farewell respects reads like a combined official and social register of the young colony. He returned to England, crossing the Isthmus of Panama by rail, arriving in Southampton in mid-October 1868.

Porcher recorded his 1865–1868 tour of duty on H.M.S. *Sparrowhawk* and his return to England in his journal contained in a notebook headed:

Cruize of H.M.S. Sparrowhawk
from 9th March 1865, to 14th October 1868
by E. A. Porcher, Commander

He also executed dozens of oblong folio watercolor drawings which illustrate the entire *Cruize*. Over half of them depict the Esquimalt-based years.[21] The journal and drawings are in the Beinecke Rare Book and Manuscript Library, Yale University, New Haven, Connecticut.[22]

Porcher's journal is a running account of his duties and activities, usually in his capacity as commander of H.M.S. *Sparrowhawk*, but in other contexts as well.[23] These emphases have determined the thrust of the editing of this document. Available and appropriate information and data are used to confirm, support, or elaborate on Porcher's account. Because the journal frequently mentions persons who do not figure importantly herein beyond their mention, they are not further identified. Editorials and articles in the *Daily British Colonist* (later named *Daily British Colonist and Victoria Chronicle*) concerning Porcher or his ship are always noted or used. This affords a measure of the role of the Royal Navy and the visibility of Porcher and H.M.S. *Sparrowhawk* in the life of the colony.

Porcher's account is an uninterrupted continuum. It is a succession of paragraphs only sometimes distinguished from others as entries for particular days, but not for every day. His running heads in the journal serve as approximate signposts for the frequent changes of subject matter; they do not necessarily apply to all of the contents of a manuscript page. To include them would be further confusing, except in a facsimile reproduction.

To organize the journal and make it more manageable for the reader, the entire manuscript is arbitrarily subdivided into nine chapters, each with a bracketed editorial introduction. Within the chapters themselves, italicized editoral marginal headings flag each cluster of paragraphs as Porcher's account moves from one subject to another.

Porcher was a well educated, articulate man. The unevenness of the flow of ink from his pen poses some difficulty in making a literal transcription of his otherwise reasonably readable penmanship.[24] Beyond the editorial devices explained above, however, a minimum of others have been introduced. Two, in particular, need to be singled out: the names of all ships are italicized; and ditto marks are either expanded or ignored, depending on the need to clarify or the desirability of uncluttering. Other generally accepted editorial practices require no explanation.

Notes to the Introduction

1. Despite the date of its publication, J.K. Laughton, "The Study of Naval History," *Journal of the Royal United Services Institution* 40, part 2 (1896): 795–820, still gives a good general introduction to the study of British naval history.

Barry M. Gough is the principal contemporary historian of the Royal Navy in the Canadian Pacific Northwest Coast. His three monographs: *Distant Dominion: Britain and the Northwest Coast of North America, 1579–1809* (Vancouver: University of British Columbia Press, 1980); *The Royal Navy and the Northwest Coast of North America, 1810–1914: A Study of British Maritime Ascendancy* (Vancouver: University of British Columbia Press, 1971); and *Gunboat Frontier: British Maritime Authority and Northwest Coast Indians, 1846–1890* (Vancouver: University of British Columbia Press, 1984) are the essential starting point for research on the area.

Gough provides additional information in: "Sea Power and Canada: The Long View of History," *Canadian Defence Quarterly* 20 (Winter 1990): 41–49; "Sea Power and the History of Western Canada," *Journal of Canadian Studies* 8 (May 1973): 50–59; "'Turbulent Frontiers' and British Expansion: Governor James Douglas, the Royal Navy, and the British Columbia Gold Rushes," *Pacific Historical Review* 41 (February 1972): 15–32; "Send a Gunboat! Checking Slavery and Controlling Liquor Traffic among Coast Indians of British Columbia in the 1860s," *Pacific Northwest Quarterly* 69 (October 1978): 159–168; "Official Uses of Violence against Northwest Coastal Indians in Colonial British Columbia," in *Pacific Northwest Themes: Historical Essays in Honor of Keith A. Murray*, ed. James W. Scott (Bellingham: Center for Pacific Northwest Studies, Western Washington University, 1978): 43–69. Gough's "The Records of the Royal Navy's Pacific Station," *Journal of Pacific History* 4 (1969): 146–153, is a very useful introduction to the manuscript documentation.

Glynn Barratt, *Russian Shadows on the British Northwest Coast of North America, 1810–1890: A Study of Rejection of Defence Responsibilities* (Vancouver: University of British Columbia Press, 1983) is the best study of Russian involvement. Chapter 3 is the most directly relevant segment. There is nothing comparable from the American perspective. Although cast in a larger setting, Antony Preston and John Major, *Send a Gunboat! A Study of the Gunboat and Its Role in British Policy, 1854–1904* (London: Longmans, Green and Co., 1967) is informative.

See also *Dictionary of Canadian Biography*, vol. 4, s.v. "Cook, James," by Glyndwr Williams; *Dictionary of Canadian Biography*, vol. 4. s.v. "Vancouver, George," by W. Kaye Lamb; *Dictionary of Canadian Biography*, vol. 4, s.v. "Hearne, Samuel," by Clarence Stuart Mackinnon; Stuart R. Tompkins, "After Bering: Mapping the North Pacific," *British Columbia Historical Quarterly* 19 (January–April 1955): 26–27, 42–43, 47, 49–50; Freeman M. Tovell, "The Other Side of the Coin: The Viceroy, Bodega y Quadra, Vancouver and the Nootka Crisis," *BC Studies* 93 (Spring 1992): 3–29; James P. Ronda, *Astoria & Empire* (Lincoln: University of Nebraska Press, 1990); James R. Gibson, *Otter Skins, Boston Ships, and China Goods: The Maritime Fur Trade of the Northwest Coast, 1785–1841* (Seattle: University of Washington Press, 1992), especially chapters 3 and 4; James R. Gibson, "The Maritime Trade of the North Pacific Coast," in William C. Sturtevant, ed., *Handbook of North American Indians*, vol. 4: Wilcomb E. Washburn, ed., *History of Indian-White Relations* (Washington, D.C., Smithsonian Institution, 1988), 379–381; Norman A. Graebner, "Maritime Factors in the Oregon Compromise," *Pacific Historical Review* 20 (November 1951): 331–345; Wilber D. Jones and J. Chal Vinson, "British Preparedness and the Oregon Settlement," *Pacific Historical Review* 22 (November 1953): 353–364; W. K. Lamb, "Correspondence Relating to the Establishment of a Naval Base at Esquimalt, 1851–57," *British Columbia Historical Quarterly* 6 (October 1942): 277–296; D. M. Schurman, "Esquimalt: Defence Problem, 1865–1887," *British Columbia Historical Quarterly* 19 (January–April 1955): 57–69; Frederick V. Longstaff, *Esquimalt Naval Base: A History of Its Work and Its Defences* (Victoria, British Columbia: Victoria Book & Stationery Co., 1941), especially Chapter 2; "Pacific Squadron," Victoria *Daily British Colonist*, 31 October 1865; "The British Squadron in the Pacific," *Daily British Colonist*, 25 January 1866.

For a somewhat different emphasis, see Roger Flynn Sarty, "Silent Sentry: A Military and Political History of Canadian Coast Defence 1860–1945" (Ph.D. thesis, University of Toronto, 1982), especially the introduction and chapter 1. He gives some bibliographic suggestions in "'There will be trouble in the North Pacific:' The Defence of British Columbia in the Early Twentieth Century," *BC Studies* 61 (Spring 1984): 4n3.

A direct effect of the presence in British Columbia waters of Royal Navy ships such as the *Sparrowhawk* is illustrated by a comment in the daily Victoria press. "Owing to the infrequency in the visits of the men-of-war the Indians around the Fort [Simpson] have become quite insolent and exacting of late." "The Northern Whisky Traffic," *Daily British Colonist*, 27 November 1865.

For a brief perspective consideration of the naval role in the region's history, albeit in the post-Porcher years, see W. A. B. Douglas, "The Seaward Flank: Defending the Indefensible," *Journal of the West* 32 (October 1993): 19–32; William Glover, "The Politics of Nation Building and the Defense of British Columbia, 1871–1939," *Journal of the West* 32: 31–37.

2. William R. O'Byrne, *A Naval Biographical Dictionary: Comprising the Life and Services of Every Living Officer in Her Majesty's Navy, From the Rank of Admiral of the Fleet to That of Lieutenant, Inclusive. Compiled from Family and Authentic Documents* (London: John Murray, 1849), 915; P. H. Ditchfield and William Page, *The Victoria History of Berkshire*, 4 vols. (London: Archibald Constable and Company, 1906–1924), 3:211, 217; J. Russel Harper, *Early Painters and Engravers in Canada* (Toronto: University of Toronto Press, 1970), 255.

Josias Du Pre Porcher (1761?–1820), Porcher's paternal grandfather, was of South Carolina Huguenot ancestry, a mayor of Madras, India, and a successful merchant in the East India trade. He served in the House of Commons (1802–1818) for the constituencies of Bodmin (Cornwall County), Dundalk (County Louth, Ireland), Bletchingley (Surrey County), and Old Sarum (Wiltshire County). Gerrit P. Judd, IV, *Members of Parliament, 1734–1832* (New Haven: Yale University Press, 1955), 310; R. G. Thorne, *The History of Parliament: The House of Commons, 1790–1820*, 5 vols. (London: Published for the History of Parliament Trust by Secker & Warburg, 1986), 1:326; 2:42–45, 379–380, 424–426; 4:870–871.

Henry Porcher (1795–1857), Porcher's paternal uncle, served in the House of Commons (1822–1826) for the constituency of Clitheroe (Lancashire County). Judd, *Members of Parliament*, 309; "Deaths," *Gentleman's Magazine and Historical Review*, January 1858, p. 113.

3. Provenance materials with the Porcher manuscripts, Beinecke Rare Book and Manuscript Library, Yale University.

The title of the published narrative of the expedition of the *Fly* indicates the nature and the extent of Porcher's travels. Joseph Beete Jukes, *Narrative of the Surveying Voyage of H.M.S. Fly, Commanded by Captain F. P. Blackwood, R.N., in Torres Strait, New Guinea, and Other Islands of the Eastern Archipelago, During the Years 1842–1846: Together with an Excursion into the Interior of the Eastern Part of Java*, 2 vols. (London: T. & W. Boone, 1847). As a sailor, Porcher is not mentioned in the volume.

4. O'Byrne, *A Naval Biographical Dictionary*, 915.

5. Porcher made a passing reference to this service in his remarks for 28 July 1865. The *Sidon* had returned to its home port of Portsmouth and as of 20 March 1849, no officers were listed as assigned to it. *Navy List* (April 1849): 157; (July 1849): 133. *Navy List* (London: John Murray, 1815–) issued quarterly and sometimes monthly, under slightly variant names, is particularly useful for tracing the tours of Royal Navy ships, and for rosters of their officers.

6. *Navy List* (July 1849–October 1853); "Mechanics' Institute," *Daily British Colonist*, 1 February 1867. In his remarks for 13 May 1865, Porcher mentioned that the *Cleopatra* had stopped at Rio de Janeiro en route to the East Indies assignment.

7. *Navy List* (April 1854–July 1856).

8. *Navy List* (April 1857): 154; (July 1857): 46.

9. Nathan Davis, *Carthage and Her Remains: Being an Account of the Excavations and Researches on the Site of the Phoenician Metropolis in Africa, and Other Adjacent Places. Conducted under the Auspices of Her Majesty's Government* (London: Richard Bentley, 1861), ix; Provenance materials, Porcher manuscripts.

10. Robert Murdoch Smith and Edmund A. Porcher, *History of Recent Discoveries at Cyrne, Made during an Expedition to the Cyrenaica in 1860–61, under the Auspices of Her Majesty's Government* (London: Day & Son, 1864); "The Grouse Creek Difficulty," *Daily British Colonist*, 31 July 1867; George Hills, "1865 and 1866. Notes and Incidents of Mission Work. Extracts from the Bishop's Journal," Columbia Mission, *Eighth Annual Report of the Columbia Mission [of the Church of England], for the year 1866* (London: Rivingstons, 1867), 21–22; Edwin Yamauchi, "The Archaeology of Biblical Africa: Cyrene in Libya," *Archaeology in the Biblical World* 2 (Fall 1992): 13.

11. *Navy List*, 1857–1861, especially (April 1857): 142; (October 1857): 166; (July 1861): 171.

12. *Navy List* (April 1862): 19, 197, 216.

13. *Navy List* (July 1862–April 1865).

14. "Mechanics' Institute," *Daily British Colonist*, 1 February 1867; "The Grouse Creek Difficulty," *Daily British Colonist*, 31 July 1867; "Death of Captain Porcher, R.N.," *Daily British Colonist*, 25 October 1878.

His Esquimalt-based years were the subject of a Sunday feature article. James K. Nesbitt, "Capt. Porcher of Sparrowhawk Studied Indians and Coral," Victoria *Daily Colonist*, 3 September 1967.

This article apparently served as the basis for a paraphrased, briefer version several years later in another newspaper. Tom Patterson, "Capt. Porcher, RN—among the happy elite," *The Victorian*, 16 September 1974.

15. Porcher Island is described as an island about twenty miles long and eighteen miles broad. It is at 54° north latitude and longitude 130°30' west. R. G. Large, 27 August 1965, Porcher Island, Clippings File Folder, Provincial Archives of British Columbia, Victoria.

See also William B. Hamilton, *The Macmillan Book of Canadian Place Names* (Toronto: Macmillan of Canada, 1978), 57; Lynn Middleton, *Place Names of the Pacific Northwest Coast* (Seattle: Superior Publishing Company, 1969), 46, 66, 89, 164, 196; Longstaff, *Esquimalt Naval Base*, 177.

16. His letter of appointment and commendations accompany his journal and watercolors in the Beinecke Rare Book and Manuscript Library.

17. *Navy List* (January 1869): 13; (July 1872): 267; (October 1878): 581. See also Provenance materials, Porcher manuscripts; John T. Walbran, *British Columbia Coast Names, 1592–1906, to Which Are Added a Few Names in Adjacent United States Territory, Their Origin and History, with Map and Illustrations* (Ottawa: Government Printing Bureau, 1909), 385.

It was reported in Victoria that he died in England. "Death of Captain Porcher, R.N.," *Daily British Colonist*, 25 October 1878. What the relationship to "Mrs. Porcher" who made annual contributions of £2 to the Columbia Mission was can only be a matter of conjecture. The name "Mrs. F. A. Porcher" is listed for 1868. Was this a typographical error for "Mrs. E. A. Porcher?" *Seventh [-Tenth] Annual Report of the Columbia Mission [of the Church of England], for the Year 1865[–1868]* (London: Rivingtons, 1866–1869).

18. The service of H.M.S. *Sparrowhawk* under the command of Henry W. Mist can be traced in the three Master's logbooks. 18 August 1868–3 May 1870, Adm. 53/10023; 4 May 1870–13 January 1872, Adm. 53/10024; 14 January 1872–5 October 1872, Adm. 53/10025, Admiralty and Secretariat, Log Books, Etc., Ships' Logs, Public Record Office, Kew. See also Joseph W. Trutch, *Report and Journal by the Hon. the Chief Commissioner of Lands and Works, of the Proceedings in Connection with the Visit of His Excellency the Late Governor Seymour to the North-west Coast, in Her Majesty's Ship Sparrowhawk* (Victoria: Government Printing Office, 1869).

19. The bulk of this history of H.M.S. Sparrowhawk is derived from P. W. Brock, "Dossier: H.M.S. Sparrowhawk, 1856–1872," Maritime Museum of British Columbia, Victoria. See also *Navy List* (February 1872): 180; (September 1872): 180; Preston and Major, Send a Gunboat, 199; James Joseph Colledge, Ships of the Royal Navy: An Historical Index, 2 vols. (Newton Abbot, Devon: David & Charles Publishers, 1969–1970), 1:517; Walbran, British Columbia Coast Names, 466–467; F. W. Howay, "Early Settlement on Burrard Inlet," British Columbia Historical Quarterly 1 (April 1937): 114; Longstaff, Esquimalt Naval Base, 177–178, 180, plates IV, VI; G. P. V. Akrigg and Helen B. Akrigg, British Columbia Chronicle, 1847–1871: Gold & Colonist (Vancouver: Discovery Press, 1977), 379.

20. Porcher's manuscript journal pages 175–180, 261–264 contain detailed statistical data about the ship. See also Brock, "Dossier: H.M.S. Sparrowhawk."

21. The drawings are dated and labeled. They are also numbered 1–102, but not necessarily in chronological order. Fifty-three are in the Porcher manuscripts. Numbers 2, 9, 17, 36, 44, 50, 54–96 are missing. The missing numbers may be accounted for in part by their reproduction as illustrations in the published reports of the resident Anglican bishop. See, for example, George Hills, "1866 and 1867. Notes and Incidents of Mission Work. Extracts from the Bishop's Journal," Columbia Mission, *Ninth Annual Report of the Columbia Mission [of the Church of England], for the Year 1867* (London: Rivingtons, 1868), frontispiece (Yale), facing 17 (Alexandra Suspension Bridge, Fraser River). See also Frank A. Peake, *The Anglican Church in British Columbia* (Vancouver: Mitchell Press, 1959), 15 (mission village of Metlakatlah), 75 (Angela College, Victoria).

22. In addition to the journal, the notebook contains several pages of statistical data about the vessel, and some forty pages of Porcher's log of the *Sparrowhawk* and of his return voyages to England. Not reproduced in this volume, these data are sometimes cited to explain or to flesh out his journal entries. See note 20 above.

23. Not all of the period covered by Porcher's journal is covered by specific or general entries. Some of the gaps can be filled in, partially at least, from the Master's Logbooks, newspaper accounts, or other evidence. Other days or intervals were generally at anchor, often at Esquimalt, with nothing deemed worthy of notice occurring.

In a few instances, an added comment of what happened later than the time of the events of that particular entry, but related to it, seems to indicate he was writing at that later date. Such comments as "the 2 men that we met there were recalled shortly afterwards," or "a longer account...was published...on our return" do not detract from the immediacy of the events which the journal conveys.

24. Porcher's spellings have been followed as nearly as can be determined. Place names, especially those of Indian origin that did not yet have orthographic standardization, and some of the names of persons posed the most difficulty in transcription. Further, Porcher himself was not always consistent in these spellings.

Chapter One

The Atlantic Transit

9 March–3 July 1865

[H.M.S. *Sparrowhawk* was commissioned 9 March 1865 for service along the west coast of British North America. After three weeks of further fittings, provisioning, trial runs, and final inspection at Portsmouth, she steamed for Plymouth, England, under her commander Edmund A. Porcher. Departing England 1 April, the *Sparrowhawk*'s voyage—under sail and steam—to Rio de Janeiro by way of Madeira, the Canary Islands, and Cape Verde Islands, was uneventful and routine. Porcher, who had not been there for seventeen years, made good use of the stay. He observed and commented on shipyards, the sewer system, hospitals, scenery, museums, and whatever else interested him in the Rio area. This was in contrast to the next port of call, Stanley, in the bleak Falkland Islands. The *Sparrowhawk* arrived there at the beginning of the winter season. Then, two months out of England, Porcher steered his ship into the Strait of Magellan. On 2 July he rounded the southernmost tip of the mainland of South America.]

Preparations for departure

On the 9th March 1865, the *Sparrowhawk* was commissioned at Portsmouth for service in the Pacific, and to be employed principally about Vancouver's Island. Being in the first class Steam Reserves, she was nearly ready for sea, and only required to take in the Warrant Officer's stores, complete with Provisions for 3 months, and a few additional fittings put in by the Dockyard, which was all finished by the 27 inst., when we steamed out of the harbour, and anchored at Spithead where we took in the Powder & shell the same afternoon. The next day we tried our speed in Stoke's Bay under the Superintendence of Commander Brett, of the Steam Reserve.

Six runs were made over the mile with Full power, which gave the mean speed of the ship 10.4 knots per hour. The revolutions of the Engines were maximum 94, minimum 89½. With Half Boiler power (using the High Boiler alone) four runs were made over the mile, which gave the mean speed 9.124 knots, and the revolutions of the Engines maximum 80, minimum 74.

In making circles with full Power, and the vessel turning to starboard, the Half circle was made in 2 minutes 29 seconds, and the full completed in 4 minutes 46 seconds. Turning to Port, the times were respectively 2 minutes 51 sec. and 5 min. 56 seconds. With half Power, and turning to Port, the half circle was made in 2 min. 34 seconds, and the full in 5 minutes, and to starboard in 2 min. 40 seconds and 5 min. 9 seconds. The Engines were stopped, started ahead and astern in 10 seconds in each instance.

At full Power and burning 24 Tons a day, a Ton of Coals will send the ship through the water 10 knots, and at Half Power (using the High Boiler alone) and burning 9 Tons a day, a Ton of Coals will send the ship on 19 knots.

In condensing from the High Boiler we used 15 cwt of Coals in getting the steam up, and the expenditure in completing the 10 Tons was 2¾ Tons of Coals, or a little more than 3½ Tons of Water for every Ton of Coals. In the 24 hours we could condense 1440 Gallons, or 6.85 Tons, or a gallon every minute.

The Draught of Water, when the light was Forward 10 ft. 6 in. Aft 11 ft. 0 in.

Deep was Forward 11 ft. 4 in. Aft 11 ft. 9 in.

The greatest number of Revolutions when light were 108, and deep 94. The Coal boxes contain 115 Tons, and consumption per Nominal Horse Power per hour at Full power 11.4 lbs. The Pressure on Safety Valve 20 lbs. The diameter of Griffith's Lever is 11 feet, and the Pitch 14½ feet. This latter can be allowed from 13 to 15 feet.

The following day after the trial (29th March), Captain F. Scott C.B. A.D.C. came on board, and mustered the Ship's Company and Inspected the ship, and after taking leave of the Admiral Sir Michael Seymour, we weighed at Noon[1] and steamed through the Needles for Plymouth where we arrived the next morning, making the distance in 19 hours.

Here we remained during the day, completing with Coals and getting a few additional stores from the Dockyard.

1. On 30 March. Porcher's log, 265. Porcher's log is recorded on pages 265–307 in the notebook.

MADEIRA. The Town of FUNCHAL, and the Loo rock, looking to the Westward. April 11th 1865.

(original watercolor size: 14 x 9.75 in./35.5 x 24.5 cm)

The Corcovado, Sugar Loaf, and the entrance of Rio de Janeiro, from the Praia Grande. May 17, 1865.

(original watercolor size: 14 x 9 in./35.5 x 23 cm)

Rio de Janeiro. The Botanical Gardens, with the Corcovado, and Sugar Loaf. May 16, 1865.

(original watercolor size: 14 x 9.375 in./35.5 x 24 cm)

Bennett's Hotel at Tejuca, 10 miles from Rio de Janeiro. May 19, 1865.

(original watercolor size: 10 x 6.375 in./25.5 x 16 cm)

Falkland Islands. The Settlement of Stanley, from the Government House. June 19th 1865.

(original watercolor size: 14 x 8 in./35.5 x 20 cm)

Patagonia. The Chilian settlement at Sandy Point, in the Straits of Magellan. June 29, 1865.

(original watercolor size: 14 x 8.5 in./35.5 x 21.5 cm)

PORT FAMINE, in the Straits of MAGELLAN, looking towards MOUNT TARN. June 30, 1865.

(original watercolor size: 13.75 x 8.75 in./35 x 22 cm)

Port Famine, looking towards Mount St. Felipe, & the head of the Bay. July 1, 1865.

(original watercolor size: 10 x 6.375 in./25.5 x 16 cm)

Plymouth to Rio de Janeiro

We left England finally the next morning (1st April), and arrived at Madeira on the 10th. On the day we left the wind was very light, which made us use our steam till the next morning, which enabled us to get well clear of the Channel. It then came on to blow hard from the S.W. which lasted two days, and shook every thing down in their places, the wind then shifted to the N.E. that lasted four days, and brought us into fine weather and within 200 miles of Madeira. The wind then became light and baffling, which made us light the fires, and steam nearly the remainder of the way.

We anchored off Funchal on the morning of the 10th, only about ¼ hour after the African Mail steamer *Ethiope* had arrived from the Southward, which remained here 5 hours, and then left for England.

We took advantage of the fine weather after our arrival, by taking in 33 Tons of Coals, at the Contract price of 37/6. The next day a heavy swell set in, which made the landing very bad, and the ship to roll a great deal, which made us leave a day sooner than we intended.

On the 12th April, after taking leave of the Consul Mr. Erskine, we weighed at 2 PM, and steamed out clear of the land, when having a light breeze in our favour we put the fires out and lifted the screw. Before leaving the *Megaera* (Store ship) arrived from Plymouth being 6 days out on her way to Rio [de Janeiro], and brought us a few days later news.

After leaving Madeira the wind was variable until we passed the Canary Islands, when we got into the N.E. trade which brought us down into Latitude 5. N[2] on the 25th April, having passed down inshore of the Cape de Verd Islands, and kept a steady breeze the whole way. As soon as the trade wind entirely died away, we got the steam up in the High boiler, and passed through the Equatorial calms in 2½ days, crossing the line in 19. W. A light breeze then sprung up from the Southward which took us into the S.E. trade, that lasted until the 7th May when we were in Latitude 19. S. The wind then shifted to the N.W. and became variable for the remainder of the way to Rio, where we arrived on the 13th May.

The length of our passage between Plymouth and Rio was 41 days (excluding the 2 days we stopped at Madeira,) whilst the time we took in the *Cleopatra* (a sailing Frigate in 1849) was 45. This we made up in this vessel by steaming 5¼ days.

Rio sojourn

On arriving at Rio we found the *Megaera* at anchor, having been here 4 days, and as she started from Madeira 3 days after us, beat us by a week, which was easily explained by her steaming half the way. She had brought out Stores for the *Egmont*, and was to return to England in about three weeks, touching on her way at Ascension, for which place she had also Stores and Supernumeraries.

The Senior Officer Captain Crawford had his flag flying on board the *Egmont,* an old line of battle ship (72), which class of vessels being now obsolete & no further

2. Porcher's latitude and longitude designations are usually expressed by using periods, thus 49.30 for 49°30'. In some instances he uses degree and minute signs in addition to periods. To avoid unnecessary confusion this transcription will use only periods.

use for active service, has been made a Store ship of, for the use of the squadron on the Brazilian station.

After calling on the Consul Mr. Hunt, I went with Dr. Comrie[3] to see the Dry dock on the Isla de Cobras, which was certainly a very fine one, as it measured 300 feet in length, and hewn out of the solid granite, and would allow vessels drawing 30 feet of water to enter it. About 50 yards from this another Dock of the same dimensions has been commenced, but the work is now stopped for want of funds. They belong to the Brazilian government who derive a small Revenue from the vessels using them.

We afterwards crossed over to the Brazilian Arsenal, and inspected their building slips, as well as a great deal of massive machinery that is required to repair the engines of their ships. We saw a great deal of activity going on in building an armour plated ship that was to be plated with 4 inch iron. She had only been commenced 2 months, and was nearly ready to receive her armour. The Government wanted her as soon as possible to ascend the La Plata, and assist in the war that was being carried on against the Paraguayans.

Since my last visit here in 1849, there has been a great improvement in the whole city, as it is now lighted with Gas and which is carried out as far as 10 miles into the country, and has a very imposing effect from the water. It seems also to be well managed in a Commercial point of view, as the Company received last year a Dividend of 47 per cent.

The greatest nuisance still remaining in the city is the open sewers that run down the centre of every street, and as they are not kept particularly clean in other parts become very offensive in hot and close weather.

To deviate this an English Company has lately been formed to Deodorize the sew[e]rage, instead of letting it pollute the harbour, adjoining the Quays, Bays, &c. They commenced by building an establishment on the East end of the town, between the Public gardens and Botafogo Bay, and is the first of three that are going to be built to compromise the whole metropolis. This first building was completed about a year ago. Steam engines and all the necessary apparatus have been placed in it, and the Company have made a contract with the Government to guarantee them the sum of £7 for each house. For this sum they have led to Sew[e]rage down in closed pipes, built cisterns for a supply of water in every house, and made it fall into 4 Recevoirs [reservoirs] a few feet above the level of the sea, where it is purified by having lime, powdered charcoal, and chloride of lime filtered through it. The water is then allowed to run off, or pumped up, and the sediment is given to the inhabitants for manure, who send carts for it. After a time, and when the people are aware of the value of it, this will be sold by the Company. In this locality at the East end of the city, there are about 2000 houses, so they receive £14.000 annually.

The City is well supplied with Hospitals, and in many of them the poor are received without any charge. The largest and the one that attracts most attention seems to be the Mesiricordia, or Hospital for the Poor, and fronting the water is a

---

3. Peter Comrie served as Surgeon on the *Sparrowhawk* during the tenure of Porcher and under his successor. *Navy List* (April 1865): 208; (January 1869): 218.

conspicuous object to vessels laying in the Harbour. It runs back some distance from the street, and is cut up by a number of open courts which are laid out in gardens, giving a very pleasant effect from the windows.

Another front is being added which will give a great deal of additional space. At present there is room for about 1500 Beds which are generally full. The Wards are well proportioned being about 100 feet in length, of good height, and the Beds are not at all crowded. In order to keep the Floors dry, they are waxed, which gives them a clean & polished appearance. A small recess is let into the walls between the beds, to hold Bottles and small articles. The internal arrangements are well managed by 44 Sisters of Charity, who seemed to be very zealous and attentive in the discharge of their duties. Only one of the Sisters spoke English, and she remained with us the whole time.

We made an ineffectual attempt to see the Museum, that is said to be worth seeing, and situated at the head of the Rua d'Ouvidor opposite the New Opera house. It is only open to the Public on Sundays in the middle of the day, but as it was intended for the use of Students, and others that wish to study the Collections on other days, we called there on one of the week days, but had a great difficulty in getting an entrance at all, as the Doors like most of them in the country had neither bells or knockers, and when we did get in at a side entrance after a great delay, were told that the Director had gone into the country and would not be back for the day, so we had to give it up with a good grace.

As we had a few days to see a little of the country, I and Dr. Comrie took advantage of the time and fine weather to visit the Botanical Gardens, Tejuca, and the Barro do Pirahy, which are the excursions which can be most easily accomplished during the day.

The first day we started by the steamer that leaves frequently for Botafogo Bay at the entrance of the harbour, and from there walked to the Botanical Gardens, which in a cool day is a pleasant walk of 3 miles. The sides of the road were ornamented by the Quintas of the Brazilian gentry which are prettily surrounded by gardens and pleasure grounds, and some small pretensions are made in them, by imitating the sculpture of the ancients.

On arriving at the gardens we were rather disappointed as they were not so extensive as we were led to expect, but the most striking part were the rows of the Cabbage Palm trees, that line the principal paths, and are effective in looking down upon them, but the grounds themselves are not kept in good order, and few of the trees classified, and being without flowers, or little to interest the eye, there is not sufficient inducement to attract people here very often, as they are 7 miles away from Rio. The prettiest walk in the gardens is by the side of a watercourse that leads through the upper part of the gardens, and communicates with the lower grounds by artificial cascades. This path is very refreshing on a warm day, and it is entirely shaded by rows of Bamboo that grow luxuriantly on each side of the stream to a great height. After spending the afternoon there, and making a view of the gardens with the surrounding scenery, we returned to Rio in an Omnibus.

On another day we left early in the morning to see the scenery at Tejuca, which is situated at an elevation of 3316 feet, about 10 miles to the South-west of Rio. A kind of Street Railway propelled by a Locomotive leads to the foot of the hill about 6 miles distant, and the train consists of a long carriage cut up into several compartments, and capable of holding 84 people. It had an Upper tier of seats which in fine and warm weather is by far the most agreeable. At the terminus where the train stops we hired horses, and rode up to Bennett's Hotel that is situated high up in a very pretty spot surrounded by hills, near which a mountain stream rushes down amongst Plantations of Coffee, Orange, and other fruit trees. Here we stopped to refresh ourselves, for several hours in the middle of the day, and returned in the Afternoon.

On the last day we could devote to these excursions we rose early, and left by the train on the Don Pedro II. Railway at 6.30 AM, for the Barro do Pirahy which is situated at the junction of the Rivers Parahiba and the Pirahy about 68 miles to the N.W. of Rio. The line takes a very romantic circuit round a range of hills 1600 feet in height, and with a very steep gradient of 6 feet in the 100, or 310 feet in the mile. It runs through virgin forests the greater part of the way, and here and there a solitary house with a little cleared land around it. The steep incline is only temporary, as a more direct and level line has been made by tunnelling through the hills, and was nearly finished.

The Barro itself has a little village growing up near the Railway station, and is well situated surrounded by thickly wooded hills. We returned at 6.30 PM, having taken 4 hours each way.[4]

Falkland Islands in winter

AFTER SPENDING 10 DAYS HERE, we left early on the morning of the 23rd May for the Falkland Islands, being at the commencement of the winter season, and took about the average time of 24 days. The passage was made under sail, the steam only being used for going in and out of harbour. It was our intention on starting to keep within 100 miles of the coast, as is advised in the Sailing Directions, in order to get a smoother sea, as well as to have the Current in our favour, but as we were blown off the land soon after leaving by the continued Westerly winds, we were not enabled to do this, and forced to make as straight a course as possible.

The prevailing winds during this season are said to be from the Westward, and mostly from the North-west, but we had the wind from the latter direction for a few hours only, and nearly the whole of the time we encountered variable winds both in strength and direction from the Westward and South-west, the latter wind prevailing; and a strong current continually against us.

A great quantity of kelp was seen in the latter part of the passage, the first piece that was obtained was found hooked on to a fishing line on the Evening of the 7th

4. The Master, sometimes referred to as the Navigating Lieutenant, was responsible, under the Commander, whether in port or at sea, for the navigation, maintenance, and repair of the ship. The terse and matter-of-fact Master's logbook entries that detailed this routine while the *Sparrowhawk* was at anchor in the harbor at Rio de Janeiro are in contrast to Porcher's narrative account of his activities at the same time. The Master's logbooks for the *Sparrowhawk* under Porcher's command are in the Public Record Office, Kew, Adm. 53/9255, Adm. 53/9256, Adm. 53/9257. The logbooks under his successor are Adm. 53/10023, Adm. 53/10024, Adm. 53/10025. The "privileged Men" were given shore leave on Sunday afternoon. Entry for 21 May 1865, Master's logbook, Adm. 53/9255.

June, being then in Latitude 39.30 S and Longitude 49.30 W, and 370 miles from the nearest land.

Birds accompanied the ship the whole way, and many were caught with a hook and line without any trouble. Cape Pigeons joined us directly we left Rio, and shortly after Albatrosses, but the latter were never seen in any numbers. Penguins are said to be often seen as far as 300 miles off the land, but we did not see or hear any the whole way.[5] On the night of the 16th June, being close in to the land we hove to till daylight, and the next morning closed the East Falkland's under steam and sail, and anchored in the safe harbour of Port Stanley a little after Noon.

A few days before our arrival, a melancholy funeral took place. During the time the *Harrier*, the last man of war that touched here, was at this port, a Sub. Lieutenant of the name of Jermingham strayed away from his party when on a shooting excursion at Sparrow Cove, and could not be found. They remained several days to search for him, but without success, and then thinking that he must have fallen over the Cliffs and was killed, left on their return to England. Shortly before our arrival he had been found by a party that happened to be at that part of the island, and who had been attracted to the particular spot by the number of birds that were hovering over the place, and on examining it found the body of the unfortunate Officer, which had been half devoured by these birds of prey. It seems that he had got into a small Cave to shelter him from the cold and wind, where after finishing a Pocket flask of spirits to afford a little artificial warmth, had lied [*sic*] down to sleep, never to awake again. His remains were removed, and buried at the Cemetery near the settlement on the 14th June.

On the day of our arrival, a nearly similar occurrence took place, but fortunately in this case without any bad results. The Colonial Surgeon of the name of MacClinton R.N. had been on board to pay a visit, and was returning to the shore with 3 of the Officers to join a small party that he had assembled at his house. They left the ship in the Gig at 7 PM, and although close to the shore managed to get drifted out of the harbour, and nearly taken out to sea, but luckily managed after a great deal of trouble to pull into Yorke Bay, where they hauled the Boat up, and walked into the settlement where they arrived at 2 o'clock in the morning, nearly all done up.

The settlement of Stanley consists of a number of straggling houses built on the slope of a hill on the South side of the harbour that is about 3 miles long by ⅓ broad. The entrance is very narrow, not being more than a cable's length across, but the shore is steep on both sides. The population of the Falkland Islands are about 500, and contains 3000 square miles. The only enterprising people here seem to be the Falkland Island Company who have bought from the Government, the Southern half of the Eastern island as a Freehold for £16000, on which there are at present a great number of wild cattle. Between this and Stanley they rent a large quantity of better land for sheep farming. The Islands seem to be the most desolate, and quite unfit for agricultural purposes, as there is not sufficient warmth in the sun to ripen any thing but a few vegetables. There is not a tree to be seen in any part of the island,

5. For whatever reason, "an Extra allowance of Chocolate" was made to the watches twice during the passage to the Falkland Islands. Entries for 14, 15 June 1865, Master's logbook, Adm. 53/9255.

and grass and a few bushes about 3 feet high comprise the whole vegetation. Coals can be obtained here at 48/. a ton, and supplies of all kinds from the Falkland Island Company, as well as from Mr. Dean who has kept a Store here for many years. It was snowing constantly during our stay, and the thermometer stood as low as 24° on the first night after our arrival.[6] We remained here 5 days to complete with coals, and then left for the Straits of Magellan.[7]

Strait of Magellan

The Passage from the Falkland Islands to the Straits we made in 6 days having had variable winds principally from the S.W. and N.W. For Two days before making the land we had thick and gloomy weather, and not able to get any sights, so that we had to run in for the land on the 27th June under steam, during a thick Fog and trusting to the Soundings. About 11 AM, this suddenly lifted, and we observed the land right ahead about 4 miles distant, and at Noon got the Meridian altitude which shewed that we were 9 miles to the Northward of Cape Virgins, which at that time we could make out distinctly, by the accurate view of the land given in the Charts, and the perfect outline of the Cape itself. This point we rounded close to, and being at the time nearly high water ran over the Sarmiento bank, and steered up for the Great Orange bank where we anchored at 5.30 PM[8] in 17 fathoms, as it was getting quite dark. Bearings of the anchorage were Cape Possession NW ¾ W, Catherine's Point ESE.

June 28th. Weighed at daylight, and steamed to the Southward of Possession Bay following the Track given in the Charts, through the First Narrows, across So. Iago Bay, and anchored as the sun was going down at 3.30 PM off Cape Gregory, in 10 fathoms. The low point of the Cape bearing S 18 W about half a mile distant.

The distance we ran over today 55 miles having had a moderate breeze against us from the S.W. but the whole of the Flood Tide was in our favour, sweeping up through the 1st Narrows very rapidly. The difficulty of finding a ship's position at the Eastern entrance of the Straits, and particularly after passing the 1st Narrows where the Barrancas Bank and the Triton shoal have to be avoided is the great similarity of the land, and the great want of a few distinguishing marks. If the Straits of Magellan ever becomes a highway for steamers which it probably will in a few years this might be easily remedied by having a few land marks built on the most prominent points, and then the only difficulty will be the violent Westerly gales that blow the whole year round, but with their greatest force during the summer.

June 29th. Steamed today through the second Narrows, passed Elizabeth Island, and anchored off the small Chilian settlement at Sandy Point at 3 PM in 10 fathoms, with the following bearings, Governor's Flag staff N 37 W. Cross of the Cemetery S 88 W, and Sandy Point N 12 E.

---

6. The *Sparrowhawk* made a contribution to counter the bad news and desolation that seemed to pervade the Falkland Islands. "Dressed ship with Mast Head Flags in commemoration of Her Majesty's accession to the Throne." Entry for 20 June 1865, Master's logbook, Adm. 53/9255.

7. On 21 June. Porcher's log, 271–272.

8. In Lomas Bay. Porcher's log, 271–272.

There was very little wind the whole day, and the atmosphere beautifully clear, so that we easily made out Mount Sarmiento at the distance of 96 miles. This is the highest land in Terra del Fuego, and rises to the height of 6800 feet in a remarkable Peak and covered with perpetual snow. After dropping the anchor the acting Governor came on board, and offered his services in any way he could be useful. Before it got dark I and Dr. Comrie went on shore to see the settlement which consisted of a number of irregularly built houses with Verandah's round them, the best of which seemed to be the Governor's house, Barracks, and wooden Fort.

The history of this little place seemed to be (from the account I could gather from the inhabitants) that in 1851, 300 Convicts were sent here from Valparaiso for political offenses, under a guard of 60 soldiers, and after being here only 3 months, mutinied, killed the Governor and the greater part of the garrison, set fire to their barracks and hospital, and then took possession of a trading vessel that was at anchor off the place. They afterwards quarrelled amongst themselves for their share of the plunder on board the vessel in which a great many of their lives were lost, and the Tragedy ended by their being taken by an English man of war, who handed over the Convicts that were spared, to the Chilian government who put them to death. Since this rather quick termination of attempting to plant a Convict establishment on these shores, it has been purely a Military settlement more for the purpose of keeping possession of the most Southern part of Patagonia than for any real good.[9] During the time of our visit it consisted of 110 souls, viz. 2 Officers, 50 Soldiers, 6 Sailors, 4 Carpenters, 2 Blacksmiths, 1 Storekeeper, 1 Priest, 44 Women, and a number of Children, who seem to live a miserable existence, only having communication with Valparaiso once in 6 months, when a sailing vessel arrives with a great supply of Provisions and Stores, and all the news they get is from the few vessels that stop here on their way through the Straits.

The following information about the Coal in this locality I received through Captain Caldbeck of the P and O company's service, from Senor Don G. Schythe who has been for the last 10 years Governor of the settlement, and only retired from it a few weeks before our arrival.

There has been some Coal discovered in the neighbourhood but up to this time has never been worked, it crops out from the side of a range of hills about 800 or 1000 feet above the level of the sea, and 8 miles distant from the settlement, the seams shew about 200 feet below the summit of the hill and are overlaid by sand and earth, so loose as to make the approach rather dangerous, this debris continually slipping away takes with it masses of coal into a mountain rivulet, and which in time

---

9. Chile occupied the Strait of Magellan in the 1840s in a wave of nationalism. A settlement was founded there in 1843 and served as a penal colony. What Porcher described here is referred to as "Cambiaso's rebellion." Simon Collier, "Chile from Independence to the War of the Pacific," in Leslie Bethell, ed., *The Cambridge History of Latin America*, vol. 3: *From Independence to c.1870* (Cambridge: Cambridge University Press, 1985), 583; Anson Uriel Hancock, *A History of Chile* (New York: AMS Press, 1971), 229; Frederick M. Nunn, *The Military in Chilean History: Essays on Civil-Military Relations, 1810–1973* (Albuquerque: University of New Mexico Press, 1976), 52; Robert D. Talbott, "The Chilean Boundary in the Strait of Magellan," *Hispanic American Historical Review*, 47 (November 1967): 520–521.

of Winter floods rolls them down to the sea where strewing the beach in lumps, having given strangers the idea of large supplies being close to.

The Dip of the seam is from N.W. to S.E. and the inclination about 30° in the latter direction, the thickness of some of the seams is stated to be nearly 3 feet. It is 9 years since the exploration was made, at which Mr. Schythe was present, and the Coal examined by two Geologists and surveyors on the Government service, Senor Don Ignacio Domeyko and Senor Pipio. The Coal is of tertiary formation, as well as the Shells and fossils found there, and is of the same description as the Chilian coal of Coronil and Lota, and requires furnaces and stoves of a peculiar construction for its combustion. Mr. Schythe thinks that great inducements in the shape of very high wages would be needed to secure labour, owing to the rigour of the climate, and the isolated position of Sandy Point, then the construction of a Wharf, 8 miles of tramway, the requisite buildings, plant and lighters together with the expense of roofing in, so as to make the working free of danger, might probably make Coaling in the Straits more expensive than in other places.

A few Patagonians come to the settlement occasionally to sell their Guanaco skins and Ostrich feathers, but the only one's we saw were two men that had taken up their abode there for some time past, and met us on our landing.

Great quantities of drift wood had been washed up along the shores round the settlement, and would be useful to any vessel that required a supply to assist in steaming, and as there was supposed to be abundance of Fish we sent a seining party away, but only returned with 10 Mullet. The Governor was very generous in giving us as many Vegetables, Milk, butter, eggs, &c as could be spared.

June 30th. The Chilian Officers came on board early to leave their letters for Valparaiso, after which we left for Port Famine where we arrived before Noon, and anchored in 8 fathoms with the extreme of Santa Anna point N 55 E, and the Rivulet N 69 W.

There was a Chilian settlement here in 1843, called San Felipe, that was abandoned in 1849, on account of the land being too steep and inconvenient, and not suited for agricultural purposes. Some of the framework of the houses are still standing, and can be clearly made out before entering the harbour, and several pieces of peat that formed the sides of the houses are still in their places. On a rising ground on the Western side of the harbour, we came upon the tomb of a seaman who had finished his days in this lonely spot. It had a wooden head board and railing. There had been a copper plate on the board which had not escaped the thievish hands of the natives, and the particulars of the inscription has been lost, but on the opposite side was written in pencil Henry Lighte, H.M.S. *Calypso*. The shores of the whole harbour were lined with drift wood, being mostly cedar and beech, and well suited for steaming purposes, as well as for Carpenters work. A party was employed cutting it up during the 1½ day we remained here, and sent on board nearly 8 fathoms. A seining party were also sent away on the Western side of the harbour, near the mouth of the River Sedger, but only succeeded in getting 4 Mullet after several hauls.

The Summer seems to be the best time for visiting these places, as the Birds and Fish are then more abundant, and the country has then quite a different aspect, the trees being out in leaf, and the ground covered with flowers. At the time we visited it every thing was saturated with moisture with great quantities of ice all round the harbour.

The evening before we left a Fuegian canoe made its appearance round the point of the harbour as it was getting dark. Instead of coming on board, they paddled up to the wooding party who had a fire burning on the beach, two of the men landed and obtained some Tobacco from our men, keeping a woman and some children in the canoe. Their fire was seen in the morning in a cove near the ship, and the canoe was coming off to us as we were steaming out of the harbour.

July 2nd. Left Port Famine at daylight, and rounded Cape Froward the most Southern point of the main land of America, and anchored in the small harbour of Borja Bay in 17 fathoms an hour after Sunset, having run 75 miles. The West extreme of Big Borja bore SE ¼ E, and the East point of the bay E ½ N.

The weather was very fine the greater part of the day, at one time quite calm, which made the bold scenery on both sides of the Straits appear very picturesque. The land rose in some parts to a height of 2 or 3000 feet, and well wooded with numerous waterfalls, but the hills were covered with snow about ½ way down, which gave it a wintry and desolate appearance. Borja Bay is very small, not more than ¼ mile wide, and surrounded by rocky hills, that on the North side being 1800 feet in height.

July 3rd. Left Borja Bay, and steamed through the Long Reach, and anchored in Port Tamar at 3.15 PM, having run 60 miles. The breadth of the Straits for the greater part of the day was about two miles, and the scenery was much wider than what we saw yesterday, the verdure having to a great extent disappeared, and the few trees that were seen grew close down to the water. At Glacier Bay we saw a very fine Glacier, that extended down to the water line, and on the opposite side of the Straits, but a little more to the Eastward were two others that did not seem to be quite so large. Till about 2 PM we had a Calm, and then a fresh breeze sprung up from the S.E. which took us into Port Tamar which appeared to be a very safe anchorage with any wind but the one that was blowing, as it blew right in without any shelter, but a shoal patch covered with kelp, having only 4½ fathoms on it. We therefore let go both anchors, the first on the edge of the patch in 13 fathoms, and the second in 24 fathoms. After veering to 72 fathoms on the Port cable, and 36 on the Starboard one, we had the following bearings: Islets in the Centre of Bay N 84 W, Western small rock off East Pte N 71 E, Eastern of group off West Pt. S 36 W. The surroundings seemed to be much deeper than what appears in the Charts, as where we had 20 and 23 fathoms, these were only marked down 12 and 13 fathoms.

Chapter Two

THE PACIFIC TRANSIT

4 July–28 October 1865

[The hazards of navigation in this virtually isolated part of the globe were substantial, but Porcher managed to complete the passage through the Strait of Magellan with minimum difficulty. A fortnight later the *Sparrowhawk* anchored in Valparaiso Bay on the Chilean coast, the southern headquarters of the Pacific British Navy. Porcher enjoyed the sights of Valparaiso and the inland capital city of Santiago before moving on. In the next port of call, Callao, Peru, the *Sparrowhawk* shared the harbor with a Spanish squadron as well as several French, Italian, American, Peruvian, and English naval vessels. After a few days of sightseeing at Callao, and the capital city of Lima, Porcher weighed anchor on 18 August for the Hawaiian Islands. The thirty-five-day voyage was void of landfall and encounter with other ships. The pleasant ambience of the Sandwich Islands was prologue to the uneventful last month of the Pacific transit. Seven months and twenty thousand miles out of Plymouth, England, ninety percent of the way under unassisted sail, H.M.S. *Sparrowhawk* entered the harbor at Esquimalt, Vancouver Island, headquarters of the Pacific station.]

Smyth Channel passage

July 4th. Left Port Tamar, crossed the Straits of Magellan, and entered Smyth's Channel during the forenoon where we threaded our way up amongst the islands, following the track laid down in the Chart, till we arrived at Fortune Bay where we arrived at 2 pm. The breadth of the Channel today was in some places not more than ¾ mile, and therefore well sheltered from the wind which was blowing hard from the Westward. Fortune Bay is a very secure and landlocked harbour, but the depth in the middle is 15 fathoms, and being only 2¼ cables across, there would not be room for a vessel to swing at single anchor. Sent a wooding party on shore, but did not succeed in finding any drift wood, the only kind worth taking being the remains of some trees that had been felled by some former vessel. The following Bearings were taken at Anchorage—South extreme of Low Island N 26 E[;] North extreme of Low Island N85 E. Fresh water creek S 82 W[;] Roget Head S 35 E.

July 5th. Left Fortune Bay at day light and steamed through the Victory Pass, passed to the Northward of the Cloyne reef which is just awash, surrounded by kelp, and would be dangerous in thick weather, and anchored in Relief harbour at 5 pm. For the greater part of the day it was blowing hard through the Channels from the N.W. with drizzling rain, which prevented us having a good view of the different mountains, particularly the Cordillera of Sarmiento which is snow capped, and has extensive glaciers, these we only partially saw. The vessel steamed well with two Boilers (having three) against the strong breezes, going between 5 and 6 knots.

Relief Harbour is a convenient stopping place, as there is no Anchorage to be had within 30 miles of it North or South, but it [is] quite open to Southerly winds, and with the ocean swell rolling through Nelson Straits, would be insecure at those times.

July 6th. Left Relief harbour and steamed through the Sarmiento Channel against a strong breeze, and moored in the excellent harbour of Puerto Bueno in 8 fathoms at 1 pm, having run today a distance of 30 miles. Continued heavy rain fell the whole day which made the fine scenery in the Channel (in some places not more than a mile wide), look rather dismal. Pulled round the harbour in the Afternoon, and found that the outline of the Bay had only been roughly sketched in, and although the Charts for these Channels are quite sufficient to guide Vessels through them in safety, but if they are to be frequently used, it would be well worth while sending a Surveying vessel down here for a few months to complete what has only been partially done.

Observed two boards nailed up to a tree on the North side of the entrance to the inner harbour, with the following writing on them:

+ P.M.S.S +
Colorado
G. H. Bradbury, Commander
May 23rd, 1865. 36 days from N.Y.
All Well.

P.R.R.Co. Str. *Parkingburgh*
Jan. 2nd. New York 1865
Capt. W. Rathmusen

July 7th. Left Puerto Bueno and steamed through the Guia Narrows which is in one place only 400 yards wide, through the Concepcion channel, and at Sunset tried to get an Anchorage at Small Craft Bight, but did not succeed in getting any soundings except very close to the shore.

All day we had a fair wind from the Southward which went down at Sunset, and having the Full Moon, and being in a wide part of the Channel there was no difficulty in keeping under weigh for the night, and therefore steamed very slowly ahead until midnight, and then stopped in midchannel until near daylight.

July 8th. This morning in a thick fog, we rounded Saumarez Island, which has high bluff cliffs, through the Indian reach, and the English Narrows which is the most intricate part of the Straits, as the passage is contracted so much by the numerous islands that in some places it is not more than 400 yards wide, and anchored in Halt Bay in 25 fathoms during the afternoon, having steamed since daylight 60 miles.

In coming up the Indian reach we saw some smoke amongst the trees, which was the first indication of any inhabitants we had seen in Smyth's Channel. A great many seals had been seen the whole day jumping and frollicking [sic] in the water, and it appeared to be the most favourite part of the Straits for their Rookeries.

The soundings in Halt Bay seemed to be also inaccurate, as in coming into the harbour we got 42 fathoms where it was marked 28 in the Chart. It is stated that the Cedar cut in this place was well adapted for steaming purposes, as it burnt easily, gave out good heat, and did not require to be freshened with Coals, but as there was no drift wood of any kind lying on the shores, and it all had to be cut down, I did not think it would suit as well, as our [we] were limited in the number of saws and axes. The harbour was half a mile wide and very picturesque, being surrounded by high steep hills covered with trees, and waterfalls dashing down in every direction.

July 9th. Left Halt Bay, and steamed to the Northward in a more open part of the Straits, and anchored in the small land locked port of Island harbour in the afternoon. This secure place is less than two cables in width, and finding that we had not many yards to spare in swinging round, secured a hawser to some trees on the Weather shore to prevent her swinging round in the same direction again.

At the end of the harbour a large cascade falls into the water, and as it can be seen from a distance it forms a good land mark. The hills around are high and thickly wooded up to their summits. It is very conveniently placed for vessels entering or leaving the Channels, and as another recommendation it is mentioned in the Sailing Directions that the Shores are lined with drift wood.

On pulling round the Harbour I certainly did not see a single piece, and it was only on leaving that I saw at the entrance at a single spot a little washed up, so that vessels coming here for the purpose of procuring drift wood, will probably be disappointed.

July 10th. Left this our last Anchorage at daylight, and on nearing the entrance of the Straits met three Canoes full of Natives, the largest having 12 in. They had fires burning in the middle of the boats, as is the custom amongst the Fuegians, and they were all naked with the exception of a Fur Cloak thrown across their shoulders. The women looked very fat and plump and not at all in a starving condition, with their faces smeared over with red earth, and all kinds of dirt. They came close alongside making a great deal of noise, but did not seem to be very anxious to board us, although we were stopped and moving ahead very little. About 3 hours after leaving, we fairly cleared Smyth's Channel, & then steered to the Westward to get a good Offing. Having now cleared both Channels with so little trouble, it is natural that I should consider steaming through them far preferable to going round Cape Horn, where vessels are frequently kept in the same position for days together in endeavouring to get to windward against the heavy Westerly gales. We certainly had the fine season, and moreover beautiful weather to assist us which must account in a great measure for our prosperous passage, and were not detained a single day from stress of weather.

With the very short days in the middle of winter, it only took us 13 days from the time we entered the Straits of Magellan to the day we cleared Smyth's Channel, including one day we stopped at Port Famine. The *Sutlej* seems to have been one of the longest ships that attempted the route by the Straits of Magellan, and they had to force their way through them during the summer when the Gales are more frequent and boisterous, and by their account it certainly seems that it would have been better if they had gone round, as they were 10 days in the Straits, during which time they lost two anchors, and were once driven on shore.

Anchorages in the Strait of Magellan and Smyth Channel

June 27th 1865.	Great Orange bank—From Cape Virgin's	28 miles
28th	Cape Gregory—Distance run	51
29th	Sandy Point	44
30th	Port Famine	28
July 2nd	Borja Bay	75
3rd	Port Tamar	61
4th	(Entrance of Smyth's Channel)	15 = 302 miles
Smyth's Channel		
4th	Fortune Bay	35 miles
5th	Relief Harbour	60
6th	Puerto Bueno	30
7th	(Remained under weigh)	85
8th	Halt Bay	60
9th	Island Harbour	51
10th	(Cleared Smyth's Channel in)	35 = 356 miles

Valparaiso/ Santiago visit

It took us a fortnight making the remainder of the Passage from the Gulf of Penas to Valparaiso, the distance being a little under 1000 miles. For the first few days we had light breezes from the N.W. which used to veer gradually round to the Westward and S.W., and not remainding [sic] long at the latter position, but shifting back again to the N.W.

On the morning of the 24th July, we got the steam up to close with the land which we saw at 9 AM, and anchored at 6.30 AM, in Valpariso Bay, in 35 fathoms.

We should have arrived a little earlier in the day, but not having had sights for 2 days and being out of our reckoning, we found on nearing it at Noon that we were 36 miles to the Southward of our Port. We therefore lighted the fires under one of the low Boilers, and steamed to the Northward with two Boilers against a NNW breeze at the rate of 6.5 knots, and anchored after it got dark in deep water. The next morning we moved further in, and anchored near the Store ship *Nereus* in 25 fathoms.

The only man of war lying here was an Italian Frigate *Principe Umberto,* which was the largest vessel of that nation that had ever been out in the Pacific. I paid a visit on board this vessel in company with our Consul Mr. Rouse, and had great pleasure in making acquaintance with her Captain of the name of Acton, a very intelligent Officer, and who was descended from English Parents.

On the evening of the 27th July, a grand Ball was given on board this vessel, at which all the principal inhabitants of Valparaiso were present. All the arrangements were very good and had been superintended by her First Lieut. Colon, a descendant of the great Columbus. Amongst them was an imitation of a Grotto that was built up aloft the mainmast, and had a jet d'eau in the middle that was worked by a donkey engine below, which threw out a continuous stream of water, and being well surrounded with large stones interspersed with water lilies, the "tout ensemble" gave a very pleasing effect.

The next morning after this party, I left Valparaiso for the capital Santiago, starting by the 10 o'clock train which arrived at 4.30 PM, the distance being 90 miles. As there is not much traffic on this line, one Passenger train is found to be sufficient every day, which starts from each end at the same time, and being a single line the trains meet at Llaillai. The first half of the route is taken through a series of Valleys with very little rise, and it was not until leaving the half way Station at Llaillai (where we stopped half an hour for luncheon at the Cafe de Smith) that any engineering difficulties had to be encountered. On arriving at Santiago we drove to the Hotel Oddo where we engaged rooms, and had every reason to be satisfied with it during our short stay of 4 days here. On dining at the Table d'hote I was very much surprised to find a Gentleman sitting next to me, that I had known in 1847, a Captain T. B. Caldbeck of the P. and O Company's service. He had then command of the *Ariel* when she was run on shore on a reef near Seymour, and to whose assistance we were sent in the *Sidon.*[1] He was now employed by a Pacific S.N. Company, who had sent him out here to see if he could make some arrangements with the Chilian government about granting a Subsidy for the use of a line of steamers that were to leave England monthly, and to touch en route at Rio de Janeiro, Mate Video, and to pass through the Straits of Magellan. In the Evening I accompanied him to a party at Mr. Charles Swinburne's, an old Merchant, where I met many of the English residents, Mr. and Mrs. Ward, Mr. and 2 Misses Haviland, Mr. Garland, and the Rev. Dundas late Bishop's Chaplain at Vancouver's Island, &c. After some very good

1. Lieutenant Porcher served on the steam frigate *Sidon*, 1846–1849. *Navy List* (January 1847): 140, 193; (January 1849): 155; (April 1849): 157.

music and singing, we finished with dancing, and wound up with the Chilian National dance Samba quaka[2] which was prettily danced by a good looking young Chilian.

The morning after our arrival, the first place I and Dr. Comrie visited was the Cathedral which was of great length, but very plain and nothing ornamental about it, and then walked over the site of the Church that was burnt in December 1862, that adjoined the Cathedral, and where between 2 and 3000 people perished, during an Illumination of the Interior. Amongst the Superstitions carried on here, was the Virgin's Post Office, where the female part of the population used to drop their letters in, when in want of any conceivable thing, and expected them to be answered.

Since that event the remains of the building that was spared by the fire has been pulled down, and the only thing remaining was part of the Eastern wall which a few men were in the act of demolishing, and the huge Bell that hung over the entrance is left on the ground where it fell.

The Pantheon or Cemetery was situated some distance outside of the town. In the Roman Catholic part, the wealthy classes have not spared any expence in placing magnificent monuments in white marble, over the remains of their departed relatives, and much time and labour has been expended in the richness of the decorations, as if they expected that would be sufficient to atone for the sins of the dead. The Protestant part was very small, and separated by a wall, and seemed to be much neglected.

One of the few sights to be seen in the City was the Museum, and I was shewn over it by the able Director of the Establishment Signor Philippe. There were several good specimens of the Natural products of the country, including the Geological, Mineralogical, and Natural history collections, but were kept in low and dingy rooms, as the Government will not go to the expense of giving a proper building to house them in. Near this, and adjoining the Government Offices there is a considerable collection of the Native curiosities of the country, including several from the islands in the Pacific. The most striking amongst them were several large gold ornaments belonging to the Incas, and the room was ornamented by flags that were taken from the Spaniards during the war of independence in 1809.

Amongst the most enterprising people here, was a Mr. Meiggs who had formerly been a Banker and a large lumber Merchant at San Francisco, but having failed there from over speculation, was obliged to decamp, and commence business in this part of the world. He was the Contractor for the Railway between Valparaiso and Santiago, and before he commenced it was bound by the Government to finish it in 3 years, or to pay $10.000 every month over that time, until it was completed. At the same time he was promised if he finished it before the 3 years, he would be given the same amount $10000 for every month before the time.[3]

---

2. Porcher put an asterisk after Samba quaka which he then footnoted as Zamecuaca. The modern spellings are samba cueca and samacueca.

3. Henry Meiggs completed the Santiago-Valparaiso line in two years. Hancock, *A History of Chile*, 241.

The hill of Santa Lucia, from the Cañada at Santiago. July 31, 1865.

(original watercolor size: 10 x 6.5 in./21.5 x 16.5 cm)

Chili. The "Quebrada de Molinas," a ravine to the Eastward of Valparaiso. August 3, 1865.

(original watercolor size: 10 x 6.63 in./21.5 x 17 cm)

Peru. The city of Lima, overlooking the river Rimac (he who speaks). August 16, 1865.

(original watercolor size: 14 x 8.88 in./35.5 x 22.5 cm)

Peruvian Fruit. Chirimoya, Granandilla, Bananas, Orange, & an Apple. August 21, 1865.

(original watercolor size: 8.25 x 7 in./21 x 17.5 cm)

Sandwich Islands. The Royal Palace of Kamehameha V, at Honolulu. Sept. 28th 1865.

(original watercolor size: 14 x 9.5 in./35.5 x 24 cm)

My Residence at Honolulu. September 29th 1865.

(original watercolor size: 10 x 6.13 in./25.5 x 15.5 cm)

Sandwich Islands. The Eastern part of Honolulu, with the Hawaiian Church, and Diamond Hill in the distance. September 26th 1865.

(original watercolor size: 14 x 9.13 in./35.5 x 23 cm)

He was advised by his friends not to accept it as it was an impossibility, but having gone over the ground he undertook to do it, and completed the whole line in 2 years, thereby pocketing $120,000.

In order to make the Chilians work who are naturally of a lasy [*sic*] disposition he used to have recourse to several devices, such as when they came to a stiff cutting, to place an equal number of men at each end of it, and in the middle bore down a deep hole, and drop a few hundred dollars, with the understanding that the party who came upon it should have the reward. In this way and other Yankee ingenuities he finished it.

One of the guest houses in the city belonged to Mr. Meiggs and overlooked the Canada,[4] and no expense was spared to make it complete. In his Drawing room he had two Prize Pianos, one from the London Exhibition of 1862, and the other from New York, and gave for each £500.

Not being contented with this house, he is now building a superb Quinta near the Railway Station, quite regardless of expence [*sic*], and every detail connected with it is being sent out from the United States. The Stables and a Conservatory are detached, and several acres are being laid out in pleasure grounds, and by the time they are finished will have cost him about £100.000.

On my return to Valparaiso, I visited the Sick Quarters that are under the Superintendence of Dr. H. Bert. It is situated in a very low locality on some rising ground at the back of the Market Place, the approaches are very bad and extremely dirty and surrounded by a Ravine where there is a small stream of very dirty water, where all kinds of Offal are thrown from the neighbouring houses, and must be a very insalubrious place for sick people to be living in, particularly during the hot weather.

The Sailors are placed in a house with two Floors the lower one being occupied by the Merchant seamen, and the upper by those from the Men of war. There are 14 Beds on each of the Floors for the seamen, and immediately above the building on a higher ground is a detached house large enough to accommodate 4 Officers. This seems comfortable enough and commands a more extensive view, but still surrounded by this unsavoury Ravine.

As this is the Head Quarters of the Southern division of the Pacific station, it would be much to the advantage of the service, if a building was taken or erected outside the town, and superintended by a Naval Surgeon, where it would not be in his interest to keep men longer than was actually required. A capital spot might be chosen somewhere between the Custom house and the Light House.

Valparaiso to Callao

After remaining in Valparaiso eleven days, during which time we took in 82 tons of Coals, and completed Provisions for 3 months, we lighted the fires on the morning of the 5th August, and steamed out of the Bay, as a Norther was commencing.

4. Precise identification of "the Canada" remains evasive. As Porcher placed a diacritical tilde over the "n" in Canada, it seems reasonable to surmise that "the Canada" was an informal local designation of Spanish for a narrow valley or glen, or perhaps a ravine or a small canyon.

Before we started a Merchant Brig was driven on shore near the Coal Wharf, and altho' some slight attempts were made to get her off, she went to pieces during the day. As soon as we got clear of the land, we lifted the screw and close reefed our sails as it came on to blow a Gale of wind from the N.W. This gradually veered round to the Westward during the Afternoon, and to the S.W. in the night, and in the next morning we had a moderate breeze from the S.E. which we kept for the remainder of the way.[5]

On the morning of the 14th August, 9 days after leaving Valparaiso, we steamed into Callao Bay, and anchored close to the [H.M.S.] *Leander* and [H.M.S.] *Shearwater*.[6] We found here a large squadron of different nations, consisting of a Spanish Admiral with 6 ships, one French, one Italian, an American Corvette, and 3 Peruvian Iron clads.[7]

Spanish Squadron Commanded by Admiral Parejia					
Villa de Madris	46	Guns (Flag ship)	800	H.P.	686 men
Revolucion	36		500		484
Blanca	36		360		409
Numancia	34	68 prs. Iron Clad	1000		650
Berenguela	28		350		393
Vencedora	3		160		180
French Frigate					
Pallas	38	Guns (Admiral)	600		600
Italian Frigate					
Principe Umberto	42		600		600
American Corvette					
St. Mary					
Peruvian					
Iron clad Frigate *Apurimac*		(Admiral)			
Iron clad Merrimac *Loa*	2	Guns			
Iron clad Monitor *Victoria*	1	(Cupola)			
Wooden paddle *Chilaco*	4				
Wooden screw *Leagundi*		Gun boat			
H.M.S. *Leander*	Commodore T. Harvey				
Shearwater	Commander Douglas				

5. An occasional notation is made, as during the Valparaiso to Callao passage, that the ship's company was issued soap and tobacco. Entry for 8 August 1865, Master's logbook, Adm. 53/9255.

6. Porcher's log, 275–276.

7. The *Sparrowhawk* arrived in Callao in a charged atmosphere. Ever interested in enhancing its prestige and perhaps gaining control over some of its former Latin American colonies, Spain moved a powerful fleet into Pacific waters in the 1860s. Spanish-Peruvian relations were strained. In early 1865, the Peruvian government had capitulated to Spanish demands. A few months after the *Sparrowhawk's* departure, a revolution established a new government which repudiated the settlement

I accompanied Commodore Harvey and Captain Acton of the Italian Frigate on board the Iron clad Frigate and Ram *Numancia* which was the first European vessel of her class that has ever floated on the waters of the Pacific, and it was considered a great feat navigating her through the Straits of Magellan. She was built in France, and her engines of 1000 horse power were also made in that country & were capable of driving the ship 13 knots an hour. She was coated throughout with 4½ inch iron, and had the name of being a bad sea-boat owing to her excessive rolling. A great defect seems to be in the manner in which her ports are cut, as they only allow the guns (68 Pounders) to be trained two or three points each way. They are also very low in the water, and has none on her upper deck, which is defended by two turrets, pierced for musketry.

The ship draws when complete with stores 31 feet of water, which would prevent her entering many good harbours. She has a top-gallant forecastle and poop: the former contains the sick bay, the latter the Captain's cabin, and offices.[8]

As our stay at the place was to be very short, I left Callao the day after we arrived for Lima with Dr. Comrie, to see as much of the place as possible. The buildings of the city can be seen in clear weather from the anchorage, and being only 7 miles distant by the railway, it only took us half an hour getting there. On arriving there we drove to the principal Hotel Maury where we engaged rooms.

The first thing that attracts a stranger's notice in this town as well as in Callao, are the great number of Vultures that are to be seen in the middle of all the streets as well as on the house tops, and are useful as being the only scavengers in the town. They are not allowed to be molested, and therefore roam about as tame as possible. At night the whole place is alive with watchmen that keep up such a continual whistling at the corners of all the streets, that I found out that it was impossible to get to sleep without shutting the windows.

The objects of most interest in this old Capital are certainly the Churches, as they were all richly ornamented and tastefully decorated, and the only European towns that were to be equal with them were Rome and Palermo. We took some time going over them the principal ones being the Cathedral in which is the tomb of the famous conqueror Pizarro, St. Pietro, St. Augustin and St. Domingo. As is generally the case with those that take so much trouble in the outward show of their religion, their morals are in an inverse ratio.

We also visited the Public Library in which there is a considerable number of old books and manuscripts, and the Museum which is in the same building. This contains many objects of Natural History, but they are badly preserved, and little trouble taken about the whole establishment.

---

with Spain, signed a defensive alliance with Bolivia, Ecuador, and Chile, and was soon at war with Spain. Robert L. Scheina, *Latin America: A Naval History, 1810–1987* (Annapolis, Maryland: Naval Institute Press, 1987), 29–31; David P. Werlich, *Peru: A Short History* (Carbondale and Edwardsville: Southern Illinois University Press, 1978), 90–91.

8. "Dressed ship in Commemoration of the birth of Napolean I" which was presumably prompted as a courtesy to the presence of a French frigate. Entry for 15 August 1865, Master's logbook, Adm. 53/9255.

We then went to see the Institution for the Industrial Arts which is in a large building and only lately been opened, and completed our tour by going over the Mint, which is at present managed by private Contract, and inspected their coining the new Peruvian Dollars, and afterwards lunched with the Manager, Mr. *[blank].*

After being at Lima a little more than a day, I was obliged to return to make preparations for our departure. I tasted there for the first time the Chirimoya and Granadilla the principal Peruvian fruits.

Callao to Honolulu

After stopping at Callao four days, we weighed on the morning of the 18th August, and steamed out of the Bay, and when clear of the land lifted the screw, and proceeded under sail with the S.E. trade which was very steady for the first 3000 miles, and set us rapidly along never making less than 100 miles during the 24 hours, and the longest run being 244 miles.

The Region of the Doldrums extended between the Latitudes 7.0 N and 9.43 N, and Longitudes 124.15 to 125.15 W, and during the whole of this distance extending over 200 miles, we had constant rain and oppressive weather, with variable winds principally from the Westward. We then experienced a second region of Variable winds that extended to Latitude 12. N and Longitude 131.30 W, when we got into the regular N.E. trade that lasted the remainder of the way. The difference between these two regions of Variable winds were that in the first the winds were very light and blowing continually from the Westward, whilst in the second the winds were stronger but frequently shifting from one beam to the other.

The Counter Equatorial Current extended from Latitude 4.0 N to 11.0 N, or about 420 miles. We first passed into it on the 3rd September at 2 PM, when we observed a ripple in the water that was strong enough to turn the ship's head round to the Westward two points against the helm, and the temperature of the water rose immediately 3½°, from 73° to 76½°, which increased the following day to 80½°, and afterwards to 83½°. On the 8th September being then in Latitude 9.40 N, we passed a line of foam extending from the NW to the SE, which seemed at first to have been the Northern limit of the Current, as the temperature of the water that had gone up to 83½° by the last observation, suddenly went down 2°.

The Counter current varied a little in its strength and direction, but principally set to the N.E. about 16 miles a day. For the 4 days before we entered it, we had been set to the Westward by a very strong Current, as shewn by the Log:

August	31st	N	9	W	32 miles
September	1st	N	77	W	30
	2nd	N	75	W	68
	3rd	N	54	W	80

Having passed into the Westerly current on the 12th September, we found that it set us daily to the W [by] S 24 miles, until we made the Sandwich Islands. After having been 35 days without seeing land or even a sail, we saw the first sign of life at 2 AM on the morning of the 22nd September, when we observed a large fire on the island of Mowee [Maui]. At day light we saw the islands distinctly the nearest part being the Eastern end of Moroloi [Molokai], 22 miles distant, and altered course to run between this island and Oahu with a strong breeze from the NE. At Noon we steamed ahead, and anchored in the safe harbour of Honolulu at 2.15 PM.

Honolulu stopover

ON ARRIVING WE FOUND THE PRINCIPAL people of the place away, the King Kamehameha V. being on a visit to the Neighbouring islands, and did not return until the morning of our departure, our Commissioner and Consul General Mr. W. W. F. Synge having left for England with Ex-Queen Emma, and the English Bishop the Rev. T. N. Staley D.D. was in the United States attending a Convention of the American Bishops. Mr. Green of the firm of Janion, Green, and Co. was doing the duty of Consul pro tem.[9]

The N.E trade wind blows over the Sandwich Islands about 9 months of the year, from March to November, and during the winter the South and West winds prevail and bring a great quantity of rain. These months are generally stormy, and during them it is unsafe to anchor in the roads. When the trade wind prevails vessels should approach the islands and run along to the Northward of Hawaii, Maui, and Molokai, about 15 to 20 miles distant, and passing through the channel between Molokai and Oahu, and run along the shore from Coco Head (the most Eastern part of Oahu) to Diamond Head, keeping the shore 2 or 3 miles distant. There are 2 Pilots belonging to the place, and a steam tug is always in readiness to tow vessels in and out of the harbour. The charges for the Pilotage is a dollar a foot, the Harbour master's fee is six dollars for doing nothing, and the use of the Tug is 50$. A water Tank supplies vessels at 2 Dollars a ton, but water can be obtained for a dollar a ton by sending a boat alongside the jetty where pipes are led into the boat.

The price of Coals when we were there were $19½ a ton delivered alongside, but no doubt would be cheaper if there were more demand for them.

The harbour is a deep basin in the coral reef, through which the fresh water from the Nuuanu stream reaches the sea, capable of accommodating 180 vessels in its present unimproved state. The depth of water varies from 4 to 6½ fathoms, and the bottom is deep, stiff mud, the best of holding ground, and vessels at anchor in the harbour are perfectly secure at all seasons of the year. In the strongest southerly gales when the wind is directly in from the sea, the harbour is well protected by the reef outside of it. About one third of the basin at the north end is filled with mud, a

9. Kamehameha V had become king in 1863. The following year he abrogated the constitution and arbitrarily replaced it with another. Dowager Queen Emma and her late husband Kamehameha IV had hoped to visit England. In 1865, at the urging of her close friends Church of England Bishop of Honolulu Thomas Nettleship Staley and Hawaiian Minister of Foreign Affairs Robert Crichton Wyllie, Queen Emma, accompanied by British Commissioner to Hawaii William W. F. Synge, sailed for England. The tour held implications for the Church of England, Queen Emma's emotional recuperation, as well as matters of state. Bishop Staley was seeking the cooperation of the American Episcopalians to strengthen the church in Hawaii which enjoyed the patronage of King Kamehameha V and other members of the royal family. William L. Green's company was prominent in Hawaiian shipping circles. King Kamehameha V's abrogation of Hawaii's constitution in 1864, and his arbitrary replacing it with another, had added an interesting dimension to the geopolitical concerns particularly of England and the United States. Ralph S. Kuykendall, *The Hawaiian Kingdom*, 3 vols. (Honolulu: University of Hawaii Press, 1947–1967), 2:94, 96–98, 164–165, 201–206, et passim.

deposit from the Nuuanu Valley stream which could be converted into a harbour for ships by dredging. The channel which includes the outer harbour, is about a mile in length, narrow and rather tortuous. The depth of water on the bar is 21½ feet, at low tide, which rises and falls about 2 feet. There are several good wharves, at which vessels of 1500 tons can discharge or take in cargo.

The site of Honolulu is good, rising gradually from the sea to an elevation of about 20 feet, and the country houses at the back, rising at a higher elevation up the Nuuanu Valley. The ground is volcanic soil, with a coral rock basis, a good foundation for building. A steamer runs to the other islands at stated times, and supplies of all kinds can be obtained at reasonable rates. The population is somewhat fluctuating; during the winter season it is as high as 10. or 12.000 caused by the influx of seamen and natives from the other islands of the group, and at other seasons of the year it may be as low as 7 or 8000. There are 6 Church Edifices, some of them substantial specimens of architecture.

During the time we remained here, I saw a great deal of the country within 6 miles of the town but had not time to go further. The best rides were to the Pali or Precipice at the end of the Nuuanu Valley where there is a magnificent view over the Northern side of the island, and will ever remain famous for being the spot where the great Kamehameha [I] routed the inhabitants of this island, and was the final victory that caused the consolidation of the whole of the islands under the same government.

Another favourite ride was to the village of Waikiki in the direction of Diamond Point where there is a very fine grove of Cocoa nut trees. I paid a visit to Mr. R. C. Wyllie the Minister for Foreign Affairs, and has been the King's principal adviser for the last 20 years. He was then dangerously ill, and not expected to live long, but quite in his senses when I saw him. A short time after we arrived at Vancouver's Island, I heard of his death, which will no doubt make a great change in the policy of these islands. I also met here an old friend and schoolfellow Commander T. B. Hanham Ret. who had been cruising about in his yacht *Themis* amongst these islands for the last 8 months. She was an iron vessel of 160 Tons, and well fitted for cruizing about in the Pacific.[10]

North Pacific navigation

After spending 8 days very pleasantly here, we left at 10 am on the 30th September for Vancouver's Island, after taking leave of Mr. Green the Acting Consul, and Messrs. Prendergast and Severance the Merchants that had supplied the ship & messes.

The distance to Vancouver's Island was 2400 miles, and we took 28 days in getting there, as we had variable winds and calms the greater part of the way.

10. An occasional notation is made, as during the stay in Honolulu, that the ship's company went ashore for church services. Sometimes the number of Roman Catholics is noted. Entries for 24 September 1865, Master's logbook, Adm. 53/9255; for 7 April 1867, Master's logbook, Adm. 53/9256. Sometimes the Master "Performed Divine Service" aboard ship. Entry for 25 March 1866, Master's logbook, Adm. 53/9255.

After leaving the Sandwich Islands we had a moderate breeze from the ESE for the first two days which took us into Latitude 25.0 N, the wind then became lighter and drew gradually to the Northward until we arrived in Lat 29.N, when it died away altogether. We steamed for 12 hours to get out of the Region of the Calms of Cancer, and for the remainder of the way to Vancouver's Island had variable winds, storm and sunshine alternately.

The winds in the strait of Juan de Fuca, Vancouver Island, have been very clearly described in the sailing directions, and therefore little need be said on that immediate locality, but as the winds differ a little a thousand miles off the coast it might be worth while saying a few words upon our experience of them in the *Sparrowhawk*.

We passed this way from the Sandwich Islands about the middle of October, being then about the change of the seasons, and we experienced some of the severe S.E. gales that are said to be so prevalent there.

At Noon on the 13th October, we had a moderate breeze from the N.W with fine weather, and the Barometer shewed 30.01, it then began to fall very gradually for the next 24 hours, when the wind that had died away for 10 hours, sprung up from the S.E which freshened before the evening. About 8 PM of the 14th inst. it began to blow very hard which obliged us to reduce the canvas to close reefed Topsails, reefed Foresail, and Inner Jib, and the weather became gloomy and squally with rain, which continued as long as the wind remained in that quarter. The Barometer continued to fall till 5 AM of the 15th inst, when it was 29.30, and it became nearly stationary for the next 12 hours. The wind blew very hard all the 15th inst, and without any warning shifted after Sunset to the S.W. when it became very light and died away during the night.

About 7 AM of the 16th inst, the S.E wind again re-commenced and before 9 was blowing a Gale with the same kind of disagre[e]able misty weather, which lasted again to the same time of the Evening, when it shifted suddenly to the S.W. and afterwards to the WNW. Nearly the whole time we were running before these S.E gales, we had the same sail set, that set us on 10 knots an hour.

As soon as the wind shifted the last time, the Barometer immediately began to rise and continued to do so during the night. The first S.E. gale lasted about 24 hours, the second only 10. About Vancouver's Island it is said when the wind shifts from the S.E to the S.W., which it invariably does, it blows heavily from the latter direction, by our few day's experience it always died away.

We made the land of Vancouver's Island shortly before Midnight of the 26th inst., and when we stood in for it the next morning under steam, we found that we had been set to the N.W 43 miles, which obliged us to steam the whole of that day and the next night, before we made Esquimalt Harbour.

Here we anchored at 6.45 AM on the 28th October,[11] and found the Admiral Hon. Joseph Denman, with the *Sutlej, Devastation, Clio, Forward*, and the U.S.S. *Suwanee* at anchor.

---

11. The arrival of the *Sparrowhawk*, a roster of its officers, and a description of the "handsome screw vessel" were reported in the local press. "Arrival of H.M.S. *Sparrowhawk*," *Daily British Colonist*, 30 October 1865.

Abstract of Passages

April 1st	Left Plymouth & arrived at Madeira in	9 ¼	days
	Remained at Madeira	2	
12th	Left Madeira, & arrived at Rio de Janeiro	31	
	Remained at Rio de Janeiro	10	
May 23rd	Left Rio & arrived at the Falkland Islands	24 ¼	
	Remained at the Falkland Islands	5	
June 21st	Left Falkland & arrived in Straits of Magellan	6 ¼	
	Running thro' Straits & Smyth's Channel	13	
July 10th	From the Gulf of Penas to Valparaiso	14 ¼	
	Remained at Valparaiso	11 ½	
August 5th	Left Valparaiso & arrived at Callao	9	
	Remained at Callao	4	
18th	Left Callao & arrived at Honolulu S.I.	35	
	Remained at Honolulu	8	
September 30th	Left Honolulu & arrived at Vancouver's Island	28	
	Total	**210 ½**	**days**
	At anchor in the different harbours	41 ½	
	Actually at Sea 5 months & 19 days or	**169**	**days**

Distances run, England to Vancouver Island

Date	Steam	Steam & Sail	Sail only	Total
March	115			115
April	551	207	2736	3494
May	41		2545	2586
June	233		2478	2711
July	579	53	1142	1774
August	41		3343	3384
September	36	58	2776	2870
October	208		2846	3054
	1804	**318**	**17866**	**19988**

Chapter Three

Routine and a Northern Tour

6 November 1865–30 May 1866

[In his first several months in the Pacific Northwest, Edmund Porcher was involved in the responsibilities and pleasures peculiar to this area, as well as normal and routine duties of a Royal Navy ship. On occasion, the *Sparrowhawk* and other of Her Majesty's ships were involved in dispensing justice amongst the coastal Indians. Sometimes the very presence of these vessels was adequate to quiet a troublesome situation. In May 1866, H.M.S. *Sparrowhawk* went on a month-long cruise to a Tsimshian Indian mission at Metlakatla and nearby Fort Simpson, a short distance to the south of the Alaska boundary, returning to Esquimalt by way of the Queen Charlotte Islands. The cruise served both missionary and police functions.]

Policing Euclataw Indians

After lying at Esquimalt Harbour for 9 days,[1] we left on the 6th November in company with the *Sutlej* and *Clio* for Comox or Port Augusta, where we arrived the next morning at 9.30 AM. The object of our coming here with such a strong force was that a request had been sent to the Governor[2] to have a troublesome tribe called the Euclataws sent back to their place of residence near Cape Mudge, as they had been robbing the settlers of their potatoes, burning their palings, &c.[3] There being a great difference of opinion amongst the settlers about this tribe, the Admiral was determined to have a meeting or War-war,[4] and invited those in the vicinity to be present on the following day, in order to hear what they had to say. The spot chosen was Mr. Cave's house, situated about 3 miles up the Courtenay river, and in a central position. There I proceeded the day after we arrived, with Mr. Philip I. Hawkins (the Superintendent of Police & Governor of the Gaol at Victoria) and Dr. Comrie, to arrange that all the settlers should be there by 11 AM, as well as to pick up other information.

At the time appointed, it was blowing a Gale of wind with continued rain, so that the meeting was put off till the following day (10th November), when everybody was assembled at the appointed time. In consequence of the heavy rain the river was swollen so much, that there was a great deal of trouble getting the canoe up against the strong current, and part of the way over the flooded prairie land, that we did not arrive at Mr. Cave's house before 1 PM.[5] Here we found many of the Settlers assembled, and after Luncheon had the War-war in the Chapel attached to the house. As we

---

1. On 31 October Porcher had left the ship for 3½ hours "to attend Court Martial." This was the first mention by the Master of Porcher's leaving the *Sparrowhawk* since it had left England. Entry for 31 October 1865, Master's logbook, Adm. 53/9255.

2. Arthur Edward Kennedy succeeded James Douglas and served as governor of Vancouver Island, 1864–1866. *Dictionary of Canadian Biography*, vol. 11, s.v. "Kennedy, Sir Arthur Edward," by Robert L. Smith; Robert L. Smith, "The Kennedy Interlude, 1864–66," *BC Studies* 47 (Autumn 1980): 66–78.

3. The Euclataw (Yuculta), presently known as the Lekwiltok, spoke a subdialect of the Kwakiutl. Among whites they seemed "a fierce race" and were reputed to be "the worst Indians." John R. Swanton, *The Indian Tribes of North America*, Bureau of American Ethnology, Bulletin 145 (Washington: Government Printing Office, 1952), 575–577; Gough, *Gunboat Frontier*, 130–137; Helen Codere, "Kwakiutl: Traditional Culture," in William C. Sturtevant, ed. *Handbook of North American Indians*, vol. 7, *Northwest Coast*, edited by Wayne Suttles (Washington: Smithsonian Institution, 1990), 359–377.

Editorial conjecture hoped that "The appearance of the fleet at the settlement ought to be sufficient to strike awe into the minds of the disaffected red skins." "Naval," *Daily British Colonist*, 7 November 1865.

4. What Porcher heard and wrote here was probably "wawa" or "wau-wau," Chinook jargon for talk or conversation. Chinook jargon was the trade language or lingua franca used over much of the Pacific Northwest. As it was essentially a spoken language, written spelling sometimes varied widely. George C. Shaw, *The Chinook Jargon and How to Use It: A Complete and Exhaustive Lexicon of the Oldest Trade Language of the American Continent* (Seattle: Rainier Printing Company, 1909); Robie L. Reid, "The Chinook Jargon and British Columbia," *British Columbia Historical Quarterly* 6 (January 1942): 5; Laurence C. Thompson and M. Dale Kinkade, "Languages," in William C. Sturtevant, ed., *Handbook of North American Indians*, vol. 7: Wayne Suttles, ed., *Northwest Coast* (Washington: Smithsonian Institution, 1990), 41.

5. The Master noted tersely: "Supplied Indians with Biscuit." Entry for 10 November 1865, Master's logbook, Adm. 53/9255.

expected they were very much divided in their opinions about the propriety of sending the Euclataws away, as the majority said they were very useful in creating a little competition with the Comox tribe, and keeping the prices down, and would suffer if they were sent away, and that the robbery that had happened was very trifling, and it had never been proved which was the guilty tribe.

The Admiral was determined to send the Tribe away, as it was the Governor's wish, but as there were 19 Settlers in favour of the tribe remaining against 11, he said they might return in the early part of the year. Before the Admiral left on the 13th inst. we had a meeting of the Euclataws on board the *Sutlej* to tell them they must go away, but that they might return soon. Their principal Chief Claylick was present, and promised that he would use his influence in getting the tribe away that day. This man had been captured and kept in irons nearly the whole time we had been there, and had been previously nearly frightened to death by the Midshipman, who had explained to him in an unmistakable manner that he was going to be hung, but he was now rewarded with presents, and given a paper to say that he had lately behaved well, and the Governor would be asked to make him a Policeman. Thus ended our warlike expedition against the Euclataws who were supposed to be the most troublesome tribe in the whole island, and the same day the Admiral with the squadron left the harbour on their return to Esquimalt.[6]

Cowichan Bay visit

On our way back we parted company with the Admiral in the Active Pass, and proceeded to Snug Creek in Cowichan Bay where we anchored on the afternoon of the 14th November. We remained here nearly 4 days,[7] during which time I had an opportunity of seeing a little of the country and several of the settlers. On the 15th inst. I and Dr. Comrie were accompanied by Mr. Moore (the only Sheep keeper in the place) to Mr. Skinner's who resided about 3 miles from the landing place higher up the river. About half way there, we visited a Convent situated in a picturesque and well sheltered spot, and seemed to be well built with an Upper floor, and looked after by 2 Sisters of Charity (an Irish woman and the other a French Canadian) who have undertaken to instruct some of the Indian girls, but it seems up to the present time with little success. We found on arriving at Mr. Skinner's that a *Bee* was going on, which consists in all the settlers in the neighbourhood assembling to assist in raising the heavy logs of wood to join the walls of the building, and set them in their places, which kind office they always perform for each other, as the Indians are totally unfit for such work. Mr. S[kinner] was formerly the Beef contractor for the Navy and lived at Esquimalt, but has lately removed to this place to commence another farm. He has chosen a very pretty spot, on a rising and cleared ground near a lake. We arrived just in time for their substantial dinner and remained for some hours afterwards.

6. "A Constable & 5 Indians came on board [the *Sparrowhawk* at 9:00 AM] for passage to Cape Mudge and left the ship off Campbell River at 3.50 P.M." Entry for 11 November 1865, Master's logbook, Adm. 53/9255.

7. The *Sparrowhawk* had apparently originally been scheduled to remain at Cowichan for the rest of November. "Naval," *Daily British Colonist*, 15 November 1865.

Checking Euclataw compliance

On the 16th inst. the Bishop of Columbia[8] arrived from Victoria in the Hudson's Bay Company steamer *Otter*, and brought me an order from the Admiral to take him to Comox and Cape Mudge, after he had made some arrangement with the Settlers here about assisting in having a Church built in the vicinity.

We left Cowichan at daylight of the 18th November, and arrived at Nanaimo at 4.15 pm, having had a strong breeze against us directly we cleared the Active Pass.

Here we remained for the Sunday which was a rainy day, and started on the 20th inst. for Comox where we arrived in the middle of the day. Our object of visiting this place again was to see if Claylick and the Euclataws had left the settlement according to their promise, and after visiting Mr. Cave and seeing several of the settlers we were led to believe that part of the tribe had left for the Northward, but several were still here working for the settlers. During our short stay here it was raining incessantly and blowing a Gale of wind, which did not prevent my accompanying the Bishop up the river in a canoe, altho we were nearly drenched to the skin. The weather having cleared up a little, we left Comox at daylight of the 22nd inst. and anchored in Gowlland Harbour before Noon. This is a well sheltered spot, and I found out afterwards, at sea, the first time a man of war had ever anchored here. In the afternoon I left with the Bishop and Dr. Comrie to ascend the Campbell river which is situated on the opposite side of the Straits, and which we did with great difficulty on account of the very strong current.

On arriving at a hut about half a mile from the mouth, we found a few of the women, but not a man was to be seen, and from what we could learn, the latter were all away some distance to the Northward. In the hut we found a tame Racoon and a Goose, and was then a few Deer that had been lately killed, which shewed that the men were not very far off. We left Gowlland Harbour the next morning (23rd November), and landed at the Euclataw village near Cape Mudge for a short time. This had been destroyed some time previously by the *Forward*, and there was no sign of any person having been here for some time. Several remains were left, such as Carved heads nailed on the transverse beams, a part of a vessel, squared pieces of timber, a 32 Pd shot, old boots, &c. In the Afternoon it came on to blow a Gale of wind from the S.E which freshened so much during the First watch, that we were obliged to get the steam up in the 3rd Boiler to give her steerage way. The next day (24th inst), we steamed ahead with the 3 Boilers making between 9 and 10 knots, and arrived at Esquimalt at 8 pm, having run since daylight 126 miles.[9]

---

8. George Hills served as the first Church of England Bishop of Columbia, 1859–1892. Son of an admiral of the Royal Navy, he maintained close official and social ties with the Esquimalt-based personnel. For a convenient biographical sketch, see *Dictionary of Canadian Biography*, vol. 12, s.v. "Hills, George," by Jean Friesen.

9. The account of the return of the *Sparrowhawk* that appeared in the press gives more detail of the mission than Porcher included in his record: "One of the murderers of the crew of the schooner Thorndyke had been arrested by two native constables belonging to Comox, and lodged in jail at Nanaimo. The Sparrowhawk went up as far as Cape Mudge, where her appearance seemed to cause considerable consternation among the Indians, and it is hoped that her visit will have the effect of preventing any further outbreak among the tribes in that vicinity."

The account goes on to editorialize: "The authorities are certainly to be commended for the alacrity with which steps are taken now-a-days to quell disturbances occurring among the natives on the

Anchors and cables

Found the *Sutlej, Forward*, and *Tribune* here,[10] the latter vessel having lost two anchors and cables a few days previously in Port San Juan. For the next 14 days we remained at Esquimalt, being the longest time we had stopped in one place since leaving England on the 1st April, or nearly 9 months. On the 8th December at 9 pm, we steamed out of the harbour for Port San Juan, having on board Mr. Bond (Master) and the Launch of the *Tribune* in tow, to endeavor to find the two anchors & cables that they had lately parted, and buoy them.[11]

Having a Westerly breeze against us the whole day, we did not arrive until Noon the next day, when we anchored close to one of the Brigs that we found watching. All that Afternoon and the next morning we were employed creeping for the cables but without success, and at Noon of the next day the *Tribune* arrived and anchored close to us. Three of her Boats and one of ours were employed creeping for the cables that afternoon and the whole of the next day, and altho' they hit upon them several times, the hawsers always slipped off when a strain was put upon them. As Lord Guilford did not think it prudent remaining in that exposed harbour any longer with her leaky Boilers, she weighed at 6 pm on the 11th December, and started for Valparaiso on her way to England. We also left at the same time for Esquimalt where we arrived the next morning at 6.15 am,[12] the thermometer during the night being down to 21°. On arriving we commenced taking in 100 Tons of Coals in order to proceed to San Francisco with the Admiral's Flag Lieutenant Sir Lambton Lor[r]aine, who was ordered to England with despatches about the Spaniards declaring war against Chile.[13]

San Francisco and return

We left at 6.30 pm on the 13th December, and arrived at San Francisco at 4.30 pm of the 17th inst. having made the passage in a little less than 4 days, the distance being 770 miles.

For the first part of the way we had Calms and light winds, and the latter a strong breeze from the Northward which set the ship on 9 knots under sail alone. The morning after arriving I landed at the Broadway Island to see the Consul Mr. Bowker, and also called on Mr. G. W. Brooks an American merchant and Owner of a line of Sailing Packets between this and the Sandwich Islands. I paid an official visit to

coast, and to bring wrong-doers to justice. Such a course will have the effect of impressing the red skins more than anything else that could be devised, with a salutary belief in the firmness and power of those who rule over them, will render the life of the white man more secure in this distant abode, and in the end be more humane to the untutored savage himself." "Return of the Sparrowhawk," *Daily British Colonist*, 25 November 1865. Bishop George Hills gives a full account of his activities and observations on this assignment, especially concerning the mission at Comox, in "1865 and 1866," 21–25.

10. The *Sparrowhawk* expected to winter at Esquimalt. "Naval," *Daily British Colonist*, 2 December 1865.

11. The anchors had been lost in a gale. "Naval," *Daily British Colonist*, 11 December 1865. The search was unsuccessful. "Naval," *Daily British Colonist*, 13 December 1865.

12. "Naval," *Daily British Colonist*, 13 December 1865.

13. The *Sparrowhawk* was also carrying the mails. "Mail," *Daily British Colonist*, 13 December 1865; "Naval," *Daily British Colonist*, 14 December 1865.

Major General H. W. Halleck, the Commander in Chief of the Army of the Pacific, and lately Secretary for War at Washington,[14] and afterwards went with Lor[r]aine to see Major General I. McDowell who had commanded the Federal Force at Bull Run. This latter Officer was more friendly, and talked of his late visit to Victoria with much pleasure.

The price of Nanaimo Coals at San Francisco was $13 or £2.12.0, $6 being the original price at the place, $5 for Freight, and $2 for the expenses here.

We left San Francisco at 2.30 PM of the 18th December on our return to Victoria with a light breeze from the N.W. and when clear of Point Reyes stopped the Engines and drew the fires. Sir L. Lor[r]aine was going to leave the next day 19th inst by the regular Mail steamer.

During the 6 days we took in returning, we had a great deal of blowy and squally weather principally from the S.W. which split nearly all our sails. We were twice drifted in rather too close to the shore, the first time being at daylight when we observed Cape Blanco and its outlying Rocks about 5 miles distant, and there being little wind at the time we loosened the screw and got the steam up, and proceeded under steam & sail for the remainder of the day, and the second time we made the land in the middle watch near Destruction Island & about 45 miles to the Southward of Cape Flattery, being foggy weather & raining at the time, but being under sail & steam, we tacked and stood off the shore until daylight. We arrived in Esquimalt Harbour at 8.30 PM. on the 24th December (Christmas Eve).[15]

Witness and prisoners

IN CONSEQUENCE OF THE *Clio* having made a mistake in bringing down to Victoria, a Whiskey seller of the name of Frank an Italian, to give evidence on murderers of the crew of the *Thorndyke* instead of his first being sent over to New Westminster to be tried on the charge of Whiskey selling,[16] we were ordered to take him on board late on Sunday night the 31st December, and leave the harbour, so to prevent a writ of Habeas Corpus being taken out on his behalf. We left at 10.20 PM, and being Full Wind, steamed all night, passing through the Active Pass at 4 AM, and anchored in

---

14. Henry W. Halleck was General in Chief, United States Armies, 1862–1864, and Chief of Staff, 1864–1865. He did not serve as Secretary of War. *Register of Graduates and Former Cadets of the United States Military Academy*, Cullum Memorial Edition (West Point, N.Y.: West Point Alumni Foundation, 1970), 230.

15. "Arrival of HMS Sparrowhawk," *Daily British Colonist*, 25 December 1865.

16. By the turn of the century, unscrupulous individual traders had introduced whisky and guns to the Indians. The impact on Indians and Indian-white relations, as well as the consequence to imperial control over the Pacific Northwest, were of great concern. Despite increasing legislative regulation and prohibition, and encouraged by bootlegging and the proximity of Alaska and American havens of safety, the trade and its debilitating consequences persisted. Means of enforcement were simply inadequate. Royal naval gunboats became increasingly involved in policing this activity. The psychological effect of gunboat presence became an important aspect of enforcement efforts as well. Gough, *Gunboat Frontier*, 13–16, 88–94, 219–223.

Burrard Inlet near the *Forward* at 10.55 AM on New Year's Day, which vessel had also a number of prisoners on board for New Westminster.[17]

On landing for the purpose of walking up by the trail from Port Moody, we had not gone many yards when we found that the shore was so deep that it was impossible to proceed that way, we therefore returned and sent the prisoners on board the *Forward*,[18] which left in the afternoon to anchor off another Trail below the 2nd Narrows, by which Lieut. Fox and the Prisoners managed to get up by. The next morning (January 2nd) we left Burrard Inlet at 7.30 AM and arrived at Nanaimo in 5¾ hours. Here we took in 106 Tons of Coals which at $7, cost £152.19.10. By going alongside the Wharf where vessels can go in fine weather with every facility, and where there is 22 feet of water, the price is reduced to $6.65, the difference being for the use of lighters.

During the time I was there, I inspected the Coal mine with our Chief Engineer Mr. Dearden.[19] After putting on an old Coat and hat, we went down the Shaft that was 110 feet deep with Mr. Bryden the Overseer. An Engine and Boiler were placed on the bottom near the Shaft to draw the Skiffs backward and forward along the rails in the Main tunnel. About 160 Tons could be sent down to the Wharf in the day. The average thickness of the seam is 4½ feet, and the dip about 22° in a S.E direction, and the shaft is sunk about half a mile from the Wharf. During the time I was in the mine, witnessed an explosion caused by ½ lb. of powder, which broke away between 2 or 3 Tons of Coals.

Left Nanaimo on January 5th, and arrived at Esquimalt at 5.15 PM, in 9¾ hours, having had calm, good & fair winds. The *Sir James Douglas* (Colonial steamer) left Nanaimo half an hour before us, and proceeded through the shorter route by Dodd's Narrows, but could not make any weigh against the strong Southerly breeze in the afternoon, and was obliged to put back & anchor under the lee of one of the islands.[20]

---

17. The Master recorded merely: "Recd a prisoner from 'Clio' for passage to Burrard Inlet." And "Sent prisoner to *Forward*." Entries for 31 December 1865 and 1 January 1866, Master's logbook, Adm. 53/9255.

"Frank" had already been sentenced for whisky trading and was brought down as a prisoner to appeal his case. He was a witness against the *Thorndyke* murder. This and other details of the incident were reported as "From the North. Cruise of the Clio. Capture of Whiskey Sellers and Murderers. Indian Ranch destroyed," *Daily British Colonist*, 29 December 1865. A fuller account was printed as "The Cruise of the Clio. Highly Interesting Diary," *Daily British Colonist*, 5 January 1866, 6 January 1866. See also, "The Northern Whiskey Traffic," *Daily British Colonist*, 27 November 1865.

18. "The Sparrowhawk was instructed to convey certain prisoners to New Westminster, but was unable to reach her destination." "From Nanaimo," *Daily British Colonist*, 6 January 1866.

19. John Dearden. *Navy List* (April 1865): 208.

20. In the interim between the arrival at Esquimalt and the next reported departure on 27 February, typically, the ship's personnel were engaged in routine duties such as repairing, painting, cleaning, carpentry, and taking on provisions, while the *Sparrowhawk* was at anchor in Esquimalt harbor. The routine was modified in this instance by sending a party ashore to attend a funeral, giving shore leave to the starboard watch, and "depriving" three of the personnel of a badge under the Articles of War and Warrants. Entries for 6 January–27 February 1866, Master's logbook, Adm. 53/9255.

Paying the marines

On the 27th February we steamed out of Esquimalt Harbour at 8 am. for Roche Harbour, San Juan [Island],[21] where we arrived in 3½ hours, for the purpose of paying the Marines their monthly wages to explode some of our Quarterly ammunition, and to cut a few trees down to build a boat shed with.

On landing at the English Camp for the first time, I inspected the Quarters, Hospital, &c at present occupied by 48 Marines, including the Officers (Captain Bazalgette, Lieut Cooper and Spanshott, and Dr. Hawbury.) Our Camp is built at the North end of the island in a perfectly landlocked bay, but is so shallow there is only sufficient water for a small Gun boat. It is pleasantly situated at the foot of a woody range of hills, and a better spot could not have been chosen. The American Camp with about the same number of men has been built at the Southern end of the island, on an open spot.[22]

Farms are scattered about all over the island, and I rode out with Spanshott to see some of them, and a Beaver's pond and Dam which was the first I had ever seen.

During our stay, the seine was hauled in the different Bays round the Camp, and enough fish were caught in a few hauls to fill half a cask, consisting of herrings, smelt, Pla[i]ce, and a few Salmon.

After remaining in Roche Harbour 2 whole days, we returned to Esquimalt on the 2nd March.[23]

Pursuing deserters

On the morning of the 7th March, I was informed that Edward Clayson (Gunner's Mate), and Alfred Brunner (Fiddler) had deserted in the Dingy during the night. We immediately made preparations for sea, and at 7.45 am. steamed out of Esquimalt for the Race Lt. House and Port Angeles. On anchoring off the latter place I called on Mr. Wilson the collector of Customs, to tell him the object of my visit, and had not been on shore more than half an hour, when I was informed that the Dingy had landed outside the Spit as we were coming round the Light house, but were obliged to pay $20 to a man called Joaquin who had seized the boat as the

---

21. The newspaper reported that the *Sparrowhawk* was to go to Nanaimo and Comox. "H.M.S. Sparrowhawk," *Daily British Colonist*, 27 February 1866.

22. The Oregon Treaty of 1846 defined the international boundary in the Pacific Northwest on the mainland as the 49th parallel. From thence it followed the channel separating Vancouver Island from the mainland to Juan de Fuca Strait and through the strait to the Pacific Ocean. The treaty did not define the channel between Vancouver Island and the mainland so both parties claimed the strategic San Juan archipelago. The matter was not settled until 1873.

The dispute festered with the gold rush to the Fraser River in the late 1850s. For the argonauts, San Juan Island was astride their route from Victoria to the mainland. This tended to emphasize the strategic value to both claimants. The deterioration of Anglo-American relations was resolved somewhat by an 1859 agreement of joint military occupation of the island. The "American Camp" was established at Griffin Bay at the south end of the island and the "English Camp" ten miles to the north at Garrison Bay.

Samuel Flagg Bemis, *A Diplomatic History of the United States, 4th ed.* (New York: Henry Holt and Company, 1955), 281–283; Gough, *Royal Navy and the Northwest Coast*, 150–165; John W. Long Jr., "The Origin and Development of the San Juan Water Boundary Controversy," *Pacific Northwest Quarterly* 43 (July 1952): 187–213.

23. They had "exercised firing at a mark" on the return trip. Porcher's log, 285–286.

men landed, before he would deliver her up.[24] The Deserters immediately took to the bush, but an American volunteered to capture them, and bring them alongside before 10 o'clock that night, for the sum of $50, but we did not see or hear any thing more of them. We remained till the following morning, when I left the description of the men with Mr. Wilson, and a list of the clothing and other articles they had stolen, and on the arrival of the *Eliza Anderson* from Victoria I saw Mr. Holmes the United States Attorney, and was informed that Joaquin had no right to claim salvage for our boat.

We left Port Angeles at 8.45 AM. and arrived at Esquimalt in 2¼ hours. On the 20th March I received a letter from Mr.Geo.F. Whitworth, the Deputy Collector of Customs at Port Angeles to say that he had seized a great many of the clothes that had been stolen by our 2 Deserters at Mr. Sacquenan's house. We therefore went over there again on the 26th inst. where we arrived at 8 AM in 2½ hours, and on landing the clothes were delivered up without any charge. It seems that the men did not approve of the clothes being taken from them, and said they were their own property, but Mr. Wilson very rightly said that he knew some of them were stolen, and as he did not know which they were, he would keep the whole of them. We returned to Esquimalt the same morning[25] and gave Mr. Wilson the Collector of Customs a passage, who was going to San Francisco on the following day. At Port Angeles we saw an English barque, the *Saint John* of New Brunswick at anchor in the harbour, that had 4 Deserters from the *Clio* on board.

Before concluding the account of these 2 Deserters, it will be interesting to know that Clayson took the opportunity of leaving the ship about 1 AM, when had charge of the Watch. The promise of higher wages on the American Territory seems to be the principal attraction, and as it is a great question if the men are ever benefitted by it, I will give this man's reasons, which he left in writing before he left the wheel.

Sparrowhawk.
March 5th
Esquimalt

Sir,

I have written these few lines to inform you that I am not leaving this Ship through any discontent on the part of the ship, but there are such temptations here for a young man that I cannot resist them any longer, although I thank you very kindly for the advice you gave me on the subject some time ago, but persuade a man against his will—he's of the same opinion still. I am sorry to find it necessary to take a few things that do not belong to me, as for the boat I shall take, I shall try my best to send it back.

E. Clayson

To Mr. Dolphin[26]

---

24. A lieutenant had been dispatched in a "Whaler" to recover the dingy. Entry for 7 March 1866, Master's logbook, Adm. 53/9255. See also "Naval," *Daily British Colonist*, 8 March 1866; "Naval," *Daily British Colonist*, 9 March 1866.

25. The *Sparrowhawk's* return was noted in the press. "Naval," *Daily British Colonist*, 27 March 1866.

26. Herbert Dolphin served as Lieutenant on the Sparrowhawk. *Navy List* (April 1865): 208.

It seems that these 2 men remained a few days at Port Angeles, and then went on to Port Townshend where they endeavored to get a few Dollars in Fiddling, and afterwards settled down at Port Gamble a few miles further down the Sound. I afterwards met Brunner in the month of October on the Pier at Port Townshend when I was there in the *Enterprise*, and he then told one of the Servants that he was getting $50 a month as a Cook and Fiddler at Port Gamble, and Clayson was receiving $60 for working on a Farm at the same place.

Escorting the governor

As Governor Kennedy wished to pay an Official as well as a private visit to Mr. Birch at New Westminster,[27] he came on board with his family and Miss Needham, at 8 AM on the 5th April, when we steamed out of the harbour.

At 2 PM we anchored off the Light vessel [lightship] at the Sand Head in 19 fathoms, till we saw the *Leviathan* coming down the river when we weighed to meet here, but on Captain Cooper the Harbour Master coming on board, he told us the water was too low for us and would be for the next hour, so we anchored again further in, in 4 fathoms. We weighed again at 3 PM as the tide was rising, but foundered several times as there was not more than 9 feet in some places, and did not succeed in getting over the Bar till 4, when we proceeded up the river at full speed, and touched the ground in going round the Sea Reach, but which did not stop our weigh, and anchored near the Government House at 7 PM, as it was getting quite dark with drizzling rain. The *Leviathan* came alongside and took the Kennedy's on shore.

We remained here 5 days, during which it rained most of the time, but between two Balls, divers parties and other amusements during the day, the time passed very pleasantly.[28] The Government House is very well situated near the banks of the river, about a mile above New Westminster. It was built by Colonel Moody[29] as his residence during the time he commanded the Royal Engineers in this country, but has been considerably added to since. The Sappers had their barracks not far from it, as well as the Officers Quarters, and was called the Camp which it has retained ever since.

Two ford roads connect the town with the Camp, one runs along the banks of the river, and the other parallel to it on a higher level, there join together in the town, and go as far as the Saw Mills at the lower end of the whole settlement. Two roads or

---

27. Arthur Nonus Birch was Colonial Secretary to Frederick Seymour who served as governor of British Columbia, 1864–1867. In Seymour's absence from the colony, 1865–1866, Birch was acting governor. On this occasion, he had invited Vancouver Island Governor Arthur Kennedy to a ball at Government House. *Dictionary of Canadian Biography*, vol. 9, s.v. "Seymour, Frederick," by Margaret A. Ormsby; Margaret A. Ormsby, *British Columbia: A History* (Toronto: The Macmillans in Canada, 1958), 200, 213, 220, et passim; *Who Was Who*, 64; "His Excellency," *Daily British Colonist*, 6 April 1866.

28. "Grand Entertainment at Government House," and "Sensation Rumors," *Daily British Colonist*, 9 April 1866.

29. Richard Clement Moody not only served as commander of the British Columbia Detachment, Royal Engineers, but also as chief commissioner of lands and works and lieutenant governor of British Columbia. For a convenient biographical sketch of his many responsibilities and activities in connection with these multifarious assignments, see *Dictionary of Canadian Biography,* vol. 11, s.v. "Moody, Richard Clement," by Margaret A. Ormsby.

An Indian Grave on Shell Island, looking towards Fort Rupert. May 8, 1866.

(original watercolor size: 14 x 8.75 in./35.5 x 22.5 cm)

Indian Graves on Shell Island, at Fort Rupert. July 19, 1868.

(original watercolor size: 10 x 6.5 in./21.5 x 16.5 cm)

The Coal mining settlement at Skidegate, Queen Charlotte's Island. May 24, 1866.

(original watercolor size: 14 x 9.25 in./35.5 x 23.5 cm)

McKenzie's Farm, near Esquimalt. June 4, 1866.

(original watercolor size: 14 x 9 in./35.5 x 22.5 cm)

trails lead through the woods to Burrard Inlet, one to Port Moody about 4 miles in length, and the other lower down below the 2nd Narrows and 3 miles in length.

Another road has been cut towards the Pitt Lake, & one to English Bay, these comprise the whole of the roads of the Capital. There is a tolerable Public Library where there is a collection of the Geological and Mineralogical specimens of the Country, and an Assay Office for the use of the Miners, where the gold dust is converted into bars, before it is sent out of the country.

On the 11th April the Governor & his family again embarked and steamed down the river at 10 AM. Stopped for a few minutes off the town to hear the Peal of Bells, that were given by Miss Burdett Coutts, and to allow Mr. A. Bisell to leave in the *Leviathan*. Captain Cooper disembarked at the Light vessel which we passed in 2 hours after leaving,[30] and arrived at Esquimalt at 5.45 PM, having made the Passage in 7 hours.[31]

Northern assignment

THE FINE WEATHER HAVING FAIRLY COMMENCED, and the days long, we left Esquimalt at 7 AM of the 2nd May, for a longer cruize to our most Northern Settlement in British Columbia, at Queen Charlotte's Island.[32] The Bishop of Columbia, Dr. Hills, being anxious to visit that part of his diocese, which he had not yet had an opportunity of doing, came on board for the cruize.[33]

Anchored in Roche Harbour in 3½ hours after leaving, and pulled in to the Camp with the Bishop and Mr. Garratt, to see Mr. Birch who wished to see me before leaving, about sending 3 Kittimat Indians up to Metlakatlah to be liberated by Mr. Duncan, and other business. After lunch, we returned to the vessel at 2 PM, when we weighed and left for Nanaimo where we anchored at 7.30 PM. The next morning we steamed alongside the Coal Wharf, and took in 103 Tons, of which we had to stow 33 Tons on Deck or in the Stake holes. We found the *Beaver* here on our arrival, and she left on the 3rd May for Fort Rupert, Mr. Pender intending if the weather permitted to examine a Rock which was said to exist in the Seymour Narrows. As it was not convenient for him to do it on his way up, he did it on his return, and found there was one with only 3 fathoms on it, well over the Western shore. The *Leviathan*

30. Cooper's fee for piloting H.M.S. *Sparrowhawk* on 5 and 11 April was $9.70. James Cooper to Acting Colonial Secretary, 2 May 1866, Colonial Correspondence, File 355, Provincial Archives of British Columbia.

31. "H.M.S. Sparrowhawk," *Daily British Colonist*, 12 April 1866.

In this interim in Esquimalt harbor between assignments "Found the remains of Mr. John Dearden Chief Engr in his bed, having departed this life during the night." Later that day, 21 April, "Sent the body of deceased on shore to Naval hospital." Three days later, "Sent Ship's Company on shore to attend the Funeral of the late Mr. John Dearden. Funeral parties landed from Scout and Alert." And after another three days, "Sold the Effects of the late Mr. John Dearden, Chief Engr. by Auction." On the day of his death, 21 April, Dearden was replaced by Nathaniel Farrant, as Chief Engineer. Entries for 21, 24, 27 April 1866, Master's logbook, Adm. 53/9255; Navy List (January 1867): 217.

Additional detail and biographic information is given in "Death on Board the Sparrowhawk," *Daily British Colonist*, 23 April 1866; "An Inquest," *Daily British Colonist*, 24 April 1866; "Funeral," *Daily British Colonist*, 25 April 1866.

32. "On a Cruise," *Daily British Colonist*, 3 May 1866.

33. Bishop George Hills kept a detailed account of this cruise, particularly about the Indian mission. *Ninth Annual Report of the Columbia Mission [of the Church of England], for the Year 1865*, preface; Hills, "1865 and 1866," 28–45.

arrived from New Westminster on the 4th May, having on board Mr. Maunsell and the 3 Kittimat Indians that were to be taken up to Metlakatlah, and as I might have some little trouble with the Northern Indians, I was sworn in as a Justice of the Peace for British Columbia.

Northward passage

MAY 5TH. LAID A STREAM ANCHOR OUT from our Port quarter and hauled the vessel off the Nanaimo Pier, and then steamed out of the harbour at 5.30 AM to the Northward, passing through the Lambert Channel, and arrived off Cape Mudge at 4 PM, when we found the Flood Tide running very strong to the Southward, which prevented our making but very little weigh, and obliged us to anchor in Duncan Bay at 6.30 PM. in 10 fathoms. On passing the Eucletaw village near Cape Mudge, we found that the natives had returned to it, and many canoes were hauled up on the beach. The wind was blowing strong against us in the first part of the morning, but afterwards lulled a great deal, but was foul the whole day.

May 6th. Left Duncan Bay at 8 AM, and steamed thro' the Seymour Narrows at slack water, where there was hardly a ripple on the water, and anchored in Forward Bay in Johnstone Strait at 4 PM, in 18 fathoms. At 3 PM communicated with a trading schooner called the *North Star* that was in want of a little leather to repair their pumps, as she was making a foot of water an hour, having been on shore and knocked a hole in her bottom. She had left Sitka on the 2nd March, and had been trading along the coast for furs. A great quantity of drift wood was piled up in endless confusion in every part of Forward Bay, and would be a good place to lay in a supply.

May 7th. Left Forward Bay at 6.15 AM, on passing Haddington Island communicated with a large war canoe, manned by 3 men and 5 women bound to Fort Rupert, and at Noon anchored close to the *Beaver*, in Beaver Harbour, to the Westward of Cattle Island. In the afternoon went on shore with the Bishop and Pender and visited Mr. Compton at Fort Rupert, who shewed us over his establishment and Fur store that consisted principally of Sea and Land Otters, Racoon's, Bears, Wolves, Fishers, Wolvereens [*sic*], Ermiens, Minks, Martens, Fur and Hair Seals. The Fort was Palisaded all round, and defended by Towers at the angles, two of them only having Guns that consisted of 4.9 Pounders each, and there was a good Garden at the back, that yielded most of the European vegetables. On the West side there was an Indian Ranch, but the greater number of the Indians were at the time away fishing. Only a few of the houses had been rebuilt since they were destroyed by the *Clio* in December last for refusing to give up some murderers, and the marks of the hatchets on the canoes were still visible.[34]

May 10th. We remained at Fort Rupert two clear days to cut fire wood, and then left at 4.30 AM for the Interior Channels to the Northward. Passed Cape James at

---

34. When the Indians refused to surrender the "culprits charged," a party went ashore to take them. Resisting, the Indians offered to exchange three suspects for two white men. They ignored a two-hour ultimatum and laughed at a shell fired over their ranch. When all their houses were burned and all but three of their canoes were destroyed, the Indians hoisted a flag of truce, surrendered their principal chiefs, the murderers, and hundreds of gallons of liquor. "From the North. Cruise of the Clio," *Daily British Colonist*, 29 December 1865.

8 AM, and were rolling about for the next 4 hours in Queen Charlotte's Sound, when we were sheltered by the land in Fitzhugh Sound.

Anchored off the site of Fort McLoughlin at Bella Bella at 8 PM, as the sun was going down, having run 100 miles. (in 15 fathoms.) Mr. Moss the Indian Agent came on board shortly afterwards, and told us that the schooner *Goldstream* had arrived from Skidegate, Queen Charlotte's Island with Mr. Stephens and Turner (Engineers), and was going to leave during the night for Victoria. He also told me that the American of the name of Lorenzo who had been accused of Whiskey Selling at Wakeeno had left the place, and there was little doing in that way, with the exception of one case at Bellakula, where he had been a fortnight before, and seized an American of the name of George Pearse, a partner of the late Antonio Loncanaje. Having received information from the Indians that he was selling Whiskey, he surrounded the house at night, and found several Gallons in his possession, but not having the means of sending him to New Westminster, he seized his Furs to the value of $150, and brought them to Bella Bella.

May 11th. Left Bella Bella at 4.30 AM, and steamed to the Northward through Milbank Sound, and along narrow channels till we arrived at Hone's Bay, where we anchored at 6.30 PM in 22 fathoms. The scenery was very fine, diversified with waterfalls falling down the steep sides of the hills the whole way. Clear places were frequently seen, where trees had been felled, and the ground completely cleared by the accumulation of [snow?] on the higher ground, and falling down the sides of the hills in avalanches. A few canoes were passed today, and the distance run 95 miles. The seine was hauled in the Evening on the sandy beach at the head of the Bay, and several fish caught.

May 12th. Left Hone's Bay at 4.30 AM, proceeded through Grenville Channel, and anchored in Duncan Bay, Metlakatlah at 2.45 PM, the last 3 hours being under sail alone with a strong breeze from the S.E. with drizzling rain and muggy weather. We came to in 6½ fathoms, at Low water 5 PM we had 4¾ fms. High water 10.30 PM we had 9 fms.

Mr. W. Duncan[35] came on board about 4 in a large canoe manned by 12 Indians.

---

35. William Duncan, to whom Porcher gives considerable attention in his journal, was an Anglican lay missionary who dedicated his life to the Coast Tsimshian Indians. He went to Tsimshian country in 1857, learned the language, and soon had a devoted following. In 1862, with some fifty converts, he established Metlakatla, several miles south of Fort Simpson. This settlement flourished for 25 years. Relations with the Anglican Church deteriorated and in 1887 he transplanted his followers to New Metlakatla in Alaska. Marjorie M. Halpin and Margaret Sequin, "Tsimshian Peoples: Southern Tsimshian, Coast Tsimshian, Nishga, and Gitksan," in William C. Sturtevant, ed., *Handbook of North American Indians*, vol. 7: *Northwest Coast,* edited by Wayne Suttles, (Washington: Smithsonian Institution, 1990), 281; M. Dale Kinkade, "History of Research in Linguistics," in *Northwest Coast*, 100; John A. Dunn and Arnold Booth, "Tsimshian of Metlakatla, Alaska," in *Northwest Coast*, 294–297; Marjorie M. Halpin, "Duncan, William," in *Handbook of North American Indians*, Wilcomb E. Washburn, ed., vol. 4: *History of Indian-White Relations* (Washington: Smithsonian Institution, 1988), 641; Clarence Bolt, *Thomas Crosby and the Tsimshian: Small Shoes for Feet Too Large* (Vancouver: University of British Columbia Press, 1992), chapter 2, especially 20–25; Ivan Doig, "The Tribe that Learned the Gospel of Capitalism," *American West* 11 (March 1974): 42–47; Robin Fisher, *Contact and Conflict: Indian-European Relations in British Columbia, 1774–1890*, 2d ed. (Vancouver: University of British Columbia Press, 1992), 125–136. For a recent perspective of historical geography on the Metlakatla mission settlement, see Daniel Clayton, "Geographies of the Lower Skeena," *BC Studies* \94 (Summer 1992): especially 41–45.

May 13th. The next day being Sunday I went on shore in the afternoon with the Bishop and Comrie, and were received on our landing by Mr. Duncan and a large number of Indians dressed in European clothes. The settlement consisted of well built houses with sloping roofs and glazed windows, and a few of them with an Upper floor. The Church was in the form of an irregular Octagon with 26 windows, and capable of holding 500 people, and a Service was performed there by the Bishop in English, and by Mr. Duncan in Tsim-she-an to a very attentive congregation of about 200. Mr. Duncan had formed this settlement about 7 years ago from Fort Simpson, this being the original home of the Tribe, and it seems quite wonderful that he had done so much during that short time for the Indians. He has laid down the following 15 Rules for the people:

1. To give up their *Ahlied*, or Indian devilry.
2. To cease calling a conjurer when sick.
3. To cease gambling.
4. To cease giving away their property for display.
5. To cease painting their faces.
6. To cease drinking intoxicating liquors.
7. To rest on the Sabbath.
8. To attend religious instruction.
9. To send their children to school.
10. To be cleanly.
11. To be industrious.
12. To be peaceful.
13. To be liberal & honest in trade.
14. To build neat houses.
15. To pay the village Tax.

May 15th. During the last 2 days when we were safely anchored in Duncan Bay, it had been blowing a Gale of wind the greater part of the time, with squalls and rain, and this morning it lulled a little, and we left at 7 AM for Fort Simpson where we arrived in 2½ hours. Went on shore with the Bishop to see Mr. Mauson the Agent for the Hudson Bay Company and there met the Rev. Robt. R. A. Doolan B.A. who had just arrived from the Naas river, on his way to Metlakatlah.

Indians, repairs, Indians

My first Magisterial business commenced here by having to try a Chief of the name of Neeshnewah for disinterring the body of an Indian of the name of [Kishon?],[36] and all the Indians drinking Whiskey round the grave, and not forgetting to give the Corpse his share, on the pretext that a relation living in the Skeenah river

36. Bishop Hills recorded this name as Kitbrone. Hills, "1865 and 1866," 30.

about 80 miles off, could not be cured of a bowel complaint, because a cloth that originally belonged to him was buried with the Corpse, and as the Chief said he knew he was doing wrong, I fined him 10 blankets to be presented to the dead man's relations.[37]

The Indian Village surrounding the Fort was the largest and best I had as yet seen, the houses being better decorated and painted, but the inhabitants were mostly smeared over with paint and dirt. The Chief I had tried this morning had his face painted black, either from anger or fear.

The Census was taken by Mr. W. Duncan when he was living here in January 1858, and consisted of 763 Men, 848 Women, 524 Boys, 432 Girls. Total 2567. No. of houses 141, No. of sick 47. They speak the Tsim-she-an language, and seem a much finer race than those from the Southward.

May 16th. Left Fort Simpson at 7.30 AM, shortly after Low water, as the rocks that line the entrance to the bay were then visible, but on endeavoring to clear the channel to the Southward of Finlayson Island, and about 3 miles from Fort Simpson, the ship grounded on a rock forward at 8.10 AM, when going at the rate of 6 knots.[38]

When we first touched, the Sounding, under bow were 1½ Fms.

Port Chains	5	Fathoms
Starbd Chains	6	
Stern	15	

The Engines were reversed, but with no effect, and then laid out a stream anchor astern, and the ship floated off at 9.45 AM, as the tide rose, having been on the rock for 1.35 hours. The following Comp. bearings were taken when aground.

South Point of Finlayson Island N 5 E. Cor[rected] for deviation N 3 E
Centre of Flat Top Island in passage N 47 E[39] N 65 E
S.E point of Passage S 22 E S 24 E[40]
West point of Finlayson Id. N 55 W Ships *[illeg.]* SW ¾ W.[41]

After the ship came off, the ship made 1¼ inch of water every hour, and continued to do so for the remainder of the cruize. There was a light breeze from the SE. during the time we were on shore, but the water was smooth without any swell.

---

37. As such, Porcher's dispensing of justice in this incident does not reflect Anglo cultural misunderstanding. Disinterment was not customary with the Coast Tsimshian. Halpin and Seguin, "Tsimshian Peoples," 277–278.

The practice was found, for example, in some peoples further south, especially the Salish, Chinook, and Tillamook. Wayne Suttles, "Central Coast Salish," in William C. Sturtevant, ed., *Handbook of North American Indians*, vol. 7: *Northwest Coast,* edited by Wayne Suttles, (Washington: Smithsonian Institution, 1990), 465; Yvonne Hajda, "Southwestern Coast Salish," *Northwest Coast*, 512; Michael Silverstein, "Chinookans of the Lower Columbia," *Northwest Coast*, 544; William R. Seaburg and Jay Miller, "Tillamook," *Northwest Coast*, 564.

38. This is now known as Sparrowhawk Rock. Middleton, *Place Names of the Pacific Northwest Coast*, 196; Walbran, *British Columbia Coast Names*, 466–467.

39. Corrected in pencil to N 67 E in the manuscript.

40. This calculation was added in pencil.

41. [N 69 W?] is written above this.

Proceeded on to Metlakatlah, and anchored in the harbour at 1.50 PM in 12½ fathoms.

Bearings of Bay—Church tower S 82 W. [Arrival Pt?] S 2 W

The Channel is very narrow, but if it was buoyed or some beacons built on the rocks that are dry at low water, there would be no difficulty, as the water is sufficiently deep.

As the ship was considerably damaged by striking the rock, and not knowing to what extent, I looked round for a level beach to ground the vessel on, and found a suitable place on the Eastern side of the settlement, and which could be done with little risk, as the tides rose between 18 and 21 feet. After cutting down 12 trees to act as shores 23 feet in length, which were fitted to rest against the Ships side under the chain plates, and set the Topmasts Lower and Topsail yards, and Gaffs on deck, letting go both lower anchors and slipping their cables, we steamed in for the settlement at 4.30 AM on the 18th May, grounded the vessel, and were left high and dry at 10 AM. Two shores were used for each of the chains, which kept the ship upright without any difficulty, but some of them were obliged to be weighted at the lower end with 1 or 2 68 Pd shot to make them sink to take the ground. The bottom was flat and muddy mixed with the sand, so that the vessel's keel sank into it. We found about 3 feet of the Gripe gone, 15 or 20 feet of the Keel carried away part of the Starboard streak damaged, and about 24 sheets of Copper off.[42] The Carpenters repaired as much as they could get at. The ship touched the ground about 6.15 AM, when all hands were sent on shore, and after being aground for 7½ hours, floated again at 1.50 PM, when she steamed back to our former anchorage, and took in the cables.

During the few days we had been here, the Bishop of Columbia had examined many of the Indians on their knowledge of the Christian religion, and on Whitsunday, May 20th, baptized 64 Adults, 35 Women and 29 men, and the following day a number of children.

On May 21st, we dressed ship in honour of H.M. Birthday, as we were going to leave before the proper day, and kept on this occasion by the particular request of the Bishop and Mr. Duncan. Fired a Royal Salute at Noon, and in the Afternoon the Indians amused us and themselves by canoe races, first by men and afterwards by women, jumping in sacks, foot racing, cat & mouse to please the girls, and 18 of the constables were drawn up in uniform and put thro' their facings. Prizes being given for the winners of the different games. In the Evening all the inhabitants assembled in the Meeting house, and the Bishop and myself made speeches which were eloquently answered by the Chiefs and the Indian Council, and concluded by a display of the Magic lantern.

May 22. At daylight took in 50 Cords of Maple wood, which were paid for at \$2¾, being delivered alongside. Left Metlakatlah at 8 AM, Mr. Duncan and Doolan

---

42. For public consumption, the damage was characterized as minimal: "The Sparrowhawk got on a rock near Fort Rupert and knocked away part of her keel, but received no serious damage. The necessity of a dry dock is much felt in such cases." "From the North," *Daily British Colonist*, 31 May 1866.

remaining on board till we were clear of the harbour, and then steered to the Southward, the wind all day being from the S.E. with thick weather and drizzling rain. At 2.30 PM anchored close to the *Beaver* in Alpha Bay, Ogden Channel, where we also found the Hudson Bay Company's trading schooner the *Petrel*.

Queen Charlotte Islands visit

MAY 23RD. LEFT ALPHA BAY AT 5 AM, in company with the *Beaver*, and steamed across to Queen Charlotte's Island with a fair breeze from the S.E., crossed the Skidegate bar in 3¼ fathoms, and anchored off the Mining settlement in Cowlitz Harbour in 9 fathoms at 6.15 PM.

May 24th. This morning I visited the Coal mines with the Bishop and Comrie, and after a hard tramp over fallen trees and along steep & difficult trails came upon the spot where the coal was first found. The Seam was first seen cropping out of the side of a range of hills, about 1¼ mile from the settlement, and 600 feet above the level of the sea, and although the outside was hard Anthracite Coal, it became to be crushed up as if by pressure as they advanced into the hill. They had made tunnels in several places to a distance of 50 feet or more, and found the coal to be all in the same state soft and useless, and when we were there the Miners were employed tunnelling into the hill about 200 feet lower down to endeavour to strike the same seam again, which dipped down at an angle of 80°, and had then advanced 100 feet without having met it.[43]

A great number of workmen had lately left as their time of agreement was up, and as the Company had gone to a great expense in commencing a Tram way and sending a considerable number of stores, they thought a few would be sufficient until they found out a workable seam. The number remaining amounted to 12, consisting of Mr. Brown the Manager, Mr. Wilkes, Firemen both with the pay of $100 a month, 4 Miners at $70 each, 2 Axemen at $50, 1 Cook at $50, and 3 Labourers at $40.

The rock surrounding the Coal seams was slate and sand stone, and the seam was in the direction of due North and South.

Before leaving I went with the Bishop to the Head of the Inlet, about 3 miles from the Mining settlement, where there was a fine fresh water river, and saw the scaffolding of houses, that had probably been used by the Indians during the fishing season. Mountainous land ran at the back of the river and divided the Inlet from the one that runs in from the Western side of the Island. The length of the Skidegate Inlet from the Entrance Island is about 15 miles. I investigated a Magisterial case here with Pender, about the right of the Indians remaining at the settlement, as the Manager considered them a great nuisance and complained of the noise they made throughout the night, when they were enabled to get Whiskey, and finding by their written agreement that the Chiefs were bound not to allow any of the Indians to encamp here, we decided they should all go away in 2 days. After they had left the miners no doubt suffered, as they were not able to get Fish or other fresh food, altho' they might have gained in other ways as these Haida Indians had lower ideas of

43. Ibid.

morality than any we had yet seen.[44] As there was no Coal to be obtained here for the use of the ship, we supplied the *Beaver* with 28 Tons of Coals, and 14 Cords of wood.

Return to Esquimalt

PARTED COMPANY FROM THE *Beaver* THAT was going to remain to make a Survey of the Harbour, and steamed out of Skidegate harbour at daylight. I went on shore with the Bishop to see the Village at the entrance which was the finest I had as yet seen, and beat those on the Main land, as the houses were better built, the interiors much cleaner and more neatly kept. Every house had an ornamental Pole in front of it, with figures cut in high relief on it, and all surmounted with Crests.

Crossed the Bar a little after 8 AM, in 4¾ fathoms, and a moderate breeze from the N.W sent the ship on 7½ knots under steam and sail, and carried a line of soundings down the whole way to Cape Scott.

May 27th. The wind died away during the night, and had a moderate breeze from the S.E in the morning which reduced our speed, but succeeded in crossing the Nahwitti Bar in 9 fathoms at 6 PM, and anchored off Fort Rupert at 9.30 PM in 15 fathoms. Mr. Compton of the H.B.C. came on board.

May 28th. Left Fort Rupert at 4.30 AM, and on passing Alert Bay landed with the Bishop and Comrie to see a fine cemetery of Indians that had died of the small pox about 4 years before, having 9 canoes hauled up close to it, and the enclosure hung round with white and red blankets that had a pleasing effect.

Steamed thro' the Seymour Narrows at slack water & passed Cape Mudge before the Ebb tide set in strong, remained under weigh during the night, and steamed alongside the Coal Wharf at Nanaimo at 7.30 AM, having taken 27 hours from Fort Rupert. Took in 93 Tons of Coals.

May 30th. Left Nanaimo at 5 AM at the same time as the *Alert*, and arrived at Esquimalt at 4 PM.[45]

---

44. In the 1830s after the sea otter trade with Americans and Europeans declined, the Haida had come under the influence of Hudson's Bay Company. With the Fraser River gold rush, they began to expand their trading horizons, particularly to Victoria where alcohol and prostitution exacted a toll. From here, in 1862, they carried smallpox back to their settlements that soon decimated their numbers. The remnant who survived gradually abandoned their towns and were resettling at Skidegate and Masset. This is the context for Porcher's comments. Margaret B. Blackman, "Haida: Traditional Culture," in William C. Sturtevant, ed., *Handbook of North American Indians*, vol. 7: *Northwest Coast,* edtied by Wayne Suttles, (Washington: Smithsonian Institution, 1990), 240–260.

45. "From the North," *Daily British Colonist*, 31 May 1866. Bishop Hills "left the vessel" at Esquimalt. Porcher's log, 287–288.

Distances run, northern cruise

	From	To	By Chart	By Log
May 2 nd	Esquimalt	Roche Harbour	24	30
	Roche Harbour	Nanaimo	55	47
5 th	Nanaimo	Duncan Bay	80	94
6 th	Duncan Bay	Forward Bay	55	46
7 th	Forward Bay	Fort Rupert	43	34
10 th	Fort Rupert	Port McLouchlin	101	99
11 th	Port McLouchlin	Hone's Bay	93	90
12 th	Hone's Bay	Metlakatlah	87	70
15 th	Metlakatlah, Duncan Bay	Fort Simpson	19	17
16 th	Fort Simpson	Metlakatlah Harbour	24	31
22 nd	Metlakatlah	Alpha Bay, Ogden Channel	34	38
23 rd	Alpha Bay	Skidegate (Queen Charlotte's Id.)	87	79
26 th, 27 th	Skidegate Hr.	Fort Rupert	253	254
28 th, 29 th	Fort Rupert	Nanaimo	180	180
30 th	Nanaimo	Esquimalt	80	73
		TOTAL	**1215**	**1182**

Chapter Four

Fenians, San Francisco, and Winter Activities

9 June 1866–6 January 1867

[The troublesome Fenians were Irish-Americans who advocated attacking Canada from bases in the United States in an attempt to end Britain's hold on Ireland. When another flare-up began back East in mid-1866, rumors spread that a San Francisco-based Fenian attempt against British Columbia was planned. Her Majesty's ships on station at Esquimalt were running errands and serving as police to maintain law and order amongst the Northwest Pacific coastal Indians and the traders. They also constituted a presence that served the interests of Empire and any perceived threat thereto. Accordingly, the ships were deployed prudently, the *Sparrowhawk* to protect New Westminster, the capital. This threat soon evaporated. Other than this, and two voyages to San Francisco for repairs and mail, the *Sparrowhawk's* duties were generally routine.]

Precautions against Fenians

Admiral Denman arrived in the *Sutlej* from Valparaiso on the 9th June, having made the passage in 54 days, and nearly 6 months since she left this place. On the same day there was a great excitement in the Colony, caused by large meetings of the Fenians having taken place at San Francisco a few days before, and threatening to make a raid in this direction, if their brotherhood were successful in Canada. The *Alert* was ordered to anchor off the entrance to Victoria and board all vessels entering the port, the *Forward* was sent to Cadboro Bay, and on the 13th June we left to protect the neighbouring Capital.[1]

We started from Esquimalt at 7.35 AM, stopped off the Light vessel at the Sand Head at 2.45 PM to take Captain Cooper on board, and anchored off the Camp at New Westminster at 6.20 PM, having made the passage in 10.45 hours with very little wind the whole way, and the Tide in our favour. Here we remained a month, and gave us the first opportunity of putting the ship thoroughly to rights.

Some magnificent Timber grows about here, being well suited for Spars, plank and building purposes, and as Captain Stamp had a contract with the French Government to supply them with 70 large Spars, he invited me to go over to Burrard's Inlet to see them on the 18th June.

Dolphin, Boys[2] and myself breakfasted with him at the Colonial Hotel, and then drove out with him by the long road, the distance being 9 miles (less 4 chains.) His Son met us on the beach, and we all embarked in a Canoe to see his new Saw Mills that are situated between the 1st and 2nd Narrows, which are not yet completed owing to some of the Machinery not having arrived from England, but when every thing is in order are expected to saw 60.000 feet daily, employ upwards of 100 men, and will be the largest in the Colony. A substantial Pier has been built out from the Mills, so that vessels of any Tonnage could lie alongside, and embark their lumber without any trouble. We then went on in the Canoe to English Bay, to see the Spars that have been felled for the French Government, which are on the average from 110 to 120 feet in length, and 36 to 39 inches in diameter. One very fine one we saw measured 111 feet and 38 inches in diameter, that had only one very small knot in its

---

1. From 1866 to 1870, the Fenians, using Irish veterans of the Union Army of the American Civil War, harassed the Canadian border, hoping to seize Canada as hostage for Irish freedom. In the June 1866 incident, Canadian militia battled 1500 Irishmen who had crossed the Niagara River; both fled the scene and the Fenians were arrested and released by New York authorities. Gough, *The Royal Navy and the Northwest Coast*, 210–214; Hereward Senior, *The Fenians and Canada* (Toronto: Macmillan of Canada, 1978); Brian Jenkins, *Fenians and Anglo-American Relations during Reconstruction* (Ithaca: Cornell University Press, 1969).

Fenian activities were frequently reported in the Victoria press. The 2 June invasion was carried as "Important News. The Fenians Invade Canada," *Daily British Colonist*, 6 June 1866. See also other editorials and news items in *Daily British Colonist*, 8, 9 June 1866.

With a breakdown in the telegraph, dispatches were soon replaced by the "circulation of all kinds of unauthorized rumors." Under the circumstances, the deployment of naval vessels and other prudent steps were taken. The *Sparrowhawk* was "to lay off Race Rocks." "The Fenians," *Daily British Colonist*, 11 June 1866. The direct San Francisco-based threat appeared in an excerpt of an undated and unsigned "Letter from San Francisco. The Projected Fenian Raid," *Daily British Colonist*, 27 June 1866.

2. Alfred Boys was Paymaster on the *Sparrowhawk*. *Navy List* (April 1865): 208.

entire length. 35 were already on the beach, squared and ready for shipment, besides many more in the same state in the wood, and all generally clear of knots. The trees in this Inlet make better Spars than those growing in Vancouver Island, as they are better protected from the wind, and consequently straighter and not so tough, as those that are directly exposed to the strong Westerly winds the whole year round. A Carpenter of the name of Rogers was superintending the work with 9 men, and seemed to get through their work very quick. The distances we had to go in the Canoe was about 9 miles each way, making the distance we had to go by land and water the same. We were shewn some Coal cropping out from the sandy beach, that seemed to be a kind of lignite, but has never been worked.

Several Beaver dams exist in the vicinity of New Westminster, and not having seen one properly, I started on the 20th June, with Mr. Birch, Ball and Kingscote to see if we could capture one. We started in the forenoon and rode along a good road in the direction of the Pitt river for about 6 miles, and then branched off on a very bad trail for about 2 miles, when we secured our horses to the trees, and walked the remainder of the way. On arriving there, the Dam was cut in several places, and the water soon drained out of the lake, when we commenced dismantling the Beaver house, which was of considerable size and built half under water, with loose sticks and earth, and with a series of passages, shewing the great ingenuity of the Beaver. After being half devoured by the Mosquitoes and sand flies, drenched by the rain and thoroughly wet up to our knees by being obliged to wade about in the water and mud, and expending a deal of labour, we were forced to give it up without seeing any thing, except 2 snakes, an eel, and several small fish that were left on the mud by the water leaving.

On the 11th July I accompanied Mr. Arthur N. Birch and Mr. D. C. Maunsell in the *Leviathan*, and proceeded up to New Langley to witness a Rifle contest between the Volunteers. Most of the inhabitants of New Westminster with their wives and families started before us in the *Lilloett* a stern wheel river steamer, which was kindly placed at their disposal by Captain Fleming. The distance was 15 miles, and we took 3 hours in getting there, and one in returning with the strong current. The site for the town was well chosen, as there was a good deal of open ground around it, but the houses that are still in good order are now all abandoned, particularly the Church that was large enough to accommodate 200. For a few miles below Langley there were some cleared spots where there were a few settlers.

After having been an entire month at anchor in the Fraser, we left New Westminster at 1.30 PM of the 12th July, took 2 hours in getting down to the Light ship [at Sand Head], and anchored at Esquimalt at 10 PM, having made the passage in 8½ hours.[3]

---

3. The return was noted in "H.M.S. Sparrowhawk," *Daily British Colonist*, 13 July 1866.

The *Sparrowhawk* had missed the Admiral's inspection of the fleet in Esquimalt harbor, 2 July 1866. "Inspection of the Fleet," *Daily British Colonist*, 3 July 1866.

San Francisco assignment

We remained at Esquimalt 3 weeks,[4] and then left on the 2nd August for San Francisco to be docked,[5] taking as Passengers Commander Fox who was lately promoted from the *Forward*,[6] and Lieut. Barclay of the Swedish Navy.

For the first two days we had very light breezes from the Westward, but after that it came on to blow hard from the Northward that lasted nearly 2 days, sending the ship on under sail alone 9.8 knots. The weather had been beautifully clear up to the time of our attempting to pass in the middle watch between Point Reyes and the Farallon's, when a thick fog suddenly came on, which obliged us to stop for 8 hours. At 9 AM it began to lift now and then, so that we were able to steam ahead again with a light breeze from the S.E. and made Point Reyes at 11 AM of the 7th August, and then had little difficulty in steering for San Francisco, where we anchored off Meigg's Pier at 2 PM, having made the Passage including the stoppage from the Fog in 4 days and 16 hours.[7]

Landed as soon as we were anchored, and called on General Halleck, and Mr. Charles Mason the Acting British Consul, in the room of Mr. Burke who had gone home on a year's leave of absence. The Mail steamers leave San Francisco for Panama on the 10th, 18th, and 30th of every month, and the Mails leave New York on the 1st, 11th, and 21st of the month, that take about 22 days before they reach San Francisco.

August 8th. The next morning at 10 AM, Captain Harrison the Navy yard Pilot came on board, when we weighed and steamed up to Mare Island, situated 22 miles up the Sacramento river where we made fast to a Buoy at 0.40 PM. A river steamer called the *Amelia* had hard work to beat us, as we were under steam and sail with a fresh breeze after us the greater part of the way.

Found the following American men of war at Mare Island:

Saranac,	13 Guns,	1446 Tons,	Captain Scott & Flag of R. Admiral Thatcher
Vanderbilt	15	3360	Captain Sanford
Monadnock (Monitor)	4	1564	Out of Commission
James Town & *Cyane*, Store ships			Out of Commission
Independence (Receiving ship)			Captain Packer.

On arriving called on Captain Scott aboard the *Saranac*, Captain David McDougal, Commandant of the Navy Yard, Captain Packer of the *Independence*, and Mr. Philip Hichbone, the Acting Constructor of the Yard came on board to take the dimensions of the vessel.

4. The *Sparrowhawk's* inspection 16 July by Admiral Joseph Denman was noted in "H.M.S. Sparrowhawk," *Daily British Colonist*, 17 July 1866.

5. While the *Sparrowhawk* was carrying the mail, the purpose of the trip was to be put into dock for examination, "to ascertain what repairs are necessary." "For San Francisco," *Daily British Colonist*, 1 August 1866.

6. "Going Home," *Daily British Colonist*, 1 August 1866; "Departure of Commander Fox," *Daily British Colonist*, 6 August 1866.

7. One seaman, a sailmaker, was given a "Reduction" in rank "for Conduct" on the Esquimalt-San Francisco cruise. Entry for 4 August 1866, Master's logbook, Adm. 53/9256.

August 9th. The following morning at 8 AM, being slack water, we warped up to the Sectional Dock, and was taken up on it. It was 325 feet by 105, and divided into 10 Sections of 32 feet each, secured together by wooden stringers, and the mooring chains above, the mechanism of all being the same. The Floor of the Dock was formed of Wooden Tanks 12 feet deep, which are filled with water by opening sluice valves a foot square on each side, and are fitted with 3 bulkheads to prevent the water seeping from one side to the other. On each side of this flooring there are wooden boxes, drawing 2 feet water, and 6 feet above it, which are used to balance the Dock. They always remain in the same position and are connected with the Dock by an Iron rod which is fitted with Gearing, and worked by the steam power above, so as to allow the Dock to rise or fall without altering the position of the boxes. On the top of these there is strong scaffolding 40 feet high, over which there are wooden houses in which the 4 Engines and Boilers (2 on each side) are placed, and from which the Pumps, valves and other Gear are worked. There are 6 Pumps to each Section, or 3 on each side, which can be worked together or separately.

We found that 27 feet of the keel which was 5½ inches deep, was more or less damaged, and several planks required shifting. The number of men that were employed on the vessel varied every day, but the average number was about 30, and the repairs took 6 days. The expenses of Docking, Labour and materials amounted to £410.11.10, and the Pilotage from San Francisco to Mare Island & back £48.10.0 at the rate of $10 a foot. The charges were excessively high, but at the same rate that were paid by the American Government. The Carpenters and Caulkers received $5.50 each, and the lowest sum that was paid to a few Helpers being $2.50. They were employed for 10 hours a day, while the hired men from San Francisco that merchant vessels are obliged to take got $6 for 8 hours labour.

During the time I was here, I went all round the *Monadnock*, a formidable Monitor with 2 Turrets. Each of them were armed with 2, 15 inch Guns throwing 450 lbs. shot, had Engines of 700 horse power with a double screw, and was 260 feet long by 51 feet beam. The upper deck was about 2 feet above the water without any bulwarks, and the only place where the Officers could walk about at sea was on an iron grating placed between the Turrets about 8 feet above the deck. The heat and closeness in the Stoke holes and other places must be very great, and to obviate this a great deal [of] ventilating appliances are worked all over the vessel by steam. I was shewn all over her by the Chief Engineer, who had been in her since she was launched, and was engaged against the Southern ports at the latter end of the war.

During the week we were at Mare Island I was shewn every civility and hospitality by Captain McDougal and all the Officers of the Yard, and had every reason to be satisfied with the work that was done on the vessel by the workmen employed by the Government. The Repairs being completed by 4 PM of the 16th August, the Dock was sunk, and Captain Harrison, the Pilot, took us out of the harbour, and anchored off San Francisco at 7 PM, having made the passage down in 2½ hours.

We remained close to the city off the Broadway Wharf two days, during which time we took in 28½ tons of Sydney Coals, at $14½, which burnt much better & less smoke than the Nanaimo Coals. I drove out with Captain Harrison to the

Cemetery built on a rising ground about 2 miles from the town, which is very extensive and has many fine monuments, and afterwards went onto the Cliff house that is situated immediately opposite to the Seal rocks on the South side of the entrance of the harbour, that are covered with Sea Lions. The barking of these animals resemble dogs, and as they are not allowed to be shot or disturbed, are as tame as possible, and not frightened away by any number of people collected there.

We steamed out of San Francisco at daylight of the 19th August,[8] with a light breeze from the Southward. As soon as we got clear of Point Reyes it came on to blow hard from the N.W. which obliged us to stop the engines and stand off the land to the W.S.W. We first attempted to beat up within a reasonable distance of the land, but we soon found out that we could make nothing to windward against the strong Southerly currents, and forced us to stand off the land for 300 miles when we got into clear weather and calms, which enabled us with the assistance of our steam, to make over Northerly.[9]

We arrived at Esquimalt at 10 AM of the 31st August, and after communicating with the Admiral, left again for Nanaimo at 11.30 AM without anchoring.[10] As the night was very dark and not able to make out Entrance Island, we hove to for the night, and steamed in at daylight, and secured alongside the Coaling Wharf at 5.45 AM.[11]

Coal consumption

WE LEFT ESQUIMALT WITH 108½ TONS OF Coals on board, and as we had a strong breeze in our favour the greater part of the way down to San Francisco, we only burnt 46 tons. With the 28½ tons that we took in at that place, it made the quantity we had on board up to 80. The following lines shew what was burnt:

From Esquimalt to San Francisco	46 Tons
San Francisco to Mare Island & back	10
San Francisco to Esquimalt	64 = **120 Tons**

On our arrival at Nanaimo we had only 3½ tons left. On the 1st September we took in 97 tons, and as soon as we had finished at 4.30 PM, we steamed out to an anchorage.

Things did not look very prosperous with the Nanaimo Coal Company, as they had stacked on the surface 10.000 tons, and no vessels had arrived during the last

---

8. It was mistakenly noted in the Victoria newspaper that the *Sparrowhawk* had departed San Francisco on the following day. "H.M.S. Sparrowhawk," *Daily British Colonist*, 22 August 1866.

9. According to the Victoria newspaper: "This man-of-war is now out ten days from San Francisco. Her non-appearance is accounted for by the fact that she had orders not to steam on the upward passage." "The 'Sparrowhawk'," *Daily British Colonist*, 29 August 1866.

10. "The war-steamer Sparrowhawk...brought no papers and came up under sail." Her arrival and departure were duly noted. "The 'Sparrowhawk'," *Daily British Colonist*, 1 September 1866.

11. Two seamen received "Disrating" sentences "for Conduct" on the return to Esquimalt cruise. Entry for 21 August 1866, Master's logbook, Adm. 53/9256.

The Government House at New Westminster, B.C. June 19, 1866.

(original watercolor size: 14 x 9.13 in./35.5 x 23 cm)

Esquimalt. V.I. from the Hospital grounds. June 6, 1866.

(original watercolor size: 14 x 9.13 in./35.5 x 23 cm)

H.M.S. Sparrowhawk in the Fraser. July 7, 1866.

(original watercolor size: 14 x 8.5 in./35.5 x 21.5 cm)

The Navy yard, and sectional Dock at Mare Island, California. August 13, 1866.

(original watercolor size: 14 x 8.5 in./35.5 x 21.5 cm)

The Coaling station of NANAIMO. Sept. 3, 1866.

(original watercolor size: 14 x 9.25 in./35.5 x 23.5 cm)

Bridge over the Dead-man's river, near Esquimalt. Sept. 10, 1866.

(original watercolor size: 14 x 9.88 in./35.5 x 25 cm)

Hudson Bay Company's Post at Nisqually, in Puget Sound. Oct. 5, 1866.

(original watercolor size: 14 x 8.5 in./35.5 x 21.5 cm)

The Church at Esquimalt. June 28, 1867.

(original watercolor size: 10 x 6.75 in./21.5 x 17 cm)

month to take any away, and they were being undersold by the Bellingham Bay Company. They had lately been boring about a quarter of a mile to the Southward of their shaft for the same seam that crops out at the Harwood Mine, as it was of better quality, but had not yet reached it, although they had gone down 350 feet, and bored thro' the same seam they are at present working. Six men had been employed at this work for the last 5 months, receiving 7/. a day each, or £2.2.0 for the party, which had amounted up to the present time to 300 Guineas.

The *Sutlej* and *Scout* arrived at Nanaimo at sunset of the 4th September on their way to Comox, and we left at 10 AM, on the following morning for Esquimalt where we arrived in 8 ½ hours.[12]

As we steamed through the Active Pass at 2.15 PM, we exercised the men in firing shot and shell at marks on the Cliffs, and on our arrival anchored between Inskip and Cole Islands for the purpose of building a slip for the Serjeant in charge of the Magazine to haul his boat by.

San Francisco mail call

As THE *Active* (MAIL STEAMER) DID NOT bring up the Admiral's or Ship Mails on the 12th September, we were ordered the next morning to take in 30 Tons additional Coal on deck, and go down to San Francisco for them,[13] and take a Mail down with us which would be in time for the steamer that leaves for Panama on the 18th instant.

Having made up our stock of Coals to 120 Tons, we left at 9 PM of the 13th September, the night being so foggy that we did not see the Race Light until we had passed it, and bore nearly North. For the first 1½ day we had very little wind, and then a fresh N.W[ester]ly wind sprung up that lasted 24 hours, and then died away for the remainder of the way.

After leaving Cape Flattery the weather was clear and remained so until we arrived at San Francisco which we did at 7 PM of the 17th September, after making the passage in 3 days & 22 hours.

The next day we took in 50 Tons of Sydney Coals which filled our Bunkers up and 10 Tons in addition, and also received 19 Bags of Mails for Victoria and New Westminster.

We left again at 6 AM of the 19th September, and arrived at Esquimalt at 1.30 AM of the 24th Sept., having made the passage in 4 days and 19 hours.[14] We had very

12. This "good run" was noted in "From Nanaimo," *Daily British Colonist*, 6 September 1866.

13. The "colonial mail and Admiralty despatch bags, which had been carelessly or wilfully left behind by the steamer Active when she left this port [San Francisco]." "California," *Daily British Colonist*, 19 September 1866. "The Navy mail,...by some inadvertence, was left behind" by the *Active*. The *Sparrowhawk* might also return with "an English mail." "An Extra Mail," *Daily British Colonist*, 14 September 1866. See also, "Union Rumours," *Daily British Colonist*, 15 September 1866; "H.M.S. Sparrowhawk..." and "A list of passengers...," *Daily British Colonist*, 19 September 1866.

14. "The Sparrowhawk," *Daily British Colonist*, 22 September 1866.

The *Sparrowhawk* had not returned on schedule. "There were no news...," *Daily British Colonist*, 24 September 1866. "Severe weather" had lengthened the return passage. "The 'Sparrowhawk'," *Daily British Colonist*, 25 September 1866.

little wind the whole way, but after the first 2 days, a heavy head sea kept us back, and reduced our speed from 7½ knots to 4. Every day on our way up we saw several Whales and shoals of Porpoises. We found that when near the land, the Current invariably set us towards it, so that during dark nights or foggy weather it would be advisable to give it a good offing. We burnt on our passage to San Francisco and back 160 Tons, which cost £317.

Lime and coal

AFTER REMAINING AT ESQUIMALT 3 DAYS we left before daylight of the 27th September, and anchored in Roche Harbour, San Juan, at 8.10 AM (in 3 hours and 20 minutes). After landing 50 empty Casks to be filled with 250 Bushels of Lime, we proceeded on to Nanaimo where we anchored off the entrance of the Harbour at 7.45 PM. The next morning we steamed alongside the Coal Wharf where we took in 102 Tons of Coals.

Being a fine day I rode out with Mr. Nicholl to see the Harewood Coal Mine, that took us 1½ hour before we got there, as it was about 5 miles by the road from Nanaimo, and 2½ by a trail. The Coal crops out from the side of a rocky hill at a moderate elevation above the sea, and dips down in a SE[aster]ly direction, and is about 4½ feet in thickness.

From the few Tons that have been tried, it is considered better burning Coal and not so dirty as the Douglas seam, but it would cost a large sum of money before it could be opened out, as a railroad would have to be made through a thick Forest and over an undulating Country for 5 miles to Departure Bay, and a Jetty built there. A few Tunnels have been cut into the hill, and 100 Tons taken out for trial, but it cost a considerable sum, as it had to be carted the whole way over an indifferent road to Nanaimo.

We left Nanaimo at daylight of the 29th September, and anchored in Roche Harbour at 0.20 PM, having taken 6 hours and 20 minutes. Here we took in 20 Casks of Lime, and landed some Provisions for the use of the Camp. We returned to Esquimalt on the morning of the 1st October.[15]

Puget Sound excursion

ON THE 4TH OCTOBER I LEFT IN THE *Enterprise* at 10 AM, with a large Picnic party of 70, for a visit to the different American Ports in Puget Sound, having been invited by Dr. Tolmie[16] of the Hudson Bay Company, and by whom the whole affair was managed.[17]

15. "Naval," *Daily British Colonist*, 2 October 1866.

16. William Fraser Tolmie was a surgeon who served Hudson's Bay Company (HBC) in various capacities, eventually as ranking member on the management board of the Western Department. While still with HBC, he was a member of the house of assembly of Vancouver Island, 1863–1866, and later in the British Columbia provincial legislature. *Dictionary of Canadian Biography*, vol. 11, s.v. "Tolmie, William Fraser," by W. Kaye Lamb.

17. "Excursion," *Daily British Colonist*, 5 October 1866.

The Company consisted of Governor Kennedy and daughter, Sir James Douglas[18] & daughter, Chief Justice Needham[19] and family, Dr. and Mrs. Tolmie, Mr. & Mrs. Finlayson (Chief Factor),[20] Mr. & Mrs. Nestor, Mrs. Wallace, Mr. & Mrs. Charles Wallace, Mrs. & Miss *[illeg.]*, Mrs. Monat, Miss Work, Archdeacon Gillson, Admiral & Mrs. Denman, Captain Price, Commander Sullivan, Dr. & Mrs. Patrick, Rev. J. Ca*[illeg.]*, Rev. A. Buckley, Mr. Sharp, Donald, Dr. Comrie, Lieut. Barclay (Swedish Navy), Lieut. Com. Franklin (U.S.S. *Saginaw*), Mr. Vereker, Cransford, &c. &c.

We first went over to Port Angeles where we remained a short time to get a clearance, and then went on to Port Townshend where we landed to see the Town, which is soon to be the Port of Entry instead of the former place, and then anchored under the lee of the land for the evening.

October 5th. Weighed during the night, and about 8 AM, went alongside the Pier at Seattle where we landed to see the town, which is well situated on a rising ground, and has a University, Telegraph station, Saw Mill and about 300 inhabitants. We then went on to Steilacoom where we secured alongside the Pier at 11 AM, and remained during the day. Drove out with a large party in a wood Cart to Fort Nisqually, the only Hudson Bay Post in Puget Sound where we spent all the afternoon. The distance was 5 miles, and we took an hour in driving there, the first part of the road being cut through the wood, and the remainder over prairie land. This Post is situated about 2 miles from the Sound, and is principally a Pastoral settlement, although furs are collected as the principal source of traffic. There is a Fort at St[e]ilacoom about 1½ mile from the town, where there is kept a Company of soldiers, for the purpose of keeping the Indians in order.

October 6th. Started during the night, and went alongside the Pier at Port Townshend at 8.30 AM, where we remained a couple of hours, and had plenty of time to walk all over the place. Met on the Pier Brunner, our late Fiddler who had deserted in our Dingy with Clayson on the 7th March, and came on board the *Enterprise*, and remained near her the greater part of our stay. The whole party were photographed by Mr. Dally in a group at the end of the Pier.

---

18. With thirty years' service in Hudson's Bay Company, having become chief factor of the Columbia Department in 1839, and having founded in 1843 the first HBC post on the island at the future site of Victoria, in 1851 James Douglas was appointed governor of Vancouver Island. He resigned his position with HBC in 1858 and accepted appointment as governor of the newly created colony of British Columbia. He held the two governorships until 1864. *Dictionary of Canadian Biography*, vol. 10, s.v. "Douglas, Sir James," by Margaret A. Ormsby.

19. Joseph Needham, appointed chief justice of Vancouver Island in 1865, continued in that office and title even after the 1866 union of Vancouver Island and British Columbia, until 1870. *Dictionary of Canadian Biography*, vol. 10, s.v. "Cameron, David," by William R. Sampson; *Dictionary of Canadian Biography*, vol. 12, s.v. "Begbie, Sir Matthew Baillie," by David Ricardo Williams; *Dictionary of Canadian Biography*, vol. 9, s.v. "Brew, Chartres," by Margaret A. Ormsby. A biographical sketch of Needham in *Dictionary of Canadian Biography* is forthcoming.

20. Roderick Finlayson was a career Hudson's Bay Company employee. He became chief factor at Victoria in 1859 and served in the legislative council of Vancouver Island, 1852–1863, and was presently superintendent of HBC affairs in the British Columbia interior. *Dictionary of Canadian Biography*, vol. 12, s.v. "Finlayson, Roderick," by Eleanor Stardom.

We arrived at Esquimalt at 3.45 PM, where the Naval part of the Company disembarked, after having enjoyed a very pleasant trip for 3 days. This was an Annual excursion given by the Hudson Bay Company, and was managed exceedingly well, and with great liberality.[21] From what we saw, it seemed that the whole of the settlements in Puget Sound were going down hill, as they were kept up at first by the Fraser river excitement, but the lumber trade is now the principal employment.

Duties and pleasures

NOVEMBER 2ND.[22] AS THE MARINES WERE nearly out of Provisions at San Juan, we left this morning at 9.30 AM to supply them, as well as with money. I gave a passage to Capt. Franklin of the *Saginaw*, Dr. Brown and Lt. Moore R.N. of the *Sutlej*, and Mr. Dally, (Photographer). We anchored in Roche Harbour at Noon, and went on shore to see Capt. Bazalgette, where we met Captain Grey of the American Camp, and Captain James of the U.S. Army, who had come across from Point Adams at the entrance of the Columbia River, where he was stationed. After having spent a short time at the Camp, we returned on board, and left Roche Harbour at 3.15 PM, and anchored at Esquimalt at 6 PM, having taken 2.45 hrs each way. This was the quickest passage we had as yet made, as the distance by the Inlet Channels was 24 miles, being at the rate of 8.7 knots an hour, the tide being in our favour.

Governor Kennedy and his family left Victoria on the 23rd October for England, and Governor and Mrs. Seymour arrived on the 7th November to take charge of the United Colonies.[23]

He only remained at Victoria till the 10th inst. when he left in the *Sir James Douglas* for New Westminster. The same afternoon at 4 PM, we left for the same place, taking on board before starting Mr. Titcombe as a Pilot, being the same man that got the *Tribune* into trouble on the bar of the Fraser.

As the night was pretty clear, we remained under weigh all night, passing through the Ship passage between Saturna and Waldron Islands (for the first time), and when in the Strait of Georgia going very easy till daylight, reducing the speed from 78 to 26 and 20 Revolutions, which sent us on about a knot an hour. At break of day, we crossed the Bar of the Fraser, where we had 16 feet at nearly high water, and anchored off the Government House at New Westminster on Sunday morning at 9.45 AM.

When we were last here in July, the ship never swung to the Flood, as the river was then high on account of the melting of the snow in the upper country, and the

---

21. "The Excursion," *Daily British Colonist*, 8 October 1866.

22. The day before, the Victoria newspaper carried a one sentence item of interest: "The Prince of Wales [a Hudson's Bay Company ship] brought out a new suit of sails for H.M.S. Sparrowhawk." *Daily British Colonist,* 1 November 1866.

23. Frederick Seymour was governor of the crown colony of British Columbia, 1864–1866. When it was combined with the colony of Vancouver Island into the united colony of British Columbia, Seymour became its first governor. He served in this capacity, 1866–1869. *Dictionary of Canadian Biography*, "Seymour."

"Dressed ship to celebrate the Union of the Colonies of British Columbia and Vancouver Island....Fired a Royal salute." Entry for 19 November 1866, Master's logbook, Adm. 53/9256.

current ran down very strong during the first part of the summer, but at this time in November, the Flood tide ran up as high as the Sumass river, 60 miles from the mouth of the river.

The Flood was very feeble compared to the ebb, and the ship only felt the influence of it for 3 hours out of the 24.

After the Governor had spent 19 days at New Westminster, we embarked him and Mrs. Seymour on the 29th November, and brought them down to Victoria, leaving at 10.30 AM, and making the passage in 7 hours.[24]

They gave their first Ball on the 11th December, when nearly every body from both Colonies were present.[25]

On the 12th December, the Bishop consecrated the new Church of St. Paul at Esquimalt, after having taken only 3 months in building, and was completed with good taste, in the Gothic style. It was well filled at the ceremony, and the collection amounted to $117. The building was completed for $3000, and will seat about 200 people. Its dimensions are 50 feet long by 26 feet wide, and 40 feet in height, surmounted by a steeple 24 feet above the roof. The chancel is 18 x 16 feet, and the vestry is 12 x 10.

The Admiral and Mrs. Denman left in the *Sutlej* at Sunset on the 13th December on their way home. She was accompanied by the *Clio* a short distance, and then separated, the former going on to San Francisco, and the latter to the Sandwich Islands.

On the 15th December, we embarked Governor Seymour, with Mr. Pearse (Surveyor General), Mr. Brew (Stipendiary Magistrate at New Westminster), and Lieut. Cooper Roll as Interpreter, for Cowichan and Nanaimo. We steamed out of Esquimalt at 10.30 PM and anchored in Snug Creek (Cowichan) at 3.30 PM, the *Leviathan* arriving 2 hours afterwards with Maunsell.

That night we had the first fall of snow, and the next day (16th December) steamed up the Cowichan river in the *Leviathan* with Mr. Seymour and party, and landed at Mr. Brennan's house, where we had a Hyas War war with the Indian Chiefs, about their Reserves in the vicinity.

They were promised that the land would be surveyed in the Spring, and the Government would assist them in staking it out. On returning down the river, the *Leviathan* grounded on one of the banks, where she remained till the next day. Mr. Pearse & Maunsell left us in the evening, to return in her to Victoria, but in consequence of continued blowy weather, did not arrive till some days after us.

---

24. For the time being, the *Sparrowhawk* was assigned to the governor. "H.M.S. Sparrowhawk...," *Daily British Colonist*, 15 November 1866. See also, "Governor Seymour...," *Daily British Colonist*, 24 November 1866; "There Were No Signs," *Daily British Colonist*, 26 November 1866; "Governor Seymour," *Daily British Colonist*, 29 November 1866; "Arrival of Governor Seymour," *Daily British Colonist*, 30 November 1866. The *Sparrowhawk* anchored in Esquimalt harbor with several other British and American ships. "Lively Times at Esquimalt," *Daily British Colonist*, 3 December 1866. The harbormaster filed a charge of $10.00 for piloting the *Sparrowhawk* to and from New Westminster. James Cooper to Colonial Secretary, 29 December 1866, Colonial Correspondence, File 355, Provincial Archives of British Columbia.

25. Not mentioned by name, it is assumed that "by...many of the officers of the Fleet," included Porcher's attendance. "The First Ball," *Daily British Colonist*, 12 December 1866; "Ball at the Government House," *Daily British Colonist*, 13 December 1866.

On the morning of the 17th December, we left Cowichan at 7.30 AM, and arrived at Nanaimo at 1.0 PM, where we lashed alongside the Pier, and took in 44 Tons of Coals.

At 7.45 PM of the 18th inst., we cast off from the Pier, and steamed down to Esquimalt where we arrived in 9 ¼ hours. Governor Seymour and his party then left the vessel, having been on board 4 days.[26]

The next day, the water rose to an unusual height in the harbour, and washed up nearly all the Piers at Esquimalt, as well as the foundations of the Serjeant's house at Cole Island.

On the 27th December, left Esquimalt at 8.15 AM, and steamed round to Cadboro Bay, where we embarked Governor & Mrs. Seymour, Stapleton and servants, and proceeded on to New Westminster, where we moored off the Government House at 6.15 PM.[27]

1867. Mrs. Seymour gave her first Ball at New Westminster on New Years night, where there were nearly all the inhabitants of the place, amounting to about 60. On the evening of the 2nd January, Mrs. Seymour gave away the Prizes to the Volunteers won during the last year. The Ceremony took place in the Drill hall, where there was a dance afterwards.

On the evening of the 3rd inst., there was a Team meeting given to the school children in the same hall.

On the 4th January, we left New Westminster with Captain Oldfield, after having been there 8 days, and anchored in Roche Harbour, San Juan, at 2.0 PM, having taken 5½ hours. Landed and took a walk on the island, and afterward dined at the Marines Mess.

January 5th. As Captain Oldfield wanted to see the Governor again, about Capt. Bazalgette wishing a Deserter of their's being delivered up from the American Camp, we left Roche Harbour at 7.40 AM, and anchored off the short Trail at Port Moody, Burrard's Inlet in 7 hours,[28] when Oldfield and Dolphin started to walk in to New Westminster, the distance being 4 miles, and returned during the night. There were several patches of thin ice along the shores between the North Arms and Port Moody.

January 6th. Left at 7.30 AM during a thick Fog, which cleared away gradually, entered the Active Pass at Noon, picked up Captain Bazalgette and party in their boat off San Juan, and anchored at Esquimalt at 4.30 PM, having taken 9 hours in steaming 90 miles.[29]

---

26. "Return of the Governor," *Daily British Colonist*, 19 December 1866.

27. "The Governor," *Daily British Colonist*, 27 December 1866; "H.M.S. Sparrowhawk," *Daily British Colonist*, 28 December 1866; "New Westminster Items," *Daily British Colonist*, 31 December 1866.

28. This concerned "extradition of a criminal from Victoria, who had claimed the protection of the American authorities on San Juan Island." "New Westminster," *Daily British Colonist*, 9 January 1867.

29. "The Sparrowhawk...," *Daily British Colonist*, 5 January 1867.

Chapter Five

On Duty and Off Duty Potpourri

9 January–6 June 1867

[H.M.S. *Sparrowhawk* and its personnel were variously occupied in the first six months of 1867. In early February, the body of one seaman was fished out of the harbor, probably the victim of overindulgence on his Christmas leave. Several weeks later another lost a mid-harbor fight with an inebriated companion and met the same fate. Porcher's routine was punctuated with social obligations and pleasures, including a ball and a trip up the Fraser River to a mining town. He and the ship's doctor gave well received lectures to the Victoria Mechanics' Institute. Aside from another San Francisco mail call, the *Sparrowhawk's* most noteworthy mission in these months was to rescue the crew of a wrecked Hawaiian bark, the *Mauna Kea*, along the northwest coast of Vancouver Island.]

Rescue mission

JANUARY 9TH. NEWS ARRIVED AT VICTORIA today that the Hawaiian Barque *Mauna Kea* had been wrecked near Klaskino on the West Coast of the island, and that the crew were suffering from want of food and exposure, and if not speedily relieved would most probably perish.

We were accordingly ordered to complete with coals the next day, and go in search of them. At 9.20 PM of the 10th Jan. we steamed out of Esquimalt, and passed thro' the Ship passage in the middle watch, and at daylight were a little to the Southward of Nanaimo, and anchored at 2.30 PM of the 11th January, in Tribune Bay, Hornby Island.

There was little or no wind during the day, but the Barometer was low and falling. Landed with Comrie at the head of the Bay, and visited a Comox Indian who was living in his portable house on the beach with his family fishing. He had shot a seal that day, and I bought a joint of it and had it for dinner, which tasted very much like Pork, and not at all bad.[1]

January 12th. The Barometer at daylight was 29.03, having been gradually going down since leaving Esquimalt, and was now blowing very hard from the Eastward right into the Bay. Steamed out of Tribune Bay at 7.30 AM, with some difficulty, as when we were going with Full Power, and making 90 Revolutions, it only gave us but little headway, and just steerage way at times. As soon as we were clear of the Bay, made sail when going thro' the Lambert Channel, but when clear of it, the wind suddenly dropped, and came on to snow very hard, which lasted for 4 hours, during which time we could only see a few yards from the ship, but cleared up before reaching Cape Mudge. Found that the Eucletaws were living at their Ranch close to the Cape. Passed thro' the Seymour Narrows as it was getting dark, and find that we were making very little headway when going 6.5 knots, we were obliged to increase our speed, when we easily passed thro' it, and came to an anchor in Plumper Bay at 5.30 PM, in 12 fathoms. Ran today 58 miles.

January 13th. The Thermometer at 8 AM was 23°, and remained so the greater part of the day. Left Plumper Bay at 7.25 AM, with the tide in our favour, which we kept during the day, and the wind was fair in the afternoon. Steamed at the rate of 7.5 knots with 65 revolutions, and consumed 7 tons of Coal, in going 88 miles. In passing Alert Bay, found the Indians had a large Rancherie there, which seems to be their winter quarters, as there were none there when we passed it in May.[2] It is a well

---

1. "This Island, on the anchorage side, appears to be formed of a recent sandstone, interspersed with black shale, offering fair indications of the presence of coal; and along the eastern side is sparsely wooded with dwarf oak [*quercus garryana*] presenting a park-like appearance, and holding out considerable inducements for a settlement, as there would be no great difficulty in clearing the land, the soil appearing to be good and the water supply plentiful." "The Wreck of the Mauna Kea. Rescue of the Captain, Five Seamen, and a Kanaka Woman, by H.M.S. Sparrowhawk," *Daily British Colonist*, 26 January 1867.

2. Kwakiutl bands customarily clustered together in winter encampments or villages such as Porcher noted at Alert Bay. In a few years, a canning factory and a mission school marked its ascendancy. With the decline of Fort Rupert in the latter half of the century, Alert Bay would become the center for the Indians of Queen Charlotte Strait. Helen Codere, "Kwakiutl: Traditional Culture," in William C. Sturtevant, ed., *Handbook of North American Indians*, vol. 7: *Northwest Coast*, edited by Wayne Suttles, (Washington: Smithsonian Institution, 1990), 361–364. See also note 18 below.

sheltered spot, and a good anchorage as it has a moderate depth of water. Anchored off Cattle Island, at Fort Rupert[3] at 5.45 PM in 9 fathoms.

Mr. [Weynton?] of the Fort called on board.[4]

January 14th. Landed at Fort Rupert after breakfast, and called on Captain Monat, from whom I obtained an Interpreter, Joe Seaweed, for 3 Red blankets and a shirt, value $9, and found that nothing more was known of the shipwrecked crew, but he had sent some provisions across to them to Quatsino Sound, and expected them to arrive at the Fort every day. The distance by Trail from Rupert Arms, Quatsino Sound to Fort Rupert was only 7 miles, and therefore accomplished in half a day.[5] Steamed out of Fort Rupert at 11.30 AM, and when clear of the harbour, it came on to snow hard which lasted 4 hours, and was so thick that we could hardly see the land when passing thro' the Goletas Channel, altho' only a few cables length from it. About Sunset it cleared up, and made out Cape Scott and the islands off it, which we passed shortly after 6. During the night we had violent squalls and shifts of wind, with a heavy rolling sea.

January 15th. At daylight, bore up for Quatsino Sound, which we entered without trouble, and anchored in Winter Harbour at 10.20 AM. Left the ship for the purpose of visiting the village situated at the head of the inlet, but on meeting 5 canoes coming off from it, and telling us that there were 20 white men there, returned, and weighed at 11.25 AM, and steamed up to Hecate Cove, near the Quatsino Narrows, where we anchored at 2.50 PM.[6]

The distance
From Fort Rupert, to Entrance Id, Quatsino Sound, is 75 miles
From Entrance Island to Winter Harbour 6 miles,
From Winter Harbour to Hecate Cove 19 having run exactly 100 miles yesterday.

January 16th. After breakfast, landed to see the large Rancherie at the entrance of Hecate Cove, where there were 15 lodges, and between 3 and 400 inhabitants. It seems to have been much better built and more waterproof than any we had as yet seen. In many of them there were sleeping rooms, looking like large boxes about 15

3. Attracted by the Hudson's Bay Company post there, Fort Rupert became the largest Kwakiutl settlement and a principal ceremonial center. A smallpox epidemic in 1862 and the destruction of the village by the Royal Navy three years later began Fort Rupert's decline and the ascendancy of the Alert Bay settlement. Codere, "Kwakiutl," 361–364.

4. He "reported that the wrecked party, consisting of 6 men and 1 woman, were supposed to be at Quatsino, but had no certain intelligence, as the Indians that had been sent to their assistance with provisions and blankets from the Fort had not yet returned." "The Wreck of the Mauna Kea," *Daily British Colonist*, 26 January 1867.

5. "[T]he Indians of the village, close to the Fort, were somewhat excited, being engaged in their medicine rites, and preparing for a magnificent 'potlach', at which, amongst the numerous things to be given away, were some very fine canoes, displayed, hauled up on the beach. They were, however, peaceable, and a marked improvement was observable in their deportment since the visit of H.M.S. Clio last year, the punishment then inflicted having had a very salutary effect." Ibid.

6. "[T]he Quatsino…Indians…are a very small tribe and number about forty; compress the head into a conical shape, and speak the Qua-Qua language, which dialect prevails from Fort Rupert round to Kyuquot." Ibid.

feet in length & 7 feet high, and roofed over, so that they must have been much warmer and drier than those that had not that additional protection.[7]

In this Sound, we saw for the first time the Conical heads to perfection, and the women were considered much greater beauties in consequence.[8] This village and the one we saw yesterday in Winter Harbour seem to be the only Villages occupied during the Winter season, but during the summer they spread themselves in other parts for the purpose of fishing such as at Koskeemo, and opposite Russia Island.

From the Indians at this place, we were informed that the shipwrecked men had not been in this Sound at all, but had gone round to Kyuquot Sound, where they were living at a White man's house.

Had a heavy gale of snow during the night, and continued rain all today, which prevented our sending a boarding party away, so we left this snug and safe anchorage at 1.45 PM. It was perfectly calm in the harbour, but when we got clear of it, it came on to blow very hard from the S.E. with violent squalls off the high land, and were at times obliged to put on all our power to be enabled to steam against it.

At 4.10 PM, we moored in Koprino harbour in 9½ fathoms, the distance from Hecate Cove being 12 miles.

January 17th. Still blowing hard from the S.E. so we employed the men cutting fire wood, of which they sent on board 8 fathoms and filled up with water.[9]

January 18th. The Barometer having gone up during the night, and the weather looking finer, unmoored at daylight, and steamed out of Koprino Harbour at 7.45 AM, but as soon as we got into the open part of the Sound, it came on to blow hard from the Southward, with squalls off the high land, so we were obliged to find shelter again, and steamed into North Harbour, inside of Ro*[illeg.]* Island,[10] where

---

7. "The natives appeared a vigorous and fine race, cheerful and intelligent, the juvenile population healthy and numerous—a good feature in the community. The tribe number about 400, of which 120 are adult males." "The Wreck of the Mauna Kea," *Daily British Colonist*, 26 January 1867.

8. "[T]he head of one…measured in diameter, fore and aft, 17 inches side to side 14 inches, circular 24 inches, and across the zygomotic [sic] arch 11 inches. Several infants were seen undergoing the process, lashed up in cradles in the shape of a small canoe, with a cavity just large enough to admit the body of a child and the head also, giving it room to expand in length. The pressure is applied by means of two lateral pads of cedar bound to each side of the head by a circular bandage, and after leaving the cradle up to the age puberty a circular band of cedar is worn, which the girls sometimes render ornamental by coquettishly placing in it a sprig of pine above the right ear. Another feature also attended to in the infantile development is keeping the feet bandaged with the toes turned in. The compression of the head seems to have no prejudicial effect on the intellect, and is, perhaps, on the whole, less injurious than squeezing the waist, which we do know interferes with the vital functions. As regards the 'toeing in,' it has been proved in the late American war that 'a man walks faster and longer with his feet in this position than with the toes turned out, as it enables him to avail himself more completely of the action of the muscles of the leg and foot.'" Ibid.

9. "The formation both here and at Hecate Cove appeared to consist of red metamorphic sandstone, much colored by oxide of iron and overlaid in some places by a coarse conglomerate, the whole reposing on a bed of clay, slate and trap. No coal was observed in this neighborhood, although the formation is decidedly carboniferous. Coal, however, I am told crops out in considerable quantity higher up the arm. The timber found to exist here consisted of Menzies Spruce (Abies Mengesli), Hemlock Spruce (Abies Canadensis), Cedar (Thuga Cigantea), with dense undergrowth of crab, alder, and sal lal (gaulethera shallon)." Ibid.

10. In Quatsino Sound. Porcher's log, 293–294.

we anchored at 9.30 AM, in 7 fathoms, the distance from Koprino Harbour being 9½ miles.

We had taken a Siwash away from the Rancherie at Hecate Cove, as an Interpreter, and to shew us the place at Kyuquot Sound where the white men were living, but this afternoon he began to be doubtful, if he ever should ever be brought [home] again, and he took advantage of several canoes being alongside, to jump over the bows into one when nobody was looking, and was paddling away quietly, when he was detected by Police Serjeant Ferrale, and brought back in rather an ignominious manner.

January 19th. The Barometer went down in the middle watch to 29.10, and we had a continual succession of heavy squalls all night, with constant rain from the S.E. At daylight it was still blowing hard from the same quarter to S.W. which prevented our moving. In the afternoon the weather cleared up, when we finally left Quatsino Sound at 4 PM, with a light breeze from the Westward, and ran down to the Southward the greater part of the night under the foresail, going about 4 knots.

January 20th. At daylight we stood in for Kyuquot Sound, but before we could close with it, it came on to blow a Gale of wind from the S.E. with thick and rainy weather, which prevented our seeing the entrance and forced us to stand off the land, under the fore and aft sails.

At 4 PM, the wind suddenly shifted to the S.W. and afterwards became light. The Barometer having gone down to 29.20, when it rose immediately.

January 21st. At 2 AM, work round and stood in for the land, under the foresail and main topsail. At daylight made out the entrance to Kyuquot Sound, and ran in for it under sail and easy steam, and anchored in Fair Harbour exactly at Noon in 20 fathoms, close to an Indian ranch.[11]

On arriving here we found out from the Indians, that the shipwrecked crew we were in search of, were living with a white man of the name of Charles Carlton, a Village Island Aktese situated off the Blind entrance to the Sound.

The Serjeant of Police started in a Canoe shortly after we anchored to inform them of our arrival, in case they had not seen us, or heard our guns that we fired on entering the Sound, the distance being about 10 miles.[12] He returned at night, having been away 10 hours, and found the whole party there, very anxious to leave, but had only a small canoe on the island.

---

11. "The Sound is surrounded by an abrupt range of high mountains, evidently of an igneous nature and at the entrance is obstructed by numerous dangerous reefs and hidden rocks, on one of which some Indian canoes we passed, thinking we were going to strike, made most violent pantomimic signs with their paddles to warn us. This tribe, the Kyuquot, number about 200, are very poor, live in low dirty hovels, go about almost naked with the exception of wearing tippets of cedar bark, and altogether are engaged in rather a severe Darwinian 'struggle for existence.' They speak a separate language of their own and do not compress the head." "The Wreck of the Mauna Kea," *Daily British Colonist,* 26 January 1867.

12. "Sergeant Ferrel of the Victoria Police [is] a most energetic and intelligent officer, who accompanied the ship as interpreter and was of very great service in communicating with and obtaining information from the natives." Ibid.

January 22nd. At daylight the 2nd Cutter left for Aktese with Lieut. Harrison,[13] who returned at 6 PM with the whole of the shipwrecked crew, consisting of the Captain (Robinson) Mate, Steward, 3 seamen, and a Kanaka woman.

Mauna Kea *saga*

THE PARTICULARS OF THE LOSS OF THE VESSEL, and their subsequent adventures may be very briefly told. The *Mauna Kea* sailed from Puget Sound for Honolulu with a cargo of lumber on the 10th November, 1866, and in consequence of continued heavy weather, the vessel became waterlogged, and fell over on her beam ends, when about 150 miles from Cape Flattery, that her masts were cut away, and after righting she drifted helplessly for 13 days, during which time the crew suffered intensely from want of food and exposure, they having no shelter during this time, and all hands subsisted upon one bag of Flour, and about 25 pounds of beans. She finally stranded near Klaskino about ½ past 4 in the morning, and two of the crew were drowned, the rest landed and remained on the beach without shelter for about nine days subsisting on shell fish picked off the rocks at low water, when they were taken charge of by the Klaskino Indians, and taken to their village, where they remained about 3 weeks, when a canoe arrived from Quatsino with Indians, who on their return took one of the seamen John Cartage to Fort Rupert, and another Humphrey Leary also leaving for Fort Rupert at the same time in a canoe belonging to Klaskino. About 5 days after leaving Klaskino these two men arrived at Fort Rupert, and remained there about 6 days when they left that place for Victoria in the schooner *Gazelle* on the 2nd January, and arrived at Victoria on the night of the 8th January.

The day after the two seamen had left the party, the Captain was informed that there was a white settler living at Kyuquot Sound, and as he was getting very weak from poor living, started in a small canoe with 2 Indians for that place where he arrived in 26 hours on Christmas Day, and found an American of the name of Charles Carlton, living on the island of Aktese, who was willing to look after the whole party. Accordingly, he got a larger canoe manned by 4 Indians, to bring the whole party over, who arrived there safely on the 4th January. Since that time they had been in comparative luxury, living on Venison, Wild Fowl, Fish, Potatoes, Beans, Coffee, Tea, Sugar, &c.

It seems that Captain Robinson and his party had received every assistance from the Indians, and the only reason that they had fared rather badly at Klaskino, was that the Chief had nothing else to give them but dried salmon, but was most useful in providing them with canoes, both in bringing them to their Village, as well as taking them away.[14]

---

13. Matthew J. Harrison had replaced Napoleon A. R. Spicer, one of the initial Lieutenants on the *Sparrowhawk*, on 11 December 1866. *Navy List* (April 1867): 217.

14. "This tribe, Klaskino, appear to be a very small one and rapidly dying off, numbering about 40, of which not more than 12 are adult male, seem to have no distinct language of their own, but like other border tribes speak with equal facility the language of the Kyuquot's on one side or that of the Koskeemo's on the other, to the latter of which, however, they appear more nearly allied, as they practice conical compression of the head after the Koskeemo fashion, a custom not existing in the Kyuquot tribe." "The Wreck of the Mauna Kea," *Daily British Colonist*, 26 January 1867.

January 23rd. Steamed out of Fair Harbour, Kyuquot Sound, at 7.40 AM, cutting our way by steaming slowly thro' the ice, which was about an inch thick all over the harbour.

When clear of the Sound we had light Easterly wind, which we kept till we got into the Straits of Fuca.

January 25th. Passed the Cape Flattery light at 2 AM, and steamed up the Straits against a fresh Easterly wind, and anchored at Esquimalt at 2.35 PM.[15]

Cut and burnt 24 ½ fathoms of wood during the time we were on the West Coast, and on our arrival here had 2 Tons of Coals left in the Bunkers.

The Serjeant of Police Patrick Ferrale who accompanied us on this cruize, was most useful during the short time we were away, and would be of great service to any ship that might be sent on a similar trip.[16]

Merchant ship beached

FEBRUARY 4TH. THE QUARTERMASTER AWOKE me at 4.30 AM to give me a letter from Captain Oldfield to inform me that the *Nicholas Biddle* (American Merchant ship) was on shore at the Race rocks, and that we were to go to her assistance at daylight. This vessel had lately put into this harbour waterlogged, having taken a cargo of Coals on board at Nanaimo, and was on her way to San Francisco when she sprung a leak, and was obliged to put back here. She was then unloaded at Foster's Pier, and afterwards repaired at Victoria. Since that time she had gone over to Port Madison in Puget Sound, and filled up with Lumber, and was beating out of the Straits on her way to San Francisco, when she got on shore at the Race rocks. Shortly before 7, we steamed out of the harbour, and proceeded there, where I sent Lieut. Harrison to the Light house to make inquiries, but came back without being able to

---

15. The *Sparrowhawk* anchored at 3.40 PM. Porcher's log, 293.

16. The wreck received sketchy notice until the return of the *Sparrowhawk*. "Wreck of the Hawaiian Bark Mauna Kea," *Daily British Colonist*, 9 January 1867; "The Wreck of the Mauna Kea," *Daily British Colonist*, 20 January 1867; "The Malacca...," *Daily British Colonist*, 24 January 1867; "No Tidings," *Daily British Colonist*, 25 January 1867.

Following the lengthy report that appeared as "The Wreck of the Mauna Kea," *Daily British Colonist*, 26 January 1867, used above to augment Porcher's account, the incident was further noted in "The Loss of the Mauna Kea," *Daily British Colonist*, 28 January 1867; "Unexampled Generosity," *Daily British Colonist*, 29 January 1867; "Dead," *Daily British Colonist*, 13 February 1867. While Fred Rogers, *Shipwrecks of British Columbia* (Vancouver: J. J. Douglas, 1973) does not mention the *Mauna Kea* incident in the text, it is noted as #320 on the endmap, "Shipwreck Chart No. 2."

Porcher had been scheduled to deliver a lecture to the Mechanics' Institute in its winter series but special naval assignments had postponed it. "Mechanics' Institute—Lectures," *Daily British Colonist*, 27 November 1866; "Mechanics' Institute," *Daily British Colonist*, 3 January 1867; "Lecture," *Daily British Colonist*, 4 January 1867; "Mechanics' Institute," *Daily British Colonist*, 16 January 1867; "It Is Expected," *Daily British Colonist*, 28 January 1867; "Lecture," and Mechanics' Institute Advertisement, *Daily British Colonist*, 31 January 1867.

The well received lecture delivered 31 January 1867, concerned the formation of coral reefs of the Coral Sea between Australia, New Guinea, and New Caledonia. It was based on his study and observations while stationed in the area and was illustrated by blackboard sketches. "Mechanics' Institute," *Daily British Colonist*, 1 February 1867. Dr. Comrie gave two lectures, 7, 21 March 1867, on "Air & Water." Advertisement and "Lecture," *Daily British Colonist*, 7 March 1867; "Dr. Comrie's Lecture," *Daily British Colonist*, 8 March 1867; "Lecture," *Daily British Colonist*, 22 March 1867; "Dr. Comrie's Lecture on 'Water'," *Daily British Colonist*, 23 March 1867.

get any intelligence, we then went on to Trial Island where we had seen a vessel under bare poles, and on nearing her, found that it was the vessel herself, then in tow of the *Isabel*. The Captain and crew had abandoned the vessel during the night, and had gone in to Esquimalt for assistance, leaving only the Steward and Cook on board.

The Agent Mr. C. Wallace on hearing of the disaster, had immediately engaged the *Isabel*, and taken her out the first thing in the morning with the Crew.

About 1 PM, we saw that the *Isabel* that was only 60 Horse Power, had not sufficient power to tow her against the wind, and had run under the lee of Trial Island, we therefore bore up, took her in tow at 2 PM, and brought her into Esquimalt, where we anchored at 4.30 PM.[17]

They attempted to repair the vessel by Divers but without success, and after Captain Stamp had secured $750 for the hire of the *Isabel*, was eventually towed over to Puget Sound by the *Fideliter* and *Diana* on the 2nd March.

Drowned seaman

FEBRUARY 9TH. THE BODY OF JOHN KELLEY a Stoker, who had gone on leave on Christmas Day and had not been seen since, was found floating near the landing place at Esquimalt this afternoon, having most probably dropped overboard when in a state of drunkenness. His body had been under water 46 days or nearly 7 weeks, before it floated, and all the exposed parts the head, hands and feet, had been eaten by the fish, and nothing but the bones left.

A Coroner's Inquest was held over it on the 11th inst. by Mr. Pemberton the Stipendiary Magistrate, and a verdict of "Found drowned" was given by the Jury, and the remains were buried on the following day.

Unsuccessful duck hunting

FEBRUARY 14TH. AS WE HAD NOT VISITED the Agricultural districts to the Northward, since November 1865, nearly 15 months, we left Esquimalt this morning at 4.30 AM,[18] passed through the Active Pass at 10.30 AM, and anchored at Port Augusta (Comox) at 8 PM, the distance being 125 miles, or at the rate of 8 knots an hour.

Exercised firing shot and shell at the rocks before entering the Active Pass. The wind was fair all day, and increased to a fresh breeze from the Eastward during the afternoon, which allowed us to make sail, and sent the ship on between 9 and 10 knots.

February 15th. After breakfast the following day, left the vessel with Colonel Foster who I had invited to come for this cruize, and Dolphin, for Mr. Hart's store at Comox, where we hired a canoe to take us up the Courtenay river to the Mission

---

17. "H.M.S. Sparrowhawk...," *Daily British Colonist*, 29 January 1867; "Disaster to the Ship Nicholas Biddle," *Daily British Colonist*, 5 February 1867.

While Rogers, Shipwrecks of British Columbia does not mention the Nicholas Biddle incident in the text, it is noted as #332 on the endmap, "Shipwreck Chart No. 2." The date of the incident is erroneously indicated as 1875.

18. "Naval," *Daily British Colonist*, 13 February 1867.

that is situated about 2 miles from the mouth, where we found Mr. Philipps (the Bishop's Nephew) and Mr. Stohem (a Surveyor). After paying a short visit, and find that there was not shooting to be had in that direction, we descended the river again in the same canoe with Mr. Bailey, and landed on the beach on the right mouth of the river, near Macmillan's house for the purpose of shooting ducks, but without success, and returned on board at 5 PM. A very fine day. The wild fowl were still very numerous, but being at the end of the season, had become very wild, on account of the number of people that had been constantly firing at them.

February 16th. I went out shooting on the Goose spit, but found great difficulty in getting near any of the birds. In walking through a Trail this afternoon, I suddenly came upon a Skull and part of a Skeleton, and looking up found that it had been blowed down from its wooden coffin out of one of the branches of the tree, which is the usual place for the Indians to bury their dead in this part of the country, to preserve them from the wolves and other wild animals. The Skull being in tolerable preservation, I sent it [a]board.

February 18th. Mr. Bailey (a Comox settler) came on board with some Bags of bacon for a passage to Nanaimo. Steamed out of Comox at 7.45 AM, but before we had advanced very far, it came on to blow hard against us from the Eastward, with thick snow, which prevented our seeing but a short distance, and forced us to anchor in Fanny Bay at 9.50 AM, the distance we had run being only 10 miles.

Went on shore with Boys to shoot wild fowl, which were in great abundance, but very shy. Visited a log hut at Bare Flat on the Northern part of the bay, where we found two Americans who were left in charge of the ground, to prevent its being jumped. They told us that the Coal seam was about 5 miles off, but as the Trail did not extend the whole distance, we should have some trouble in reaching it, and as the weather was very bad, we were obliged to give up the idea of visiting it.

It had been discovered by the river passing through the seam, and cropping out of the banks on each side with little or no dip. An American Company intended to work it in the Spring, but were obliged to give up the idea for the present, as there was some doubt who the land properly belonged to, and the 2 men that we met there were recalled shortly afterwards.[19]

February 20th. The weather having improved a little, altho' still snowing, and an Easterly wind against us, we left Fanny Bay at 7.30 AM, and secured alongside the Coaling Wharf at Nanaimo at 2.20 PM, the distance being 45 miles, or at the rate of 6½ knots an hour, against a strong breeze the greater part of the way.[20]

February 21st. The next day we took in 80½ tons of Coals. We found here the American ship *Amethyst* Captain O'Reilly, that was taking in 500 tons of Coals. She was the only vessel belonging to the Bellingham Bay Company, who were at present pumping out the mine, having been obliged to flood it a few months back, to put a fire out.

---

19. Someone, perhaps Porcher, reported further comments on the settlement and economy of the Comox region when the *Sparrowhawk* returned to Victoria. "From the East Coast," *Daily British Colonist*, 28 February 1867.

20. "From the East Coast," *Daily British Colonist*, 22 February 1867.

The Coal Company at Nanaimo were not doing much business, they had between 8 or 9000 tons stacked on the surface ready for any sudden demand, and about 40 men were employed down in the mine, that sent up on the average 100 Tons daily, or between 2 or 4 tons each man, that took them generally 8 hours. For every ton they sent up $ ¼ was paid them.

The Russian Fur Company's steamer *Constantine* arrived from Victoria on the 23rd inst. for 200 tons of Coals, on their way to Sitka. Her Captain Lindfors called here, and in returning his visit, I met Captain Boucht of the Russian steamer *Alexandra* that was repairing at Victoria, and Captain Lemascheffsky belonging to another vessel of the same Company at Sitka. We remained at Nanaimo nearly 5 days, during which it was snowing the greater part of the time.

February 25th. Hauled off from the Pier at Nanaimo, and steamed out of the harbour at 8.15 AM, and anchored in Roche Harbour, San Juan at 4.30 PM, a distance of 55 miles, or at the rate of 7 knots an hour. It was blowing hard from the S.E with snow the greater part of the day. Captain Bazalgette came on board in a canoe with one Marine shortly after we anchored, bringing him our English Mails, that had been left by the *Malacca* on their way to New Westminster.

We remained at San Juan the next day, and left at 6.20 AM of the 27 February with very little wind, but before rounding Discovery Island it came on to blow hard from the S.E. which soon brought our speed down, and anchored at Esquimalt at 10.30 AM.

Altercation and drowning

THE FOLLOWING EVENING TWO OF OUR Leading Stokers Pinch and Dawson[21] had been on leave at Esquimalt with two of the Stokers of the *Malacca*, and were all returning to the ship in the middle watch in the Grappler's Dingy. When about half way to the ship the Leading Stoker and Stoker of the *Malacca* had a dispute about the boat being full of water, which ended in a fight, and caused the boat to capsize. A boat belonging to the *Forward* as well as our Dingy hearing their cries went to their assistance, and picked up Pinch and the Leading Stoker of the *Malacca* who were holding on to the boat, but the other two who could swim had struck out for the shore which was not more than 50 yards distant, and as they were not seen again were probably benumbed by the cold & went down.

The men seemed to have been all sober, with the exception of the Stoker of the *Malacca*, who commenced the fight, and was one of the two that were drowned.[22] For several days after this, a Boat was employed dragging for the 2 bodies, but without success, the men's Caps were picked up on the shore, close to the place where the boat was capsized.[23]

The bodies of these two men were afterwards found, for after the lapse of 7 weeks they both floated, which was nearly the same time our former Stoker Kelly had

21. Thos. Dawson. Entry for 1 March 1867, Master's logbook, Adm. 53/9256.

22. The published report said: "The accident occurred through carelessness." "Casualty at Esquimalt," *Daily British Colonist*, 2 March 1867.

23. "The Boat Accident at Esquimalt," *Daily British Colonist*, 4 March 1867.

taken. The Stoker of the *Malacca* first floated on the morning of the 17th April, and Dawson our Leading Stoker on the 19th inst, which gave 47 and 49 days respectively.

Cowichan Bay visit

THE EARLY PART OF MARCH USHERED in a great deal of cold weather, which prevented the foliage coming forward as early as last year. The first shrubs I saw coming into leaf were the brilliant pink Ribes or flowering currant, and the wild gooseberry on the 12th March, and the first wild flowers the chick weed on the 18th inst.

On the 23rd March, we left Esquimalt for a short cruize taking with us Mr. Stapleton, and Captain Bazalgette, and arriving in Roche Harbour at 1.30 PM, in 3 hours, where we remained till nearly Noon of the 25th inst, when we left for Snug Creek, Cowitchen, where we arrived in 2½ hours the distance being 21 miles, or at the rate of 8.4 miles an hour. Before leaving San Juan, Bazalgette, Dolphin and Christie[24] went out shooting on Henry Island, and brought on board 3 Deer.

March 25th. Landed with Stapleton at Mr. Harris's store John Bull Inn at Cowitchen, where we met Mr. Rothwell of Esquimalt. The history of Mr. Harris seems to have been that he joined the 2nd Life Guards as a Private in 1829, at the age of 18, which makes him now 56 years of age, and bought his discharge for £30, after having served 4 years. He afterwards went out to the Mosquito Coast, where he was made a J.P. at Bluefields, and has been living here for the last 9 years, keeping a Public house, and speculating in land.

March 26th. Landed at Cowitchen with Stapleton and Boys, where we met the Rev. W. S. Reece, and Mr. Wing, and not being able to obtain horses on account of the Bishop being expected in the Afternoon, we started with Wing for Skinner's Farm, about 3 miles off, calling on our way at the Convent where we examined 6 of the Indian girls in reading which they did very creditably, but slowly. The Sister of Charity, a French Canadian, told us that she had lately 20 Girls to instruct, but that they were continually leaving and running away. Mr. Skinner seems to be getting on very slowly at his Farm, as the house that we saw Commenced more than 15 months ago was only half finished, and only a few acres of land had been cultivated and staked round.

We afterwards walked on to the Quamichan Ranch, situated near the banks of the river that flows into the Bay, and is placed in a very picturesque spot, with a good deal of open ground round it, and a Salmon weir built across the river. The Rev. W. Reece had lately built a Church and Parsonage house a few hundred yards at the back of this Ranch on higher ground, and he was now employed getting the ground and place in order.[25] The Bishop was expected up today to fix on a site for a school, so as to be at a convenient distance from his house & church.

---

24. George Christie was Master on the *Sparrowhawk*. *Navy List* (April 1865): 208; Master's logbook, Adm. 53/9255, 53/9256, 53/9257.

25. The "greater portion" of the "voluntary subscription" of funds for the construction of the church "was gathered together by my kind friends on board H.M.S. *Sparrowhawk*." W. S. Reece, "Cowitchen. European and Indian Mission," Columbia Mission, *Ninth Annual Report of the Columbia Mission [of the Church of England], for the Year 1867* (London: Rivingtons, 1868), 31.

After lunching at the Parsonage, we returned to the Bay (about 2 miles) calling Mr. Nott's Store (Agent of Mr. Fell's). The day had been very fine and warm, but a great deal of snow was still lying about the woods. Mr. Wing accompanied us the whole day & was very useful in shewing us the different trails, and came on board to dinner.

March 27th. The next day we left Snug Creek at 7.15 AM, and anchored at Esquimalt in 4 hours and 20 minutes, the distance being 41 miles, or at the rate of 9.5 knots, the tide being in our favour.[26] Met the *Enterprise* off Trial Island on her way to New Westminster, stopped and put Stapleton on board.

San Francisco mail call

April 11th. As the Colony is at present $18,000 in debt to the Californian U.S.S. Company for carrying the Mails, and there being no more money in the Treasury to pay for the usual Subsidy, one or two Mails had to be left behind at San Francisco, and were likely to remain there till some arrangements were made. At the request of the Governor (Seymour) we made preparations for sea, and took on board the Colonial Mails, the one's from New Westminster arriving at 10 PM in the *Leviathan*, that small vessel having taken 16 hours in steaming down here, a fresh breeze being against her part of the way.[27] We steamed out of Esquimalt at 10.30 PM, for San Francisco the night being very fine with little wind. Passed Cape Flattery shortly after daylight, and during April 12th the forenoon, a breeze springing up from the Westward which enabled us to set all plain sail, and sent the ship on 8 knots. This fair wind only lasted 15 hours, and then shifted ahead from the SSE which lasted 26 hours, and brought the speed gradually down to 3 knots.

April 13th. Finding that we should not have sufficient coals to take us the whole way, if the wind remained much longer at the SS.E., we stopped the engines at 4 PM, and put the ship under easy sail, standing off the land to the S.W. until 4 AM the next morning, when the wind [(]April 14th[)] shifted to the W.S.W. and enabled us to lay our course under steam and sail, and sent the ship on 7 and 8 knots the whole day.

April 15th. This wind lasted 22 hours, and then shifted to the Northward with a high barometer, at 1.30 AM, and blew fresh during the day, sending the ship on during the day 10 knots, and lasted till we got into port.

April 16th. Rounded Point Reyes at 2 am going 9.5 knots, and ran in for the harbour, where we anchored off Meigg's Wharf at 5.30 am. After breakfast called on the Acting Consul Mr. Mason, and arranged with Mr. McC*[illeg.]* to send off 100

---

26. "H.M.S. Sparrowhawk...," *Daily British Colonist*, 28 March 1867. The ship stayed in the harbor for several days pending another assignment. "Esquimalt Items," *Daily British Colonist*, 5 April 1867.

27. The *Sparrowhawk* had been "provisioned and with her fires banked, prepared to start" for several days. "The Mails," *Daily British Colonist*, 8 April 1867. Three days later the readers were admonished to "Get your letters ready!" because the *Sparrowhawk* was scheduled to leave that afternoon carrying mail and express. "For San Francisco," *Daily British Colonist*, 11 April 1867. See also "The Mails. Editors Colonist." *Daily British Colonist*, 9 April 1867; "The Mails," *Daily British Colonist*, 9 April 1867; "The Strange Apathy of Government Regarding the Mail Service," *Daily British Colonist*, 10 April 1867; "For San Francisco," *Daily British Colonist*, 12 April 1867; "The Mails," *Daily British Colonist*, 12 April 1867.

Tons of Sydney Coals at $16.50. The price had risen $2 since we were here in September, when we took in 50 Tons. Made the passage for Esquimalt in 4 days & 7 hours.

April 17th. Commenced taking in the 100 Tons this morning which was brought alongside in 2 lighters, and finished at 5.40 PM, and allowing 2¼ hours for the men's meals, we took it in at the rate of 9 Tons an hour.

Called on General Halleck who was going to leave this day for Fort Yuma on the Southern extreme of the State, situated on the Rio Colorado, on a tour of Inspection.

An American young Lady Miss B. *[blank]* told me that it was so hot there, that the Fowls laid hard boiled eggs. After receiving on board 116 Bags of Mails, we steamed out of San Francisco at 9 PM, having at the time very little wind, and nearly full moon.[28]

April 18th. Little wind all day. In the afternoon had a light breeze from the Southward with drizzling rain, which increased sufficiently by 6.50 PM to enable us to make all plain sail.

April 19th. Good Friday. Blowing fresh from the Southward sending the ship under steam & sail for a great part of the day 11.2 knots with rain. Split the Fore Topsail at Sunset.

April 20th. The wind shifted to the Westward about Midnight and became lighter, but the ship still making upwards of 9 knots. At 8.25 PM sighted the Cape Flattery light which we rounded at 10.30, and steamed up the Straits against an Easterly breeze, which became lighter as we proceeded.

April 21st. Anchored at Esquimalt at 5.45 AM, having made the passage from San Francisco in 81 hours,[29] being with the exception of one the quickest passage on record, and making the passage each way, including the 2 days stoppage at San Francisco, in 9¼ days.

The quantity of Coals we burnt on this trip was 142¾ Tons, viz. or 74½ Tons in going down, and 68¼ Tons in returning:

68¼ Tons	at $16.50	=	$1122 [*sic*]	or £229. 1.6
23	9.00	=	207	42. 5.3
51½	6.65	=	342½ [*sic*]	69.18.6
142¾ Tons			**$1671½**	**£341. 5.3**

But the real expense of carrying the Mails from Esquimalt to San Francisco & back between 11th & 21st April 1867, was as follows:

100 Tons	at $16.50	@	48½	$1650	£333. 8.9
23	9.00		49	207	42. 5.3
19¾	6.65			133 [*sic*]	27. 3.1
142¾				**$1990**	**£402.17.1**

28. "The Sparrowhawk…," *Daily British Colonist*, 18 April 1867.

29. Another report said the run had been made in 79 hours. "Quick Trip," *Daily British Colonist*, 23 April 1867. See also "The Mails," *Daily British Colonist*, 22 April 1867; "Express," *Daily British Colonist*, 22 April 1867.

Lighthouse inspections

April 29th. Accompanied Governor Seymour, Mr. Birch, Young, Pearse, and Capt. Oldfield in the *Forward*, and steamed to the Race rocks, where we landed and inspected the Light House. Two men were living there to look after the light, and must spend rather a monotonous life. The Light house was built on the largest rock which was about 270 yards long, and there was so little soil on it, that only two small plots of ground about 20 feet square were cultivated, the remainder being but a little more than a bare rock. A large Fog bell was lying on the ground, having been landed there about 9 months ago with all the apparatus for ringing it. It had cost £800, but the Colony had not yet gone to the expense of putting it up. The light house was a circular tower strongly built of stone, and the quarters for the men were comfortable enough. At this season of the year when the lamp was lit after 7 pm, and put out after 5 am, the consumption was Oil was about 3 Pints. On our way back we landed to see the Fisguard Light House at the entrance of Esquimalt, which was also in good order, but the landing place had been washed up during the high tides, and wanted being put in order. Mr. Bevis, late a Purser of one of the West India steamers was living there with his Wife with a salary of $80 a month. The light was of the 4th Order, and burnt at this season 1½ Pints of Rape seed Oil. Both the lights were Dioptric, or by refractory lenses. The Race light had a white flash every ten seconds, and SEE 3 or 4 cable length is a reef, having 5 feet *[illeg.]*.[30]

Churches and fishes

On the 4th May we left Esquimalt at 5.15 am, and arrived in Cadboro Bay in a 1 hr. 25 m. where we anchored to await the arrival of the Governor,[31] who arrived at 8.15 with Birch and Maunsell, when we weighed and proceeded to New Westminster, on our way we exercised firing shot and shell at the rocks, and anchored off the Government House N.W at 4.20 pm. It was nearly calm all day. On crossing the bar of the Fraser, the water was so low, that we were just enabled to scrape over it. The Governor had only been 8 days at Victoria, having arrived there in the *Forward* on the evening of the 25th April.

When we arrived at New Westminster the ship only swung to the Flood about 3½ hours out of the 24, but became less every day, and did not swing at all after the 13th May, as the current then became stronger, on account of the water rising in the river. The water is generally at its highest point between the middle and end of June, when the drift timber gets floated off the shoal spots, and comes down the river with great velocity, often fouling the ships at anchor.

The Clergymen at present here were the Rev. Hagman, and Cave, both of whom had lately been ordained in the Colony. The average collection every Sunday at the temporary Church in the Town was $20, and at Sapperton (Town of the Sappers) $3½. At Nanaimo it is $10, which the Clergyman keeps, so as to make his Salary up to £100 a year, any thing above that goes towards the expenses of the Church.

30. There are a few clues to the other activities of the *Sparrowhawk* in these weeks. "H.M.S. Sparrowhawk...," *Daily British Colonist*, 24 April 1867; "H.M.S. Sparrowhawk," *Daily British Colonist*, 25 April 1867; "The Bark Scotland," *Daily British Colonist*, 26 April 1867; "The Governor...," *Daily British Colonist*, 30 April 1867.

31. "The Governor...," *Daily British Colonist*, 3 May 1867.

Yale, the head of navigation of the Fraser, & 125 miles from its mouth. May 16, 1867.

(original watercolor size: 14 x 9.88 in./35.5 x 25 cm)

Indian Graves at Chapman's Bar, 12 miles above Yale. May 18, 1867.

(original watercolor size: 9.13 x 6 in./23 x 15 cm)

At this time of year the Hou-li-kun[32] were coming up the river, and afforded us some sport for a week or so.

They very much resemble a smelt in size, and are extremely good eating. They are caught in the following manner: About 3 dozen sharp nails or spikes are driven into a flat piece of wood 12 to 15 feet long, and 2 or 3 inches broad, making an instrument like a rake, a man sits in the bows of the boat, and dipping this down perpendicularly under water, sweeps it along toward the after end of the boat, pinning some 6 or a dozen fish on the nails each sweep he takes, every time he brings it up, turns the points of the nails downward, gives the rake a tap on the gunwale, which knocks the fish off into the bottom of the boat. In this simple way an Indian will often half fill his canoe in an hour or so.

One afternoon (9th May) I went out in a small boat with Mr.E and Mrs. Seymour, Birch and Maunsell, and caught 4 cwt within 2 hours, or counting 10 to the pound, about 4500 fish.

Boston Bar visit

As I HAD NOT YET SEEN ANY THING OF the inland parts of the country, I was very glad to join a large party that was going up to Yale, the extreme point of navigation, and from there a day's journey by land. It was given at the expense of the Governor, the use of the steamer being offered to him by her Captain and Owner.[33]

Every thing being ready, we left New Westminster on the 15th May in the *Onward*, Captain Irving,[34] at 10.50 AM, with a party of 17, 10 Gentlemen and 7 Ladies, consisting of the Governor and Mrs. Seymour, the Chief Justice, Mrs. & 2 Misses Needham, The Bishop and Mrs. Hills, Mr. & Mrs. Trutch (Surveyor General),[35] Mrs. Pearse, Judge Begbie,[36] Mr. Etheridge, Birch, Maunsell, and Lieut. Cooper Roll.[37]

---

32. Oolachan, eulachon, eulachan, or candlefish.

33. "For Fraser River," *Daily British Colonist*, 15 May 1867; "The Gubernatorial Excursion," *Daily British Colonist*, 16 May 1867.

34. The sternwheeler *Onward* was under the command of William Irving. Norman R. Hacking, "Steamboating on the Fraser in the 'Sixties," *British Columbia Historical Quarterly* 10 (January 1946): 40.

35. After several years as a civil engineer in the United States, English-born Joseph Trutch went to British Columbia where his prominence was established in public works, particularly in the construction of the Cariboo Road and the Alexandra suspension bridge spanning the Fraser River. He was presently commissioner of lands and works, and surveyor general, and he was sitting on the colonial executive council. J. B. Kerr, *Biographical Dictionary of Well-Known British Columbians, with a Historical Sketch* (Vancouver: Kerr & Begg, 1890), 311–312; Ormsby, *British Columbia,* 251–252; *Dictionary of Canadian Biography,* vol. 13, s.v. "Trutch, Sir Joseph William," by Robin Fisher. See also note 40 below.

36. Judge Matthew Baillie Begbie was prominent in maintaining order in the gold rush years of British Columbia and in his capacity as a member of the executive council of the colony. Although the 1866 enabling legislation for the union of Vancouver Island and British Columbia had omitted any judiciary provisions, in effect Begbie became chief justice of the mainland portion of the new colony. He was to accede to this title for the entire colony in 1870. *Dictionary of Canadian Biography*, "Begbie"; Sydney G. Pettit, "'Dear Sir Matthew': A Glimpse of Judge Begbie," *British Columbia Historical Quarterly* 11 (January 1947): 2.

37. Excerpts from the journal of Bishop Hills give some added detail to Porcher's account. Hills, "1866 and 1867," 16–17.

We passed Derby or New Langley in 1¾ hours after leaving, and in an hour afterwards, stopped for ¼ hour at the Roman Catholic mission of St. Mary's, where the 2 Priests, and their scholars turned out and played "God save the Queen," and a few hymns. At 10 PM, ran in to Jeffrie's Bar, where the first Gold diggings took place, and tied the vessel up for the night, and took in some wood. The *Onward* was a Stern wheeler of 90 H.P. and built in the country, burnt 25 cords of wood in the round trip (between N.W. and Yale) which at $3½ a cord, cost $87 [sic], and drew when light 13 inches, or deep 21 inches.

May 16th. Left Jeffries Bar at 7 AM, and as the river became here contracted, the scenery was much finer, as the hills rose more precipitously from the banks, and the distant mountains in the Cascade range covered with perpetual snow. We arrived at Hope in 3 hours, where we stopped about 20 minutes to see the place, as it is pleasantly situated in more open country, and when first built was the stopping place for the steamers, as it was considered not safe for them to attempt to reach any higher, the remainder of the way being accomplished in canoes. It took us 3 hours more in reaching Yale, the distance being 14 miles, against a strong current, particularly at Emory's Bar in the Devil's Gate, and the vessel was obliged to put on all her power to enable her to get over it. The pressure the boilers were supposed to stand was 110 lbs, but on these occasions they carry 125 lbs and more.

Spent the afternoon at Yale, which is one of the Posts of the Hudson Bay Company, and situated 90 miles up the Fraser, and very pleasantly situated, the town extending for some distance along the right bank of the river, the hills rising immediately at a steep slope.[38]

May 17th. The whole of the party were all started off from Yale by 9 AM, in the regular Stage drawn by 6 horses, and kindly lent by the Proprietor Mr. Barnard, the Governor's Waggonette, a Luggage waggon for the servants, and 8 riding horses. The party were increased by the Magistrate & Gold Commissioner with his Wife, Mr. and Mrs. O'Reilly.[39] The road extended from Yale along the right bank of the river for about 12 miles where Mr. Joseph Trutch had thrown a suspension bridge across the river,[40] and then led along for the remainder of the way on the left bank. About ½ a mile above the bridge, we stopped 1¾ hour for luncheon at an Hotel at Chapman's Bar, where there were some very good Indian graves, and which I made a sketch of on my way down.

It took us 2¼ hours more in driving through the Canons, where the road was cut through a most difficult country but completed in 2 seasons, and arrived at Boston Bar at 4.30 PM. The Thompson river, Bonaparte, and other Indians had arrived here from the upper country to see the Governor, and were received by him, as well as by

38. The sketch of Yale in the volume in which Bishop Hills' journal appears is probably the work of Porcher. Columbia Mission, *Ninth Annual Report…for the Year 1867*, frontispiece.

39. In 1859, Peter O'Reilly was appointed assistant gold commissioner, stipendiary magistrate, and high sheriff of British Columbia. Four years later, he gained a seat in the legislative council, and the following year he became chief gold commissioner. Kerr, *Biographical Dictionary…*, 267.

40. The sketch of the Alexandra suspension bridge which illustrates Bishop Hills' journal is almost certainly the work of Porcher. Hills, "1866 and 1867," facing 17, 17.

the Bishop and Judge Begbie (commonly called the Hyas Tyhee, Praying Tyhee, and the Rope Tyhee).[41]

As it was getting dark I walked out with the Misses Needham to see one of the Tribes encamped round their fires. These young Ladies sat down on a log of wood, and sang some songs, on which the Indians were most attentive, and thinking they were hymns, all took their hats off, and when they were finished, all faced to the East, and knelt down, with the Chiefs in the front, and sung a hymn in capital time, and concluded with a short prayer. The Indians from the interior of the country are much finer men, and more advanced in civilization, than the fish-eating Indians on the coast, and some of the tribes have become Christians through the influence of the Roman Catholics, and on meeting them often make the sign of the cross.

The accommodations at the Inn at Boston Bar were rather limited, and the few sleeping rooms were given up to the Ladies, the Gentlemen contenting themselves with a hay loft for the night.

Return to Esquimalt

May 18th. Left Boston Bar at 11.20 pm [am], and took about the same time in returning to Yale, as we did in coming. The whole party dined at the Hudson Bay Company's Post then in charge of Mr. McKay.

May 19th. After attending the service at Yale at 9.15 am, we left in the *Onward* at 12.15 am [pm] on our return, stopping on our way down the river at Hope, Harrison river, and Sumass river where we embarked the Presbyterian minister, the Rev. White, and lastly at Langley, arriving at New Westminster about 9 pm. This picnic party that was very well managed, and lasted part of 5 days, cost the Governor $1350, or £270.[42]

May 24th. This being the Queen's birthday, it was usual for the Indians to come down from the Upper country, and partake of the festivities that were held at New Westminster on that day, at the expense of the Government.[43] About 3000 were present on this occasion, most of them having come down the Fraser in their canoes a day or two previously. At Noon the Indians paddled up in their canoes, that had a banner in the bows of each, that consisted of a red flag with the Motto, "Religion, Temperance, Civilization," in white. They first went round the ship, and landed opposite the Government House, and then walked up to the Cricket ground, where they were addressed by the Governor, and they had a potlatch in the town consisting of molasses and flour.

---

41. "Hyas tyee" is Chinook jargon for a great chief, officer, king, or anyone of superior order. The meaning of the other two names used here can be implied. Shaw, *Chinook Jargon....* In that connection, Matthew Begbie was popularly known as "the hanging judge." Over a score of Indians, for example, had met such a sentence in his court. *Dictionary of Canadian Biography*, "Begbie."

42. "The Return," *Daily British Colonist*, 24 May 1867.

43. In 1867, the government was looking for ways to save money. One economy could be made, it was proposed, by eliminating the traditional feast and gifts of the government to the thousands of Indians who usually came to New Westminster for the 24 May celebration of the Queen's birthday. This proposal was defeated and the Indians were extended the usual hospitality. Akrigg and Akrigg, *British Columbia Chronicle*, 352.

It was unfortunately a rainy day which prevented a variety of games and races coming off, only a few taking place after 4 PM. At 9 PM we burnt blue lights at the yard arms, as well as the *Malacca*. After this I embarked with a large party on board the *Llilloet* [sic] (stern wheeler) and steamed down the river opposite the town, to see the fireworks set off form a scow which was moored in the middle of the river alongside the *Onward*. The Fireworks that were very good of their kind had only arrived 6 days before in the *Princess Royal* of the Hudson Bay Company, at the cost of £160, two thirds of them were only consumed this evening. Several had arrived damp and useless.

May 25th. The next day was finer. Some horse races took place in the middle of the day in Columbia Street (the principal street in the town), and during the afternoon a variety of games took place on the Cricket ground. At 9 PM, about 150 canoes formed a torch light procession astern of the *Leviathan*, and proceeded round the ships and down the river.

May 26th. This Afternoon 10 Hydet [Haida?] Indians had a War dance on the lawn before the Government house, in the presence of 2000 Indians. They were painted and dressed up for the occasion, and accompanied by several Klootchmen sitting down playing Tamb[o]urines, &c.

May 28th. After having been lying in the Fraser 24 days, we left it [New Westminster, in the *Sparrowhawk*,][44] this morning at 11.45 AM, with Mrs. Pearse, and Mrs. and Miss Needham, arriving off the Light ship in 2 hours where we left Captain Cooper to go back in the *Leviathan*, and anchored at Esquimalt in 7 hours 50 minutes, being detained a short time at Cadboro Bay, where we put in to see if there was a carriage waiting there.[45]

Repairing the Beaver

JUNE 4TH. THE SURVEYING STEAMER *Beaver* was hauled up on Laing's ways, in Victoria Harbour to repair damages done on the 15th May when she got on shore at the Race rocks when under the charge of Mr. Calvert, the Gunner of the *Forward*. The charges for the use of the slip were $186 for the first day, and $23¼ every day afterward, that is to say a Dollar a ton for the expense of hauling the vessel up, and a bit a ton for each day afterwards.[46]

On the 6th I drove in to Victoria with Lieut. Kinahan, and the Carpenter of the *Malacca* to see what the extent of the damages were. We found that the False keel was all gone, half the Main keel, and several planks required being taken out on the Port bilge.

44. Porcher's log, 295–296.

45. "The Sparrowhawk…," Daily British Colonist, 30 May 1867.

46. Four "stragglers" from the *Sparrowhawk* were returned by the court. "Police Court," *Daily British Colonist*, 5 June 1867.

Chapter Six

A Northern Cruise and an Inland Journey

7 June–17 August 1867

[The involvement of a naval vessel and its commander in colonial affairs depended on their opportune availability, and the discretion of the governor in his capacity as colonial senior naval commander. This was demonstrated on two occasions in the summer of 1867. In early June H.M.S. *Sparrowhawk* took the governor on a two-and-a-half week mission. The press speculated it was a diplomatic assignment to Russian Alaska shortly before its transfer to the United States. At any rate, interesting details of the cruise, including visits to settlements and missions en route, were publicly reported in Victoria. The second summer highlight came for Porcher in August. He was invited to join the governor on a trouble-shooting mission into the interior to resolve what was being called "The Grouse Creek War." The press suggested that Porcher was serving in an advisory capacity to the governor. The governor's party traveled through the mining country up the Fraser River to the Cariboo mining region.]

To northern settlements

June 7th. As Governor Seymour was anxious to visit the Northern settlements of the Colony,[1] we left Esquimalt at 9.30 AM, and embarked him and Captain Cooper at Cadboro Bay, and then proceeded on to Nanaimo, where we lashed alongside the Coaling Wharf at 7.45 PM.

June 8th. Took in 124 tons of Coals to day, making up the quantity we had on board to 196 tons, of which we had 100 tons in the bunkers and stoke holes, and 96 on deck.

The draught of water being then 11 Ft. 4 in Forward, and 13 Ft. 8 Aft, which was a good trim for steaming, as the whole of the screw was immersed for the first time.

Hauled off from the Wharf, and steamed out of Nanaimo at 5 PM,[2] and as the night was calm and clear kept under weigh.

June 9th. Passed through the Seymour Narrows at 5 AM, with ease, there being but little tide, and anchored off Fort Rupert at 5.35 PM in 9 fathoms, having run 180 miles in 24½ hours. Landed with the Governor, Ketson and Boys, and visited the Roman Catholic chapel and the Priest's house, which was very small, and could hold but few people. The Priest only makes periodical visits here, as his head quarters are at *[blank.]* ["Very few Indians were left in the village, the majority being up Knight Inlet, engaged in Eulachon fishing."][3]

Saw Mrs. Moriat, her husband being absent at Victoria, attending another trial on the loss of the Lab*[illeg.]* and Mr. Hunt, trader, who is a native of Dorsetshire,

---

1. The initial press statement said the governor was to visit Metlakatla and return by way of the west coast of Vancouver Island. "The Sparrowhawk...," *Daily British Colonist*, 4 June 1867. Also, "There is some talk of the Governor extending his trip to Sitka." "The Sparrowhawk...," *Daily British Colonist*, 8 June 1867. See also "The Malacca...," *Daily British Colonist*, 6 June 1867; "The Sparrowhawk...," *Daily British Colonist*, 7 June 1867.

One purpose was "to inspect the wonderful community which the exertions of Mr. Duncan has founded there [Metlakatla] out of the rough native materials he has had to work upon." "One object...," *Daily British Colonist*, 6 June 1867.

Whatever reason or justification for the trip, the governor was severely criticized for going on this mission. "The Necessity for a Change," *Daily British Colonist*, 13 June 1867.

There was momentary speculation that the governor was on a diplomatic assignment to Russian Alaska "to make overtures for the transfer of the thirty-mile strip to British Columbia." That conjecture was dismissed as improbable because of the impending transfer of Alaska to the United States. "Sitka," *Daily British Colonist*, 24 June 1867.

2. "From the North West Coast," *Daily British Colonist*, 12 June 1867.

3. "From Victoria to Metlaktlah with Some Account of the Mission There," *Daily British Colonist*, 4 July 1867.

Except for those derived from four particular accounts, quotations extracted from the *Daily British Colonist* are located in the editorial notes that enhance or document the text itself.

The exceptions, four lengthy accounts of *Sparrowhawk* missions, were published July 1867–July 1868. While they are not signed, they were most certainly written by Porcher or Comrie. On the face of it, Porcher attributes Comrie for the 4 July 1867 piece (see entry for 13 June 1867), but that ascription is belied by the fact that this, and the other three pieces, contain considerable verbatim borrowings from Porcher's journal entries themselves. Curiously, in the 2 July 1868 piece, reference to some of the geographic features named after officers of the *Sparrowhawk* include Comrie Head but not Porcher Island. If Comrie had written the piece, he most certainly would have mentioned Porcher Island.

For another attribution to Porcher of authorship of these accounts, see James K. Nesbitt, "Capt. Porcher of Sparrowhawk Studied Indians and Coral," Victoria *Daily Colonist*, 3 September 1967. By way of explanation, as passages, sentences, and other portions of these four accounts enhance Porcher's entries, they are integrated ["in this fashion"] into the texts of Porcher's entries themselves.

and has been stationed here for the last 17½ years, out of which time he has only been absent 5 days, when on a trip to Victoria.

June 10th. Left Fort Rupert at 4.30 AM, passed thro' Queen Charlotte's Sound in 3¾ hours with little wind and swell, and anchored off the settlement of Bella Bella at 5.30 PM in 12½ fathoms, rock, having run 100 miles. Landed with the Governor, Dolphin & Capt. Cooper, at the Village, that consisted of a small Ranch of a dozen houses ["containing about 200 of a population,"][4] built on a rock about an acre in extent, and separated about 300 yards from the main island, and where they[5] are obliged to go for their wood and water.

["The men appeared robust and well made, especially the chief, a young man about twenty-four; the women were painted with a profusion of black and red bars across the face. They have slightly flattened heads (the women alone flatten the heads), broad faces and rather fair, ruddy complexions. We saw for the first time in this country an Albino, a woman with fair, rubicund complexion, white hair and reddish eyes, and on inquiring of the chief as to her genealogy, he told us she was "Sitkum." The situation of the village on an Island of about an acre in extent, where there is neither wood nor water, is rather peculiar, but chosen many years ago as a place of defence. Here was observed, among some of the old, extensive scars on the arms, the result of the custom of biting, during their medicine orgies, when the candidates in their frenzy are supposed to be inspired, and it is considered a matter of religious duty to offer them an arm to gnaw, such scars being highly honorable. Another peculiar custom also is said to prevail on the occasion of the death of a chief—a practice that somewhat resembles embalming. The body is disembowelled, the cavities filled with cedar bark, and then conveyed to a cavern on the opposite shore, where it is deposited. The chief came off in the evening, bringing with him a collection of curious masks, rattles, &c.; these he carefully brought on deck, and would not exhibit except on the after part of the ship, hid from the sight of the canoes. On some of them the carving was very well executed. One of his whistles was decidedly ingenious, consisting of a tube fitted into the neck of a bladder, which being compressed in the hand, gave out musical notes. On shore they appeared to have a plentiful supply of the necessaries of life, as numerous deer, beaver, halibut, were seen in their houses."][6]

June 11th. Left Bella Bella at 4.30 AM, and in about an hour afterwards passed through Milbank Sound, where we felt the ocean swell for a short time. On passing up Finlayson Channel, a small canoe came alongside with 3 men, having part of a bear and beaver in the boat which they had lately killed, they were bound for Bella Bella.

Yesterday and today it rained a great deal, which made the fine scenery look rather dismal. Anchored at Lowe Inlet in Grenville Channel at 6.20 PM, in 16 fathoms,

---

4. "From Victoria to Metlaktlah with Some Account of the Mission There," *Daily British Colonist*, 4 July 1867.

5. The apposition "the Indians" is inserted here in pencil by caret.

6. "From Victoria to Metlaktlah with Some Account of the Mission There," *Daily British Colonist*, 4 July 1867.

shells, about 26 miles to the Northward of Hone's Bay. It is a snug anchorage, the inlet running up about 3 miles,[7] where a stream falls into it, and where the *Clio* anchored about 18 months ago. Ran today 120 miles.

["Here some of our party who went on shore saw numerous tiny, glittering specks in the sand, brought down by the river, and fancied they had discovered valuable diggings. The specimens brought on board, however, turned out to be only iron pyrites."][8]

Metlakatla settlement

June 12th. Left Low Inlet at 4.30 am, and steamed through the Grenville Channel with drizzling rain, communicated with the *Alexandra*[9] in Lawson Harbour, and was informed by Pender that they were going to leave for Metlakatlah the next day. Anchored off the river-harbour at Metlakatlah at Noon in 7 fathoms, with the following Bearings, Carr Inlet W ¾ N, Knight Inlet S ¼ E, Observ[ati]on Pt. N ¼ E. Ran today 60 miles.

["The voyage from Fort Rupert was through a succession of shattered channels, the ocean swell being only felt for about 20 miles, in passing between Cape Scott and the entrance of Fitzhugh Sound. The rest was inland navigation, intricate, but perhaps the smoothest in the Pacific. Many of the archipelagoes passed through were of surprisingly beautiful, the scenery being almost of a highland character, the shores wooded close to the water's edge, numerous canals resembling a succession of inland lakes, dotted with many beautiful islets; the scenery ever-varying in shade and outline, and consisting of open glades and gently sloping activities, at others, of snow clad peaks and mountains, cleft by deep ravines, down whose sides thundered impetuous mountain torrents; while now and again a glimpse was caught of the snow clad Cascade range. In passing along there might be seen occasionally a long avenue cleared in the forest from the top to the bottom of the mountains—the work of some devastating snow avalanche; the result of the melting of the snow, perhaps in some instance proceeding from distant glaciers. Metlakathla is situated on the coast, about the middle of the western side of the Chympsean peninsula. This peninsula, inhabited by the Chympsean tribe, is about 40 miles long by 20 broad and is washed on three sides by Chatham Sound, Port Essington and Work's Canal. The Mission of Metlakathla is situated on a little bay protected by several small islands; the village being built on a triangular piece of land jutting out into the bay. The church, and Mr. Duncan's the missionary's house are situated at the apex, whilst two rows of houses occupy the sides."][10]

7. "further" is inserted here in pencil by caret.

8. "From Victoria to Metlaktlah with Some Account of the Mission There," *Daily British Colonist*, 4 July 1867.

9. Porcher makes an earlier reference to Russian steamer *Alexandra*. See his entry for 21 February 1867 above. The present *Alexandra*, however, is probably the Hudson's Bay Company stern wheeler of which he made a watercolor sketch on 5 July 1867.

10. "From Victoria to Metlaktlah with Some Account of the Mission There," *Daily British Colonist*, 4 July 1867.

Shortly after we anchored Mr. Duncan called on board, and after luncheon I accompanied the Governor and Ketson on shore, and were received in state by all the inhabitants, a salute of 2 Guns being fired from a 1 Pounder without a carriage, and a Volley from 13 Constables dressed in the Royal Artillery uniform. ["They all sang in a very spirited manner 'God Save the Queen.'"][11]

The Governor then walked round the settlement, ["inspected the site of the proposed saw mill, which is about to be erected on a stream at the end of the village," and][12] through the principal houses which had been greatly improved from the older one's we saw last year, having rooms partitioned off at each end for the different families, but retaining the central apartment with the fire in the middle.

["The older houses, although externally built after European fashion with doors, glass windows and shingled roofs, had no separate apartments."][13] Some of the interiors were very clean and neat, and were furnished with bedsteads, tables, chairs, matting and prints.

["There are about 32 houses, each accommodating a family and their collateral relations. The population numbers about 600. Many of them are relations, who although still heathens, have followed their christian relations to whom they have been attached, and no doubt ultimately will be gathered into the christian fold. In the meantime they conform to the regulations of the place. About 100 of the population are catechumens, and 300 more are desirous of becoming so. They all look intelligent, wear English clothing and are clean and comfortable in appearance."][14]

He afterwards went round the store which Mr. Duncan keeps for the benefit of the Mission to which the Indians sell their skins and other produce in exchange for European articles. ["This is well stored with a great variety of articles, clothing, blankets, groceries, tobacco, cutlery, including an air bed, steel collars, Eau de Cologne, kid gloves, &c. A large quantity of valuable furs received in barter are also to be seen, consisting of minx, marten, sea otter, bear, eulachon oil, salted salmon, &c."][15]

The road in front of the houses had been widened and the bank strengthened by pallisades, and near the beach a platform was being constructed to haul the canoes up on, ["and a pier where a schooner can come alongside and land her cargo at any stage of the tide."][16]

The Governor[17] then adjourned to the Mission house,[18] where the greater part of the population were assembled, and stated to them that it afforded him much pleasure to meet them in their own homes, and to see the progress they were making in the

11. Ibid.

12. Ibid.

13. Ibid.

14. Ibid.

15. Ibid.

16. Ibid.

17. Ibid. The governor was accompanied by Porcher, Comrie, Duncan, and Lt. Kitson.

18. Ibid. The mission house was an octagonal building with a capacity of about 500.

arts of the white man, ["told them that what was good for the white man was also beneficial for them,"][19] and hoped they would continue to persevere in their well doing, and at some future period to visit them again. ["They might depend on having his protection, but if on other hand, they misconducted themselves, the same punishment would be awarded to them as to white men. He should always be glad to hear of them through Mr. Duncan."][20]

In answer to this, several of the chiefs spoke, and said they were as yet weak and required protection, that they were like the eggs that a bird took care of, that they were very grateful to the Governor for his promised support and for his coming so far to see them, and also begged him to stop the potla[t]ches amongst the neighboring tribes, which they believed to be the great source of crime, ["so much so, that even Indians would prostitute their own children in order to acquire property to give away for the purpose of display, and that doing away with them would be a great leverage to raise the Indians. The Governor in reply stated that the subject of the potlatches should have his consideration and that he disapproved of them. He said no doubt although they were young and weak as a people they had advanced considerably towards an equality with the whites. They worshipped the true God, believed in the same creed, had houses constructed after the English fashion, a store, good roads, and a sawmill. That he hoped to hear of advancement, and trusted to have a favorable account from Mr. Duncan."][21]

We then went to the schoolroom, and heard some songs sung by the girls, 14 of whom reside in the house & manage all the household economy. ["They vary in age from 12 to 16, and after this initiation in house-keeping are eagerly sought after in marriage by the young men of the place. Mr. Duncan receives all the suitors, listens to their proposals and generally arranges their love affairs. They sang several Chympsean songs, one of which, to the tune of "Home, sweet home," was very pretty; and also a variety of English songs, including "Cheerful in duty winning applause," "Buttercups and Daiseys," "Tell me now, sweet little bird, who tipped thy wings with gold," Mr. Duncan accompanying them on the harmonium and concertina."][22]

The copy books were afterwards inspected, and also heard them read in English ["distinctly and intelligently. Altogether, the impressions formed of Mr. Duncan's training were very favorable, and the results in the case of these pupils would bear comparison with any of the more advanced young ladies' schools in Victoria, while in neatness, appearance and general deportment they were equally ladylike. Mr. Duncan also carries on a day school, at which about 90 pupils attend. This room is hung round with maps, illustrations, &c., and has quite an academical appearance, containing globes, electric machines, &c., while outside is a series of gymnastic appliances, swings, bars, &c. The community is composed chiefly of young persons, 200 being under 20 years of age, while about one hundred are under ten.

---

19. "From Victoria to Metlaktlah with Some Account of the Mission There," *Daily British Colonist*, 4 July 1867.

20. Ibid.

21. Ibid.

22. Ibid.

"The history of the rise and progress of this Mission is a most interesting one. Mr. Duncan, to whose exertions the present state of things is owing, was educated at the missionary college of Highbury, and arrived in this country in 1857. Almost immediately after his arrival he proceeded to Fort Simpson, the village of the Chympseans, situated at the northern end of the peninsula. Here he labored for five years, but finding the presence of the Fort and other influences against his progress, he in 1862 removed to Metlakatla, a Government Reserve, and the old home of the Chympseans before Fort Simpson was built thirty years ago. When he left Fort Simpson only fifty accompanied him, now there are six hundred.

"The secret of his success has been owing to a thorough acquaintance with the language, and carrying out civilization hand in hand with evangelization. One aid was the establishment of a store. Out of the profits of the store, a sawmill costing about $1600, and a church about $5000, are to be built; and all public works are paid from this source: A carpenter's and blacksmith's shop, a factory for making soap from Eulachon oil, and also a bakery are in progress. The management of this community rests with a Council of fifteen, selected out of the settlers, under Mr. Duncan. For the public works, such as keeping up of roads, &c., ten days' labor, or four blankets, equivalent to $8, is required annually of each inhabitant.

"Numerous gardens exist in front of the houses, in addition to which each individual has a plot of ground allotted to him on the numerous islets in front. In these plots, potatoes, onions, cabbages, turnips, carrots, &c., are grown to such an extent that the neighboring tribes come here to trade. For their convenience a market house is about to be erected. A schooner, manned and commanded by those belonging to the mission, makes passages up and down the coast for the purpose of trade. Mr. Duncan has also lately published a pamphlet in Chympsean, containing the Lord's Prayer, Creed, and a selection of Scriptural passages, the first attempt at printed Indian language on this side of the Rocky Mountains.

"Great credit is due to Mr. Duncan for his efforts, in spite of the numerous difficulties he has had to contend with; he is the right stuff of which missionaries are made—active, cheerful, energetic, possessed of great tact and good nature. He has succeeded in combining industrial training with religious instruction, and laid the foundation of a system which we hope he will remain sufficiently long to mature, more especially, as the results will entirely depend on the bringing up of the younger members, to whom in all probability we must look for the perpetuation of the Indian race on this coast.

"We have entered into a lengthened history of this mission because Mr. Duncan's aims have been misrepresented by jealous rival traders, each skin traded here being looked upon as so much loss to them. He has also brought down upon him a host of slanders from the active part he has taken in stopping the Indian liquor traffic on the coast. It may be mentioned, that on this occasion five hogsheads of villainous stuff denominated whisky, were broken up and their contents poured out upon the beach. This had been taken, some weeks previously by Mr. Duncan's forces from a schooner engaged in the nefarious traffic, and then poured out, tainted the air for a considerable distance. A fine of $400 had been imposed on the proprietor, which the Governor generously handed over to Mr. Duncan for the benefit of the Mission."][23]

After dining with Mr. Duncan on bacon, preserved mutton, potatoes, eggs & milk we returned on board at 8 PM, being escorted by 4 large canoes.

Fort Simpson settlement

JUNE 13TH. LEFT METLAKATLAH AT 5.0 AM, AND anchored off Fort Simpson at 7.50 AM in 12 fathoms, mud, the distance being 22 miles. Found two sloops here the *Thornton* & *Eagle*.

We were received on landing by Mr. Horn, trader, who was in charge of the Fort in the absence of Mr. Manson who was on a visit up the Naas river, and I am sorry to say not in a state of sobriety. Settled 2 Magistrate cases here. 10 Indians who had plundered and cut the rigging of the sloop *Thornton* were sent down to be tried by Mr. Duncan, and to pay two blankets each as a security that they would go there.

The other was an Indian of the name of Segwan who had murdered 3 people. A brother in law of one of the murdered men had been paid 20 blankets as a compensation, but was not satisfied and expected he ought to have 100. Sent him down to Mr. Duncan.

["The Fort [an]d the Chympsean village grouped round it, [oc]cupy a semicircular bay at the extreme [no]rthern point of the Peninsula. The Fort [is] a quadrangular enclosure, stockaded round [wi]th beams, about 20 feet high, driven into [th]e ground, and has a bastion at each corner, [wh]ile on the inside at the height of about [?] feet from the ground a gallery runs round. [Th]e buildings within consist of a chief [tra]der's house, stores, trading room, &c."][24]

The village stretches on each side of the Fort, the lodges being built on piles of the height of 8 or 10 feet, and at high water are inaccessible except by canoes, the tide washing underneath. The houses as regards structure, external and internal decorations are the most superior we have seen on this coast, and are only excelled by the village of Skidegate in Queen Charlotte's Island. The doorways and pillars are most elaborately carved with a great variety of the representations of animals, ["animate [and] inanimate objects. Heads of men and [ani]mals of a colossal size, beautifully [deco]rated, being the most prominent; while [occ]upying a central position is a representa[tion] of the crest or *totem* of the proprietor's [fam]ily."][25]

The principal of these were the eagle, whale, sturgeon, beaver, shark, owl, salmon, wolf, bear, and a starfish. The houses of the chiefs are distinguished by having their crests placed on the top of a long pole, the height of it corresponding to the rank of

23. "From Victoria to Metlaktlah with Some Account of the Mission There," *Daily British Colonist*, 4 July 1867.

24. "H.M.S. Sparrowhawk's Trip to Sitka," *Daily British Colonist*, 10 July 1867. The binding of this issue of the newspaper into a volume has sometimes obscured words and parts of words along the left margin. Wherein possible, these exclusions are supplied in editorial brackets from context or reasonable surmise. Failing this, the exclusion is noted simply as bracketed question marks. See also note 3 above.

25. "H.M.S. Sparrowhawk's Trip to Sitka," *Daily British Colonist*, 10 July 1867.

the owner,[26] the longest being that of Paul Legaic who has given up his position of principal Chief, and joined Mr. Duncan's force at Metlakatlah and turned Christian.[27]

["On [the] outside of the houses the pillar support[ing] the beams were in many cases carved in [imi]tation of statuary, of most artistic finish, [rese]mbling the caryatides of ancient art. The [sign]ificance of these crests is rather difficult [to a]rrive at; in one respect they subserve a [ver]y beneficial end, in preventing intermar[riag]es, those of the same crest being not [allo]wed to marry. In addition to these on [the] poles or houses, the chiefs also have their [cres]ts engraved on a large copper plate, to [whi]ch they attached a most exaggerated value, [the] worth of some being estimated as high as [?] blankets. One we saw at the Fort was [abou]t 4 feet long by about 2 feet broad, and [appe]ared to have been deposited as security [for] certain advances made to the owner.

"[The] custom of flattening the head dis[appe]ars here and another, confined to the [wom]en, takes its place. This is the labial [cir]cular piece of wood inserted into a slit [in] the lower lip, parallel with the mouth, [and] about half an inch below. The first [step] is the insertion of a small metallic [?], the aperture being gradually dilated, [and] in the case of the fine old ladies, [?]ing to 3 inches in length by one inch [wide?]. Many of their customs are very [pecu]liar; for instance, all descent is by the [moth]er side, and in the case of orphan [child]ren, they always go to the mother's [family?]. No matter how high in the social scale [the] father may be, if he marries beneath [?] his children are [culius?] *i.e.* of the [?]er's original rank in life. Their disposal [of the] dead is also peculiar. They burn the [body] and preserve the ashes in small [?], placed on stands in a cemetery. [Num]erous other peculiar customs prevail [?] to which we have not space now to [tell].

"The total population is said to [amou]nt to 1200, the community being divided [into t]en tribes, one of whom is not now re[prese]nted here, the whole tribe, Chief In[?]d, having gone to Metlakatlah with Mr. [Dunc]an. Some seven or eight years ago the [estim]ated population was 2,500, but it is now [?] decreased, they having suffered from [an e]pidemic of small pox in 1863.

"The form[ation] here consists of metamorphic slate, in[?]ted by veins of quartz. In the slate [consi]derable quantities of graphite existed, [and s]ome detached pieces of quartz were ob[serve]d containing garnets.

"The Governor [visit]ed the Fort, and also the head of the [Chy]mpseans—the Chieftainess Shoudal—who [appe]ared to be a very fine woman, in the [prim]e of life, neatly and tastefully dressed, [her h]ouse being very clean and containing [?] articles of English furniture arranged [with] considerable taste. The Chympseans [are g]reatly superior to the other coast tribes, [?] muscular and well built, with broad [?] features and fair complexions. They [are n]ow beginning to appreciate a little of [civili]zation, and are large purchasers of [Engl]ish manufactures.

26. Ibid. Some were approximately 80 feet high.

27. Bishop Hills gave a fuller account of the conversion and experience of Paul and Lydia Legaic. Hills, "1865 and 1866," 21–32.

"[The] reformed whiskey [traders] whom we met [?]d in the most ingenuous way, is cor[rabor]ation of this, that a fair profit, at[tain]ed with less risk, was now to be made [by tr]ading along the coast cheap prints, groc[erie]s, flour, &c., than by whiskey."][28]

A longer account of this place, as well as the whole cruize was published in the Victoria Colonist on our return by Dr. Comrie.[29]

Russian America

June 14th. Left Fort Simpson at 2.30 am, and entered the Russian possessions, steaming during the day thro' the Duke of Clarence's Channel, the aspect of the country being nearly the same as what we have been lately passing thro', the hills being thickly timbered to their summits, but the only sign of life we saw was a Sloop [beating?] thro' the Straits, and on nearing Point Stanhope saw some smoke thro' the trees, and shortly afterward 2 men leaving the rocks in a canoe.

Passed thro' the narrows near Bushy Island at 8 pm, when we got into 2½ fathoms near a rivulet, but deepened immediately afterwards. Went easy during the night, the twilight lasting the whole time.

June 15th. On nearing the entrance of the Duke of Clarence Straits, it came on a thick Fog, which luckily lifted sufficiently for us to see our way out, and lasted 5 or 6 hours. Observed a rock off the entrance about 10 feet high with the South point of Coronation Island bearing NEE ¾ E 3 miles distant.

Entered Sitka Sound at Sunset, and as the night was fine, the twilight good, and nearly full moon, we threaded our way through the islands, and anchored off the town of New Archangel at 11.45pm in 13 fathoms, the distance from Fort Simpson being 305 miles.

["The passage from [Fort] Simpson was through a succession of [?]ered channels, the islands being larger [and] the canals wider and deeper than those [we] had hitherto passed through, while the [scen]ery lost much of its softness as we ad[vanc]ed, becoming more rocky and desolate, [the v]egetation stunted and scrubby, the land[scape] having a dreary appearance compared [to] that to the south of Fort Simpson. Mountains, their craggy peaks covered with snow, rose in white glittering ridges against the sky, giving a savage sublimity to the scene.

"From the northward of where the eastward boundary of the Russian territory begins in 54°40' North and 131° to 133° West, (forming the 30 mile strip), no land capable of cultivation exists, and it is likely to remain only an uninhabited wilderness, occasionally penetrated into by hardy fur trappers or gold adventurers. A very scanty native population lived in some of the grassy, desolate valleys, but the vigorous climate is such that for many years to come these lords of the soil are not likely to be disturbed in the possession of these cheerless and uninviting wastes.

"Our course was through the Prince of Wales' Archipelago, Chatham Sound, Clarence Strait and Christian Sound—an extraordinary network of sheltered water communication, perhaps a little perplexing to the tyro, but greatly facilitating a passage

28. "H.M.S. Sparrowhawk's Trip to Sitka," *Daily British Colonist*, 10 July 1867.

29. See note 3 above.

when piloted by an experienced navigator. An excellent landfall to Sitka is afforded by Mount Edgecombe, a dome-shaped peak about, 2,800 feet high, of volcanic formation, distinguished by streaks of snow and bright lines of reddish clay radiating from its apex. This mountain forms the Northern boundary of the Sound, at the head of which, 14 miles up, and protected by numerous small islands, stands the town of Sitka, the capital of Russian America."][30]

Our dock load of coals was just completed leaving our bunkers full, and the Draught of water was now Forward 10 Feet 6½ in. and Aft 11 Ft. 6½ in. We arrived at Sitka on Saturday and as the Russians still keep the old style [calendar] was their Sunday.

June 16th. After church, landed with the Governor & Ketson and paid an Official visit to the Russian Prince Meksutoff Governor, and his Wife who had been confined with her second child only 9 days before. They were both very agreeable and spoke English. The Greek Bishop had only left for the A*[illeg.]* 5 days before, and as the territory was about to be transferred to the Americans that have no State religion, would probably never return. The town is built on a narrow strip of ground, ["running out from the mountains forming the extremity of the Sound, a peninsula of about a mile in breadth by half a mile in length the base being bounded by a river running into the sea,"][31] at the base of a mountainous range one of them Mount Verstoow, being about 3000 feet in height. The principal buildings are the Government House a large two storied building, with a corrugated iron roof painted red, built on a rising ground overlooking the town, with the Offices & Stores adjoining it, Hospital, Bishop's house, Club, Labourers' houses, 3 Greek churches, Lutheran church, &c., the town containing about 900 inhabitants all of whom are connected with the Fur Company.

["A considerable proportion of the population is made up of widows and orphans whose relations have died in the service and who enjoy a pension conditional on their residence here. For the orphans, excellent schools divided into an upper and lower grade exist, entirely kept up by the Company. Three Greek Churches exist, one being for the natives, for whom there is also a school. Very little progress however has been made among the natives, which may be attributed partly to the unacquaintance of the Priests with their language, who can only address them through an interpreter, and also to the savage and irreclaimable nature of the Koluschans.

"This tribe numbers about 900 of which 500 are warriors, and during our stay 300 went out on the war trail to retaliate on a neighboring tribe, the [Hudapoboo?], who had killed one of the Sitka tribe's chiefs. The tribe were all in mourning after their custom, having blackened faces and short-cut hair, marks of extreme woe. They resemble the Chympseans in their customs, such as the use of the labret and burning the dead, and to a certain extent they recognize crests. Here we noticed a decided gradation towards the Mongolian type of features, their faces being more flattened, heads globular and eye-lids oblique than any of the other tribes seen on the coast. This indicates the Asiatic origin of the Indians of this coast.

---

30. "H.M.S. Sparrowhawk's Trip to Sitka," *Daily British Colonist*, 10 July 1867.

31. Ibid.

"The coast line broken by countless inlets and channels, and the innumerable islands formed around offer a land-locked passage almost to the Asiatic coast. This change of feature was even more conspicuous in the case of Aleutian islanders, 100 of whom are here in the service of the Company, for the purpose of fishing and preparing the skins. They are also the domestic servants here and many of them are married to workmen of the Company, and some of the offspring of this union—pretty half-breeds are married to priests and officers of the Company.

"The present population of the Aleutian Islands amounts to about 6000, and owing to the existence among them for many years of a mission conducted by the present Metropolitan Bishop of the Greek Church now in Siberia, they are all Christian, and the Greek Church have printed books for their use in the Solavonic [*sic*] and Aleutian. The principal Greek Church is a very good specimen of their style of architecture, having a central dome and open porch. The interior is roomy, has two side chapels contains some very good copies of the Italian masters, the Greek pictures only being placed on the altar screen and handsomely inlaid with silver and gold.

"An hospital exists containing 40 beds under the care of Dr. Tilling, a most excellent physician and naturalist. The cases at our visit were scurvy and affections of the chest. The hospital appeared excellently arranged and had an air of comfort and cleanliness not often seen in hospitals abroad.

"The Greek Church is here represented by 7 priests and deacons, the Bishop being absent in Siberia. The priests appeared to be vastly superior to the order one sees in the Mediterranean, being better educated and gentlemanly men. The Superior was a magnificent looking man, about 6 feet 3 inches in height, and in his ample robes and flowing head looked to great advantage. They are all married men, in conformity with an ordinance of the Church—single men not being admitted into orders as parish priests. If their wives die they are not allowed to marry again, and must then either give up the clerical profession or enter a monastery. They consequently make rather indulgent husbands, and are much sought after by marriageable young ladies.

"The Government of the place rests with a Governor, appointed by the Emperor, and who is always selected from the Imperial Navy, being generally of the rank of a Post-Captain. The next in command is the Captain of the Fort, ranking as a Commander, while several masters from the Imperial service fill subordinate offices. The present Governor is Prince Macautoff."][32]

On the Northern side of the town fronting the Inner harbour, is the Indian village, which is divided from the town by a strong stockade about 20 feet in height and loopholed ["and extending from the sea to the river. On the other side of this, the village of the Koluschan is situated."][33] These Kolusches[34] generally out number the white settlers, and as they are very seldom to be trusted, a strong battery is turned

---

32. Ibid.

33. Ibid.

34. A linguistic family designation for the Tlingit Indians who dominated the area. Swanton, *The Indian Tribes of North America*, 540; Kinkade, "History of Research in Linguistics," 104.

upon them below the Government house. When they visit to bring their Furs or other goods to market, they are admitted into a railed yard with a narrow entrance, ["a sort of pen immediately outside where they bring their goods to market,"][35] so as not to allow more [than] a limited number at a time. This Indian reserve is extremely filthy, and the people are all besmeared over with paint and dirt, so that one visit to it is quite sufficient. The interior of the houses are arranged differently from what we had hitherto seen, the floor being sunk 3 or 4 feet and each side partitioned off into rooms. In the middle of the town there are some Public gardens, which are laid out with shady walks, summer houses, swings, kitchen gardens, but the constant wet weather prevents this being much used. The fur trade seems to be the principal employment, and large quantities are annually collected of Land and Sea Otters, Hair and Fur Seals, Bear, Beaver, Foxes, Martens, squirrel, ermine, muskrat, &c. ["the quantity at present in store being valued at 480,000 silver rubles."][36]

No shops exist in the town, but the necessaries of life are to be obtained from the Company's store. ["Everybody is victualled as if on board ship, obtaining everything at a fixed price frequently below prime cost. Often the victualling is entirely on salt provisions, the Indians at present being at war bring nothing in, and the place is entirely dependent on them for fresh supplies. The only article of this kind obtainable was salmon caught by the Aleutian fishermen, but in flavor were coarse and insipid and not to be compared either with those got at Esquimalt or in the Fraser."][37]

The day before we left Prince Meksutoff came on board to luncheon and remained 3 hours, he was received by the Officers and a Guard, and was saluted on leaving with 17 Guns. He had formerly held a command at Petropavloski during the Russian war, and was promoted to this position for his services on that occasion.

During the 3 days we remained here, the weather was fair, but generally had thick fog during the nights or mornings.

Return to Esquimalt

June 19th. As soon as the fog cleared away, we steamed out of Sitka at 7.30 am, and had a light Southerly wind against us the greater part of the day, which we kept the whole way to Cape Flattery, with very fine weather.

About 50 miles to the North West of Queen Charlotte's Island, we fell in with 5 Whalers, and on passing down the Westward side of that island saw several Whales & porpoises.

June 22. Steamed into Nootka Sound at 3.15 pm, and landed at Friendly Cove with the Governor and a party of 8, where we remained an hour, looking over the Indian village which was built on the site of the Spanish settlement. Saw about 20 Sea Otter skins, for which they asked 20 or 30 Blankets each, but did not buy any.

35. "H.M.S. Sparrowhawk's Trip to Sitka," *Daily British Colonist*, 10 July 1867.

36. Ibid.

37. Ibid.

Walked over the small triangular plot of ground that was offered to be ceded to the English by Spain in September 1792, it had a sandy beach in front of it about 70 yards long, and extended about the same distance on the other sides.[38]

June 23rd. Entered the Straits of Juan de Fuca at 6. AM, passed inside the Race rocks for the first time, and anchored at Esquimalt at 3.10 PM, after having been away 16 days.[39]

The Governor then disembarked. On arriving we only had 7 tons of Coals left, having burnt 200 tons in steaming 1618 miles.

Distances run, northern cruise

June 7th	From Esquimalt to Nanaimo	76 miles
8th, 9th	Nanaimo Fort Rupert	180
10th	Fort Rupert Bella Bella	100
11th	Bella Bella Low Inlet	120
12th	Low Inlet Metlakatlah	60
13th	Metlakatlah Fort Simpson	22
14th, 15th	Fort Simpson Sitka	305
19th, 20, 21, 22d	Sitka Nootka Sound	595
22d, 23d	Nootka Sound Esquimalt	165
		1623 miles

Pursuit of thieves

JULY 3RD. IN THE MIDDLE WATCH SOME OF the seamen of the *Malacca* and *Forward*, ran off with the Plunger of Mr. Rab*[illeg.]* and finding it out shortly afterwards, requested a boat to be sent in pursuit from the *Malacca*, and then started himself in a small pulling boat with his son and daughter of the age of 14 and 12 years, and came up with the thieves not far from the Race rocks about 8 miles distant, who ran the Plunger on shore and escaped through the bushes. When within 500 yards of them he fired his double barrelled gun loaded with buck shot, which accelerated their movements. A waterman also left at the same time in another boat, so as to afford assistance if required.

38. An international crisis was precipitated in 1789 when the commandant at the incipient Spanish settlement at Nootka Sound on the central west coast of Vancouver Island seized British fur trade ships. Its resolution by the 1790 and 1794 Nootka Convention resulted in Spanish withdrawal. Tovell, "The Other Side of the Coin," 3–29; Barry M. Gough, *The Northwest Coast: British Navigation, Trade, and Discoveries to 1812* (Vancouver: University of British Columbia Press, 1992), 163–166, et passim. In some respects, this volume is an expansion and revision of Gough's earlier *Distant Dominion*.

39. The governor's mission to the outpost settlements of the colony and to Russian Alaska on the *Sparrowhawk* was duly reported in the Victoria press. "News from Sitka. Return of H.M.S. Sparrowhawk," *Daily British Colonist*, 24 June 1867. Letters published in the same issue noted the *Sparrowhawk's* presence in Sitka.

July 6th. The Bishop of Columbia being anxious to hold a Confirmation and consecrate a Cemetery at Cowitchen,[40] we left Esquimalt at 6.15 am, and embarked him and Mr. Alston[41] at Cadboro Bay at 8.15, and anchored at Cowitchen off Mr. Harris' John Bull Inn in 13 fathoms at 12.45 am, having taken 6½ hours. As we were not pressed for time, we steamed slowly today at 65 Revolutions with little or no wind, and made 7.2 knots, the consumption of coals being 5 tons.

Cowichan cemetery consecration

The Rev. W. Reece came on board, and after luncheon landed with him, the Bishop, Mr. Alston & Dr. Comrie, having some difficulty in entering the river, as the water was extremely low, and had some trouble in finding the proper channel.

After seeing Mr. Brennan and Nott (trader) we walked out to Mr. Reece's parsonage a distance of two miles, where we dined and then walked back with Comrie. I have a sketch of the Quiamichan village which was well situated on the Cowitchen river.

July 7th. Landed at Cowitchen in the morning with Comrie and Boys, and walked up to the Parsonage. Attended a long service which lasted 3½ hours in consecrating the new Cemetery which adjoined the Church,[42] and concluded with the Confirmation service, when 4 Girls and 3 men were confirmed, including the 2 eldest girls of Mr. Skinner. There were 59 people present, which were as many as the Church would hold.

July 8th. Exercised firing shot and shell at the trees on the opposite side of the Bay, opposite Mr. Haris' Wharf, 1700 yards distant.

The Bishop, Mr. Alston, Skinner & Rothwell embarked, and left Cowitchen at 11.45 am, and anchored at Esquimalt in 5½ hours. Raining nearly all the Afternoon.

July 18th.[43] As the Admiral wished to pay an Official visit to the English Camp at San Juan,[44] we embarked him, Captains Dawkins & Oldfield, Commander K*[illeg.]*, Staff Commdt. Carr, Lieut. Maclean, Staff Surgeon Burton, Mr. H. Perry Secretary, Mr. Drew Assistant Paymaster, Rev. T. Hamilton, Rev. W. W. Parry, and steamed to San Juan, proceeding thro' the Mosquito Passage for the first time, and anchored at 11.30 am, nearly abreast of the entrance to Westcott Creek. Found the channel very

San Juan inspection

40. "H.M.S. Sparrowhawk," *Daily British Colonist*, 6 July 1867.

41. Mr. Alston was Registrar-General of Bishop Hills' diocese. "Arrival of H.M.S. Sparrowhawk from Cowichan," *Daily British Colonist*, 10 July 1867.

42. "The cemetery comprises about an acre in extent, surrounding the log church erected by the settlers this spring. After reading the morning prayers, the Bishop delivered a short address explanatory of the custom of the church in setting apart a place for burial. He then left the church, attended by the Rev. Mr. Reece and followed by the congregation, and went into the churchyard, where a petition from the congregation was read by Mr. Alston, the Registrar of the Diocese, praying that the ground might be consecrated. A circuit was made in procession round the ground, the Bishop and congregation singing the customary hymn, after which the sentence of consecration was read by the Registrar-General and signed by the Bishop, who then offered up the usual prayer. The church was then revisited." Ibid. See also Hills, "1866 and 1867," 19–20.

43. This entry and the following one for 12 July are accurate. For whatever reason, Porcher has misordered them. Entries for 12, 18 July 1867, Master's logbook, Adm. 53/9256.

44. "Admiral Hastings," *Daily British Colonist*, 19 July 1867.

narrow, and not sufficient room to swing without touching. Landed with the Admiral and Staff, and inspected all the Quarters and returned on board at 3. PM. Landed Provisions and the Marines were paid by Boys. Left again at 3.50 PM, and arrived at Esquimalt in 2 hours and 50 minutes.

Dispensing justice

THE *Zealous* ARRIVED AT NOON OF THE 12TH July with Rear Admiral Hon. George F. Hastings C.B. and Mrs. Hastings.[45]

Shortly after 2 Courts of Inquiry and 5 Court Martials were held. The first I sat upon with Captain Dawkins and Staff Comr. Carr, to inquire into the causes of the *Malacca* having been on shore lately 3 different times. Also an Inquiry, with the same Officers on the cause of the *Beaver* having been on shore on the Race rocks, when under the charge of Mr. Calvert Gunner of the *Forward*.

The Court Martials were on a Marine of the *Zealous* of the name of Hearne on a charge of Theft, on Mr. Crewe an Engineer of the *Malacca*, Mr. Hethesington Engineer of the *Forward*, Mr. *[blank]* Carpenter of the *Malacca*, and lastly Mr. Crewe again on a charge of drunkenness and breaking his leave.

Into the interior

JULY 30TH. AS A DISTURBANCE HAD TAKEN place at Cariboo between the Grouse Creek Bed rock Flume Company, and the Canadian Company upon a piece of ground which they both claimed,[46] I was invited by Governor Seymour to accompany him there, in order to bring them to terms, which I was very happy to do so as to be able to see a little of the interior of British Columbia.[47] I drove into Victoria with the little luggage I was obliged to take, and left in the *Leviathan* at 7.10 PM with Mr Ma[u]nsell and Moss the Pilot, and proceeded on all night.

July 31st. On crossing the Bar of the Fraser found that most of the Buoys were out of their places, the Red buoy that marked the South side of the channel being over on the opposite side. Arrived at New Westminster at 10.15 AM, 15½ hours after leaving Victoria. Called on the Governor & Mrs. Seymour, and started at 11.30 AM

---

45. "The Sparrowhawk," *Daily British Colonist*, 13 July 1867.

46. The governor's mission and the cause of the disturbance were reported and editorialized as "The Grouse Creek 'War'," *Daily British Colonist*, 2 August 1867.

Curiously, the same issue included a dispatch from Quesnelmouth, dated 1 August, that "the Canadian Company have jumped the balance of the Flume Company's ground that was not in dispute, and named it the '*Sparrowhawk*'." This is undoubtedly a coincidence as the name was probably given because J. M. Sparrow was the agent of the Grouse Creek Bed Rock Flume Company. "Grouse Creek Troubles. Great Excitement," *Daily British Colonist*, 29 July 1867.

47. An editorial notice of Porcher's inclusion on the governor's mission suggests that he was to serve the governor in at least an advisory capacity. He was given high praise as a professional and his presence assured that an impartial judgment would be rendered in the case. "The Grouse Creek Difficulty," *Daily British Colonist*, 31 July 1867. See also "Captain Porcher, R.N.," *Daily British Colonist*, 1 August 1867.

Governor Seymour deliberately included naval commanders on occasion to strengthen his hand. Further, he contemplated the potential employment of Royal Navy sailors for such inland assignments if the situation called for it. Gough, *Royal Navy and the Northwest Coast*, 148–149. Tina Loo examines "The Meaning of Law and the Limits of Authority on Grouse Creek" in her *Making Law, Order, and Authority in British Columbia, 1821–1871* (Toronto: University of Toronto Press, 1994), chapter six.

The Hudson Bay Company's stern wheeler ALEXANDRA in VICTORIA harbour. July 5, 1867.

(original watercolor size: 10 x 6.88 in./21.5 x 17.5 cm)

FORT SIMPSON, on the North extreme of BRITISH COLUMBIA. June 13, 1867.

(original watercolor size: 14 x 9.5 in./35.5 x 24 cm)

Indian Crests at Fort Simpson. June 13, 1867.

(original watercolor size: 9.88 x 6.75 in./25 x 17 cm)

The Quamichan Rancherie, on the Cowitchen river. July 6, 1867.

(original watercolor size: 14 x 9.13 in./35.5 x 17.5 cm)

The 150 mile house (from Lillooet & the same distance from Cariboo). August 12, 1867.

(original watercolor size: 10 x 7 in./25.5 x 17.5 cm)

CLINTON, the junction of the Lytton & Lillooet routes to CARIBOO, & 135 miles above YALE.
August 13, 1867.

(original watercolor size: 14 x 9 in./35.5 x 23 cm)

in the *Onward*, with our party of the Governor, Mr. Trutch and Bushby, and Dr. Black, Mr. Claudet, Hone, Dally, Barnard, Nelson, &c being also in the steamer, going to different places up the country.

At 9 PM. saw a magnificent meteor, starting from the side of one of the mountains, shooting upward at a gentle curve to about 40° above the horizon bursting and falling about 120° from where it started and remaining in sight 15 seconds. It was in the form of an half opened umbrella.

August 1st. Stopped at Hope 1½ hour, leaving it again at 5.15 AM. Friday the current was running very strong (Skokem chuck) through Emory's Bar, the vessel was tied up a few hundred yards below it, and unloaded part of the cargo to lighten the vessel, and then steamed thro' it with some difficulty. Arrived at Yale at 10 AM. The Cariboo Mail had arrived 1½ hour before us, and the *Lillooet* left with it at 11. Dined with the McKay's of the H.B.C. where I met Mrs. Sanders & her sister Miss [Morenby?]. The former was going to join her husband at Lillooet, who was the Magistrate there.

Every thing being ready we left Yale in Mr. Barnard's stage with 6 horses at 4.10 PM, and drove through the Canyons, arriving at Boston Bar in 4 hours, a distance of 25 miles, or at the rate of 6 miles an hour.

The cost of the Stage for our journey to Cariboo and back was £300, the distance being 380 miles each way.

The Fare for Passengers by Stage had lately been reduced from $130 to $85, with the addition of $8 for the steamer that runs between Soda Creek and Quesnel mouth.

August 2nd. Left Boston Bar at 6.45 AM, the road still extending along the left bank of the Fraser, but more easily made than what we went through yesterday, as the side of the hills were not so precipitous. The scenery going across the Jackass mountains about 45 miles above Yale is very grand, the road being led up to a height of 1400 feet above the level of the river, with a steep descent to Kanaka Bar, which is 10 miles to Lytton.

After passing the Jackass mountains the character of the Country varies, and different vegetation makes its appearance. Rain very seldom falls at this time of year, between this point and Ashcroft, a distance of 60 miles, beyond that it is wet again.

Wild cherries that were now ripe lined the road a great part of the way, and the principal trees were the Yellow Pine (that first makes its appearance after passing Boston Bar,) Balsam, Spruce, and Douglas Pine. Arrived at Lytton at 0.20 PM, 57 miles from Yale. The town of Lytton is nothing more than a few wooden houses, built in a very bleak situation, the trees being all cleared away, and the little grass that was left being all burnt up. It is built at the junction of the Thompson river with the Fraser, and is generally blowing a Gale of wind with clouds of dust, a pleasant place to live in.

The Government house is built at the North end of the town, and is a substantial log house, consisting of 5 or 6 rooms, now inhabited by Mr. Hale, Chief Constable, in the absence of a Magistrate. Remained at Lytton 3¾ hours, and then drove on along the Canyons of the Thompson to Spence's bridge where we arrived at 7.30 PM, having travelled today 55 miles, at the rate of 7½ miles an hour. Inspected here one of those curious places the Indians live in during the cold weather, commonly called a sweat hole. It is built underground, about 10 feet deep, being arched over with timber, and the earth thrown on top, and 30 feet in diameter where several families are huddled together for mutual warmth. The descent being effected by a knarled[48] pole.[49]

August 3rd. Left Spence's bridge at 7.0 AM, having got through the night pretty well, the mosquitoes that were very numerous and annoying when we first arrived, having gradually disappeared as the night grew on. From this place, that was formerly called Cook's Ferry, we cleared the Cascade range and the country opened out into more level plains, with a succession of benches, but as the grass was now dried up, and but few trees to be seen, it looked rather barren, but the crops that we saw, seemed to grow well, whenever they could get any irrigation. Arrived at Ashcroft, 104 miles from Yale, at 10.15 AM, having gone since leaving at the rate of 7½ miles an hour, including the stoppages.

Ashcroft is situated in a large valley, destitute of trees, but surrounded by hills scantily wooded, several hundred acres being fenced round, and 70 acres planted with Wheat, Barley, Oats, and Alfalfa or California Lucerne. The Cornwalls were both away fishing at Luna [Loon] lake, and left Mr. Horton in charge of their establishment. They had on their farm 350 head of cattle, and 40 horses. Stopped here 2¾ hours for luncheon, and then drove on, changing horses at Cache Creek, the Junction for Kamloops and the Big Bend route, and the road then extended along the Bonaparte river where Rattlesnakes are rather numerous, and through a very pretty valley filled with a succession of lakes. Arrived at Clinton at 5.15 PM, 31 miles from Ashcroft, and 135 miles from Yale. This place is the Junction with the Lillooet route, and from this town the remainder of the distance to Quesnel mouth is calculated, Clinton being 47 miles from Lillooet, and the number of inhabitants are only 32 including women and children. The cold is very intense during the winter often going down to 40° below zero, the elevation being 3200 feet above the sea.

August 4th. Left Clinton at 6.40 AM, the first part of the way through the fine valley in which the town is built, extending about 10 miles in length and cultivated with Barley and Oats, we then ascended a steep hill, and the road then extended for 50 miles through a dense wood composed of small trees, and commonly called the "Green timber." At Clinton the mosquitoes were numerous, and today were very plentiful and annoying, as it was cloudy and no wind, and had little rest from them along the whole of the road to Soda Creek. At the 59 mile house, the Cows were grouped close round several fires, that were lighted for the purpose of the smoke

48. An archaic form of gnarled.

49. Winter housing, occasionally for communal occupation, was commonly constructed in excavated semisubterranean pits. Supported by timbers, the roofs, sometimes at ground level, were poles, brush, and bark covered with a thick layer of dirt. Mats, platforms, fire pits, insulation, and other devices raised the comfort level of the occupants. Dorothy I. D. Kennedy and Randall T. Bouchard, "Northern Coast Salish," in William C. Sturtevant, ed., *Handbook of North American Indians*, vol. 7: *Northwest Coast*, edited by Wayne Suttles, (Washington: Smithsonian Institution, 1990), 446; Suttles, "Central Coast Salish," *Northwest Coast*, 462; Halpin and Seguin, "Tsimshian Peoples," *Northwest Coast*, 271.

driving them away, and found it to be a common practice along the road to give the horses a little rest, and was also used for the workmen that were repairing the roads. A mile and a half beyond this, the road led round a magnificent chasm about 3 miles in length, ¼ mile wide, and 1000 feet in depth formed by stratified rocks, and was a great contrast to the dreary wood we had to pass through on each side of it. Arrived at the Loch Lomond House (74 mile house) at 11.20, having travelled over a very indifferent road at the rate of 5.6 an hour, a little variety in the scenery being in a succession of lakes, in which we saw several wild fowl. Our halting place for the night was at the 100 mile house, Bridge Creek, where we arrived at 5.40 PM, having driven today 53 miles. The flowers were very backward owing to the elevation, and the extreme cold in the early spring, and those that had passed away at Victoria two months ago, were here in full bloom, such as the Roses, Tiger Lilies, Blue Lupine, Vetches, Camomile &c and the Strawberries were ripe and in flavor.

August 5th. Left Bridge Creek at 4.45 AM, arrived at the 117 mile house near Lac La Hache in 2 hours, and arrived at the 150 mile house (Toomey's) at Noon, having travelled exactly 50 miles before breakfast, at the rate of 6.8 miles an hour, including the stoppages. The whole of our journey today was through an open and picturesque country, more like park like scenery than any thing else, and covered with lakes, Lac La Hache being 10 miles in length. Stopped a little more than two hours, at the 150 mile house, when we started again, and soon got into a very bad road, muddy and cut up into deep ruts, which made it difficult for the heavy teams, one alone we saw had 15 yoke (30) of oxen to get it through the bad places. The Stage waggon that followed us stuck in the mud 6 times, and was only got out with the assistance of additional oxen and horses. Arrived at Soda Creek at 7.25 PM (178 miles from Lillooet) at the rate of 5½ miles an hour, and took up our quarters on board the steamer *Enterprise*.

August 6th. Left Soda Creek in the *Enterprise* at 4.0 AM. She was a small stern wheeler of 60 Horse power, drew 2 feet of water, and was commanded by Mr. Wright. The distance between Soda Creek and Quesnelmouth is 60 miles, and as the vessel has not much power takes 15 hours in getting up, and 3½ hours in returning with the Current. The river had widened out considerably from when we saw it last at Lytton, and the scenery very different to the lower Fraser by the Canyons, as hardly a rock was to be seen and the banks varied by having both open ground and wooded. Arrived at Quesnel mouth at 6.45 PM, where we met the Gold Commissioner Mr. H. M. Ball. This was at one time a thriving place, but its importance has now been eclipsed by William's Creek, where most the settlers have removed to.

August 7th. Left Quesnel mouth at 6.20 AM, passed by the Cotton wood Creek, and arrived at Hamilton's on the Lightning Creek at 1 PM, having driven 37 miles with the same horses, mostly up hill and over bad roads.

Here we stopped an hour for breakfast, and then started again. Passed several miners at work at Van Winkle, and arrived at Richfield in William's Creek at 7 PM, and put up at the Paris and London Restaurant.

The road led the whole way through woods which made it rather gloomy, and as there had been a great deal of rain lately, had to pass thro' a great deal of mud, which made it heavy for the horses. The latter part of the way, the road was rather dangerous, as it was very narrow being only 10 feet. The whole journey from New Westminster to Williams Creek has taken exactly a week.

Cariboo mining frontier

August 8th. We only remained 2 days 3 nights at Cariboo so that I had to make the most of my time in going round the principal places. The Gold mining is very extensive and employs about 2000 men, and more gold has been taken out within a given area than any other place in the world, and the only drawback is the extreme cold which prevents any real mining being done for more than 4 or 5 months in the year. The mining is worked in every conceivable way with the exception of quartz crushing, by deep shafts, tunnelling or drifting, hydraulic washing, ground sluicing, and by the common rocker. William's Creek has been partly worked over from one end to the other a distance of 3 or 4 miles, on the upper and two ditches on different levels convey the water for the use of the Penstocks for the Hydraulic washing, and the different Flumes. The usual way of washing the ground for the gold is as simple as possible, merely shovelling the earth into the flumes, and the rush of water taking the stones & light parts away leaving the gold to be collected at stated times out of the Riffles that are placed like this in the bottom of the Flumes.

The gold is principally found in the pay dirt immediately over the bed rock, and is of a much darker colour than the earth or gravel above it, and extends only for a few inches in some places, and at other times for 4 or 5 feet. I paid a visit to the Aurora claim, a little below Barkerville, which is considered at present to be richest diggings at Cariboo, and take out frequently during the week 230 ounces. They had tunnelled in upwards of 500 feet into the side of the hill, and out of the pay dirt which ranged about 5 feet I picked out with the Foreman several pieces of gold of the value of $3.18 within a few minutes. There are four towns in William's Creek, Richfield the first settled and on the highest ground, Barkerville or Middle town, 1½ mile lower down, which has now the principal business and the largest population, and Cameron town, and Mary'sville, the latter being gradually buried from the tailings of the Bed rock Flume.

All the public buildings are at Barkerville, two Banks, a Public library that takes in the principal papers and books for circulation, a Masonic Hall which is well fitted up, and Dancing saloons. These latter I visited the last evening, in one house there were 4 Hurdies, (or German dancing girls), and 7 in the one adjoining, the other making up the [dozen] not being very well at present, or in a fit state for dancing. The arrangement made for the Hurdies, are that for every dance, the gentlemen have to pay a dollar, half of which goes to the girl, and the other half to the house.

One miner is said to have paid for this amusement in one year $2300. Gambling saloons are to be found in the same and other buildings, the favourite games I saw being Keeno (a kind of Lot[t]o), Faro, and also Monte, Poker, &c and in the Chinese houses, the rather stupid game of odd & even.

A steam Saw Mill has been built at the Head of the Creek, and supplies the greater part of the lumber, the principal wood that is used being the Spruce, which is good for the Flumes &c on account of its hardness.

An execution took place during the time we were here. A miner and an Indian both for murder, and were hung together in front of the Court house early in the morning.

The Governor's two servants were sleeping in the Court House the night before, and were much surprised on waking up to find two Coffins placed by their bed sides, which made them leave a little sooner than usual.

The dispute about the Grouse Creek claims, ended by having 8 of the Canadian Company imprisoned in the Gaol for 48 hours for Contempt of the Law, and the ground was given up to the Governor, and not to be worked upon by either side, until a decision was come to by the Executive Council.

Downriver journey

August 10th. Having finished the business we came here for, we left William's Creek at 5.15 am, passed Van Winkle and Beaver Pass, and arrived at Hamilton's in 4 hours, the distance being 25 miles. Remained a couple of hours for breakfast, and arrived at Quesnel mouth in 6 hours, the whole distance of 57 miles being done in 10 hours. On arriving found there Mr. Ogden (Chief Factor) had arrived from Fort George with 105 bales of Furs in 5 bateaux manned by 40 men, that were collected at that Fort (100 miles higher up the river) as well as at Lake Stewart.

August 11th. Left Quesnel mouth in the *Enterprise* at 4.50 am, taking in the vessel as Passengers Colonel Welcker lately belonging to the Topographical Staff of the U.S.A. and afterward joined the Confederate forces, Mr. Harper, a large Cattle owner, Ladner a merchant of New Westminster, the Hangman, and one of the Hurdies that was going down to San Francisco for change of air. Arrived at Soda Creek in 3½ hours, and left again in our Stage at 10.10 am, arriving at Deep Creek house (14 miles) in 2½ hours, where we lunched. This is situated in a very fine valley, 4 miles long by½ mile wide, surrounded by hills partially wooded, and in a good resting place for travellers, being well furnished with Beds. Amused ourselves by looking at some oxen being shod. Left again at 2.15 pm, and arrived at the 150 miles house (from William's Creek as well as from Lillooet) in 2.40 hours.

August 12th. After making a sketch of the 150 mile house, left it at 9.30 am, and passed through 50 miles of the finest part of the country on this route, lunched at the 117 mile house (in charge of Mr. McKinlay who had left his home in Scotland 36 years ago to join the Hudson Bay Company's service, and was in charge of Fort Alexandria 30 years ago,) and arrived at the 100 mile house, Bridge Creek at 5.30 pm.

In the upper part of the country the charges for living were generally the same, being \$1½ for Meals, and Beds \$1, but gradually coming down as we neared Yale. The price of Eggs at the 100 mile house were \$4 a dozen.

August 13th. Left Bridge Creek at 7.10 am, and passed through 50 miles of the most dismal part of the journey, (the Green timber), stopped at the 74 mile house at

Noon for a short time, and arrived at Clinton at 4 PM, where I had a refreshing bath in the mill stream.

August 14th. Left the Clinton Hotel, W. McKinnon at 5.15 AM, arrived at Ashcroft in 4 hours, where we met Henry Cornwall, remained there 2¼ hours for breakfast, and then proceeded on to Lytton where we arrived at 6.50 PM, having travelled today 79 miles.

Passed several good Indian Tombs today, particularly near Spence's bridge where there was a very simple and effective one of a canoe being raised on supports about 4 feet above the ground, and ornamented by 3 Poles with Flags.

On our arrival at Lytton a salute was fired in a very simple way from an anvil, a

small quantity of powder was placed each time in the center that was sunk and about 2 inches square, the powder was then partly covered by a card to prevent the wind blowing it away, a plant placed on the top of this, and a heavy stone above it, which gave us loud a report as a gun would each time.

August 15th. Left Lytton at 8.0 AM, having been well entertained by the Belgian owner's of the Hotel Monsieur & Made. Gautier. Arrived at Boston Bar in 5½ hours where we stopped 1½ hour for luncheon, and arrived at Yale at 6.45 PM. Dined at the Colonial Hotel, and slept at the Commissioners house.

The length of the Stages varied during the journey, for the last two days, we went 25 miles with the same horses, and the day we arrived at Cariboo we went 37 miles, which nearly did the horses up.

August 16th. Left Yale at 11.15 AM in the *Onward*, stopped at Hope to land Mrs. McKay and her family, and arrived at the Camp New Westminster at 6.45 PM, making the distance of 105 miles in 7½ hours, including the stoppages, or at the rate of 14 miles an hour.

Distances traveled

July	31st	From New Westminster to Yale	105 miles	By Steamer
August	1st	Yale to Boston Bar	25	Stage
	2nd	Boston Bar to Spence's bridge	55	
	3rd	Spence's bridge to Clinton	55	
	4th	Clinton to Bridge Creek	53	
	5th	Bridge Creek to Soda Creek	78	
	6th	Soda Creek to Quesnel mouth	60	Steamer
	7th	Quesnel mouth to William's Creek	57	Stage
			488 miles	

August 1867. Ashcroft. Lytton

5.15 A.M., arrived at Ashcroft in 4 hours, where we met Bishop Cornwall, remained there 2¼ hours for breakfast, and then proceeded on to Lytton where we arrived at 6.50 P.M. having travelled to day 79 miles.

Passed several good Indian Tombs to day, particularly [illegible] Species [illegible] then there was a very simple and effective one of a Canoe being raised on supports about 4 feet above the ground, and surmounted by 3 Poles with Flags.

On our arrival at Lytton a salute was fired in a very simple way from an anvil, a small quantity of powder was placed each time in the centre where was sunk an about 2 inches square, the powder was then partly covered by a card to prevent the train running in more, a plank placed on the top of this, and a heavy stone above it, which gave as loud a report as a gun would each time.

August 15th. Left Lytton at 8.0 A.M., having been well entertained by the Belgian [illegible] of the Hotel, [illegible], arrived at Boston Bar in 5½ hours.

A sample page from Porcher's journal. Yale University Library

Return journey from Cariboo

August	10 th	From William's Creek to Quesnel mouth	57 miles	By Stage
	11 th	Quesnel mouth to Soda Creek & to the 150 [mile] house	88	Steamer & stage
	12 th	150 mile house to the 100 [mile] house	50	Stage
	13 th	100 mile house to Clinton	53	
	14 th	Clinton to Lytton	78	
	15 th	Lytton to Yale	57	
	16 th	Yale to New Westminster	105	Steamer
			488 miles	

August 17th. Left in the *Sir James Douglas* at 3.30 PM, with the Governor, Mr. Trutch, Goring, Bushby, Maunsell, and Captain Cooper, and arrived at Victoria at 11.45 PM, making the passage in 8¼ hours, and the Trip to Cariboo and back to Victoria having taken only 18 days.[50]

Very few visitors get as far as Cariboo on account of the expense, the travelling alone being as follows:

From Victoria to New Westminster,	By steamer	$ 4
New Westminster to Yale		5
Yale to Cariboo By Barnard's	Stage	85
Soda Creek to Quesnel mouth	By Steamer	8

The living also being very expensive as you came up the country.

50. "The Sir James Douglas...," *Daily British Colonist*, 19 August 1867.

Chapter Seven

Activities of Circumstances and Official Responsibilities

14 September 1867–18 May 1868

[Edmund Porcher's final winter and spring at Esquimalt included several short trips and errands to nearby destinations. Repairs on the *Sparrowhawk*, participation in courts martial, gunnery practice, an occasional ceremonial appearance, and other routine activities absorbed much of the time. Another Fenian alert induced prudent precautions but it produced little excitement beyond press coverage. In mid-April, the admiral used the *Sparrowhawk* to make a tour of principal towns and sights of Puget Sound. The capital of British Columbia was moved from New Westminster on the mainland, to Victoria on Vancouver Island. Porcher escorted the governor and his official party in the move.]

Sooke harbor launching

September 14th.[1] As the *Forward* was going to Sooke to see a vessel launched, I took the opportunity of taking a passage by her for the purpose of seeing the place. We left at 10.30 am with the Rhodes's, Spark's, Mrs. Foster, Captain Dawkins, Dr. Burton, Rev. Thos. R. Hamilton, Mr. Robinson, Christie, &c and steamed round the Race rocks, and anchored in Sooke harbour at 2 pm opposite the Muir's building yard, where the Brigantine was ready for launching. The company then landed to see the vessel christened by Mrs. Rhodes, before she reached her proper element. The keel of the vessel was perfectly level, although the ways for some distance were of the proper incline, but after many unsuccessful attempts to start the vessel, were at last obliged to *[illeg.]* to abandon her, after using jack screws, hammering, and the strongest hawser they had taken out to the *Forward* that went ahead with it at full speed till the rope parted. The party then walked out to the Muir's Farm that is situated about ¾ mile from the building yard and steam saw mills, in a cleared valley which is open to the Straits of Juan de Fuca.

Here there were living under the same roof four generations of the family, that occupy their time between building vessels, sawing timber, and farming. On our first landing the vessel was christened the *Robert Cowan* after the head of the family, and was the largest vessel that had yet been built on the island. Her length being 110 feet, beams 28 feet: 9½ feet depth of hold, which made the tonnage 458 and was intended to run between Victoria and the Sandwich Islands. She was successfully launched 4 days afterwards, and taken round to Victoria to be fitted out.

There was another building yard in Sooke harbour, opposite the entrance, where a smaller vessel was in course of construction.

We left Sooke on our return at 5.30 pm, and took 3½ hours each way, the distance being 18 miles.[2]

New Westminster visit

As the Admiral, Hon. Geo. F. Hastings, was anxious to pay a visit to the Capital before the bad weather regularly set in,[3] he came on board accompanied by his Secretary and Flag Lieutenant, Staff Commr. Carr, and The Rev. T. R. Hamilton, on the morning of the 8th October, and we then steamed out of Esquimalt at 7.15 am for Nanaimo, where we secured alongside the Coaling Wharf at 2.30 pm, after

1. Porcher followed his entry for 17 August with a page of anecdotal accounts, using "Quantity of Mud in the Country" as the running head. He then wrote four pages headed "Carrying Freight on the Coast of Mexico." After this he included six pages of dimensions and other statistical data of the *Sparrowhawk*, which are repeated in an appendix to his journal. The mud and Mexican accounts are of no relevance to Porcher's entries. The data of the *Sparrowhawk* are technical beyond the needs of understanding his entries. These digressions are all omitted herein.

For whatever reasons, Porcher did not make entries for the period 16 August–13 September. He traveled in the party of Governor Frederick Seymour, who was intervening in the Grouse Creek affair—a dispute between two mining companies. Ching Foo to Editor, 15 August 1867, *Daily British Colonist*, 3 September 1867; *Dictionary of Canadian Biography*, "Seymour;" Akrigg and Akrigg, *British Columbia Chronicle*, 349–350.

2. The *Sparrowhawk* had left Esquimalt harbor for a short time on 25 September 1867, to engage in target practice. Porcher's log, 297–298.

3. One of the admiral's apparent reasons was to examine Burrard Inlet to determine a practical location for a dockyard. "We understand that Admiral Hastings…," *Daily British Colonist*, 1 October 1867.

making a quick passage of 7¼ hours. We had thick drizzling rain the whole day. As soon as the vessel was secured, we took in 38½ tons of Coals, and during this was going on, I called on the Spalding's with the Admiral, and looked over the different hotels to see if there were any of them fit for the Admiral to put up at, but found them all very indifferent, and only fit for the lower class of Miners.

October 9th. Cast off from the Wharf at Nanaimo, and steamed out of the harbour at 7.55 AM, for Burrard's Inlet, stopped off New Brighton situated at the end of the long road from New Westminster to make enquiries, and then steamed up to Port Moody, and then returned to the 2nd Narrows and anchored off New Brighton (Hocking's) at 1.30 PM. Here the Admiral and Staff landed, and went up to New Westminster by the Stage Cart at 3 PM. As our stern had swung into 2 fathoms, we weighed at 3.30, and steamed round to Stamp's Saw Mills where we anchored in 9 fathoms at 4.0 PM. Landed with Dolphin and were over the Saw Mills, and brought off a piece of Lignum Vitae to make some balls for the Bowling Alley, that weighed 390 lbs, which being worth half a dollar a pound would have cost $195. It rained nearly the whole day.

October 10th. Raining the greater part of the night & day. Left Stamp's Saw Mills at 10.55 AM, and steamed out of Burrard's Inlet against the Flood Tide, exercised firing at a Target near the Light vessel, and then crossed the Bar of the Fraser at nearly High water, having at the shoal[i]est part 16 feet, and anchored off the Government house at 4.50.

October 12th. The Admiral and Staff embarked at 10.30 AM, and we left New Westminster at 11 AM, on attempting to cross the Bar of the Fraser, we ran aground on the Northern bank near No. 4 buoy where we remained an hour, we then hauled the ship off by a stream anchor, the tide being half flood, passed the Light vessel at 2.30 PM, and entered Esquimalt at 7.30 when the Admiral disembarked.[4]

Burnt on our passage down 10.6 tons of Coals, going at the rate of 10.2 knots an hour, between the Lt. vessel & Esquimalt.

Fraser River entrance

ON ATTEMPTING TO CROSS THE BAR OF THE Fraser on the 12th October 1867, when the Admiral Hon. Geo. F. Hastings was on board, we grounded on one of the banks near No. 4 buoy, where we remained an hour, and then hauled the vessel by the stream anchor into the middle of the channel where there was 5 fathoms, as the tide rose.[5]

4. The Victoria newspaper corrected its earlier report that the *Sparrowhawk* had crossed the bar of the Fraser River successfully. "Admiral Hastings...," *Daily British Colonist*, 14 October 1867.

It was not the fault of Captain Cooper, regarded as the most skillful pilot on the coast. "It is an unfortunate and generally admitted fact that the main channel of the Fraser is rapidly shoaling, and that in a few years, at farthest, it will be entirely closed to navigation by all but flatbottomed steamers and scows." "The Sparrowhawk on the Sandheads," *Daily British Colonist*, 15 October 1867.

The potential difficulty had been anticipated because the *Sparrowhawk* was "a very light-draught vessel" and because of "the shifting of the sands" at the mouth of the Fraser River. "Admiral Hastings...," *Daily British Colonist*, 8 October 1867.

5. This paragraph and the remainder of this entry are relocated here from a position before the 14 September entry in the manuscript. Porcher had probably intended the misordered remarks as an aside or afterthought to his regular entry.

The channel of this river is frequently changing, and the Buoys are constantly being drifted out of their places, or if they remain in their positions, the sand forms round them, which makes it equally dangerous to them for marks.

If the Fraser was ever likely to be a highway for commerce, the same attention might be paid to the Buoys as is done in other places, and a fresh Survey ought to be made every year, but at present it is very seldom a ship enters the river, as it would occasion too much delay, and there being no market for the goods.

If this was not enough to deter vessels from entering the river, the Colonial Government passed a law on the 2nd November 1867, obliging vessels to take Pilots at the following exorbitant rates, which is quite sufficient to prevent vessels from entering at all:

From the Light ship to New Westminster.

Sailing vessels under 10 feet draught, $6 per foot.

Sailing vessels 10 feet and upwards, $7 per foot.

Sailing vessels in tow of steamer, under 10 feet, $5 per foot.

Sailing vessels in tow of steamer, 10 feet and upwards, $6 per foot.

Steamers under 10 feet $4 per foot.

Steamers 10 feet and upwards $5 per foot.

New Westminster interlude

October 15th. Left Esquimalt at 9.0 am for New Westminster[6] with Captains Price and Dawkins, Lord George Campbell, Mr. Foley, Naylor, and Mr. [Bushby?].

The water not being high enough for crossing the Bar, exercised the men firing at a Target, and then passed the light vessel at 3.30, made fast alongside the Wharf at New Westminster at 5.40 pm, as it was getting quite dark, and discharged the 24 pr. howitzers with the ammunition, we then cast off and steamed up to the Camp where we anchored at 7.0 pm.

Our guns fired this afternoon were heard distinctly at Esquimalt, a distance of 40 miles in a straight line, and the smoke of the guns were seen from San Juan.

October 16th. This afternoon the Governor laid the foundation stone of the first stone church that had been erected in the Colony, the service being read by Rev. W. Hayman. We then went on to see the Industrial Exhibition that was being held at the Drill Hall, and where there was a good display of the fruits and vegetables that had been grown in the Colony. Some of the Cabbages weighed 42 lbs.

During this week, the ship swung round to the Flood for two hours out of the 24, between 10.30 am and 12.30. The water of the river being much less muddy than it is in the summer.

October 19th. All the Officers living at the Government House, and Pooley, Walker, Mr. Gamble of the Telegraph Company, Uriah Nelson, several Miners and 2 Wives, embarked at 7 am, and then weighed and left the Camp, but a dense fog

6. "H.M.S. Sparrowhawk, with a number...," *Daily British Colonist*, 16 October 1867.

coming on, obliged us to anchor again near the town, on clearing again at 8.40 AM, we weighed and steamed down the Fraser, arriving at Esquimalt at 3.20 PM, having taken only 3¾ hours, or at the rate of 10.5 an hour.[7]

Repairing the ship

For the next four months we remained at Esquimalt, and as it inlcuded the whole of the winter when gales and bad weather are to be expected, we moored the ship on the 20th November for the first time in this harbour. On the following day we completed our coals from the Stores.

In raising the screw on the morning of the 2nd December, for our monthly inspection, the purchase fall carried away, and broke the cross piece on its going down.

A new one was made by Mesrs. Spratt and Kriember for $245 in 12 days, and was fitted by our Engineers afterwards in the Dockyard Factory who took 14 days more before it was secured in its place on the 31st December.

The Diver of the *Zealous* went down on the 3rd December to see if he could find the two broken pieces of the cross piece, but owing to the mud being very soft they could not be found, the deep sea lead sinking into the mud for about a foot. A short distance from the spot where the pieces went down, the bottom was hard, so that it varied a great deal in different parts of the harbour, a sheathed knife was brought up in good preservation.

Esquimalt winter

The first snow appeared on the hills round Esquimalt harbour on the 16th December, and on the low ground on the 20th December.

The harbour of Esquimalt is one of the safest in the world, the depth varying from 6 to 7 fathoms at low water, and the wind never blows with any strength, owing to the hills breaking its force in the vicinity. The Barometer is very lively and varies a great deal, often shewing there is bad weather not far off, though hardly perceptible in the harbour. On the 22nd December there was very little wind all day, but the Barometer went down half a tenth every hour. It came on to rain at 2 PM, and continued till 8 PM when it nearly ceased. The Barometer was then at its lowest point 28.65, after which it began to rise at the same rate it went down, and at Midnight shewed 28.85. Shortly before this it came on to blow in squalls from the S.W. and at 8 AM of the 23rd Dec. there was a light breeze from the Eastward with the Barometer at 29.05. It was nearly calm all day, but the Bar. very low. At 10 PM it was 28.96.

The weather this winter was much colder than we had experienced the two previous years. It came on in the first week of January, and lasted the greater part of the month. The first really cold day was on the 5th January, when the Thermometer at 6 AM shewed 13°, at 8 AM 17°, and did not rise higher than 19° during the day.

7. "H.M.S. Sparrowhawk is expected...," *Daily British Colonist*, 19 October 1867; "H.M.S. Sparrowhawk returned...," *Daily British Colonist*, 21 October 1867.

On the 6th January the Ther. at 6 AM was 10°, and at 8 AM 16°, and very piercing all day. The Ponds & most of the inland waters were frozen over, and afforded capital skating, some of the ice I saw was 10 inches in thickness.[8]

February 10th. Our Bowling Alley was completed today, and I played 3 games there for the first time. The first lumber for it was received from the *Nicholas Biddle* on the 2nd March last year, and the exterior was commenced and completed shortly afterwards, and took nearly 7000 feet, the quantity we had received from that vessel, for towing her when waterlogged from Trial Island into Esquimalt, and afterwards lending her a hawser to take her over to the Sound. We received 6500 feet from Captain Stamp to finish the interior, as well as sufficient Lignum Vitae to make 13 Balls, the largest being 8 inches in diameter. The Alley was 90 feet long by 12 feet in breadth, as well as in height, the length of the Bowling part being 75 feet, by 3 feet in width, which was made by the boards being placed on end 1½ inch wide.[9]

Secret dispatch delivery

FEBRUARY 28TH. A SECRET DESPATCH HAVING arrived in the *Reindeer* yesterday from the Secretary of State for the Colonies, directed to the Governor, we steamed out of Esquimalt with it at 2.45 AM, passed over the Bar of the Fraser at nearly High water, the least water we had being 17 feet and anchored off the Government House at New Westminster at 0.30 PM, having taken 9¾ hours.[10] Very little wind the whole time, and burnt 9 tons 14 cwt.

Delivered the Despatch to the Governor, and embarked 30 iron bedsteads for the new Marines that had arrived in the *Reindeer* for San Juan.

February 29th. Left New Westminster at 7.5 AM, exercised firing at a Target near the Light vessel, and anchored in Roche Harbour at 2.30 PM. Met the *Diana* coming away from the Camp, the American Officers with their wives having been there on a visit.

---

8. A crew member found another diversion that lasted for a few weeks: "A young blade belonging to H.M.S. Sparrowhawk, having become smitten with the charms of a youthful maid of the forest, deserted his vessel about a month ago and took up his abode at the Indian village, where he basked in the smiles of his red inamorata until Sunday, when a cruel-hearted, practical policeman, having neither poetry in his soul or the milk of Human Kindness in his heart, broke in upon the blissful scene and escorted the amorous young sailor to the Barracks. Yesterday Mr. Pemberton ordered him back to his ship." "'Oh, for a Lodge in some vast Wilderness!'," *Daily British Colonist*, 14 January 1868.

It was also reported that: "Cabins have been constructed on H.M.S. Sparrowhawk for the accommodation of Admiral Hastings. We hope that the appearance of the symmetrical little vessel will not be detracted from by the addition." "Cabins have been constructed…," *Daily British Colonist*, 14 January 1868.

John Millan, deserted from the Sparrowhawk was brought before the police court on 20 January and "given up to the naval authorities." "Deserter," *Daily British Colonist*, 21 January 1868.

9. This may have been in connection with the Naval Club House for the naval officers which was described as "76 feet long by 30 feet wide,…The interior is divided into separate apartments for billiards, library, reading room, dining room, lavatory, kitchen, pantries, &c. On the upper floor are six bedrooms. Without, stabling will be provided for animals, and boats are ready at any hour to carry officers and others to the ships." "Naval Club House," *Daily British Colonist*, 22 June 1867; "Naval Club House, Esquimalt," *Daily British Colonist*, 2 September 1867. See also entry for 9 October 1867, above.

10. "The Sparrowhawk…," *Daily British Colonist*, 29 February 1868.

March 2nd.[11] Left Roche Harbour at 8.15 AM, with Capt. Delacombe and Hoffmeister, exercised firing at a Target near Trial Island, and anchored at Esquimalt at 0.15 PM. Burnt today 4 Tons 16 cwt.

Fenian alert

IN THE BEGINNING OF MARCH A LITTLE EXCITEMENT took place here in consequence of Mr. Bowker the Consul at San Francisco, having written to Mr. W. A. G. Young the Acting Colonial Secretary, to say that a Fenian Head centre had left in the Mail steamer for Victoria, and that he had better be on his guard.[12]

The *Forward* was ordered into Victoria Harbour, the Guards were doubled at the Dockyard, sentries were placed at the Hospital as well as at the Magazine at Cole Island, and the Guard boat was sent away twice during the night. An additional force of 10 Marines were sent to the *Forward* from the *Zealous*, to guard the Banks as well as the Gaol, special Constables were called out to keep watch at Victoria during the night, and threatening anonymous letters were sent to the Admiral and Governor.

This excitement went on during the greater part of the month, but as nothing took place, things went back to their usual routine.[13]

Court martial

MARCH 9TH. TRIED CHARLES MURPHY AN AB [able-bodied seaman] of this ship, by a Court Martial, for deserting from the ship on the 16th November last, and leaving the place in the U.S.S. *Ossipee* for San Francisco. In consequence of his having shewn some desire to return to the vessel, desertion was not proved but only absence without leave, for which he was awarded 10 weeks imprisonment with hard labour.

Ceremonial appearance

MARCH 20TH. AS THE LEGISLATIVE COUNCIL WAS going to be opened at New Westminster tomorrow, the Governor requested that the *Sparrowhawk* might be sent up to be present on the occasion.[14] In the morning it was blowing very hard from the S.W. the Aneroid having fallen 0.7 inches during the night.

---

11. The *Sparrowhawk* had returned that morning from New Westminster by way of San Juan. "H.M.S. Sparrowhawk returned...," *Daily British Colonist*, 3 March 1868.

12. "Local Centre," "State Centre," and "Head Centre," were ascending titles of officers of the Fenian movement. Jenkins, *Fenians and Anglo-American Relations*, 26–32.

13. "A number of absurd rumors were afloat yesterday concerning an anticipated Fenian raid, not one of which, we are happy to say, is correct...every precaution has been taken...in the face of which he must be a fool or madman who would attempt an outrage. No doubt is entertained, however, by the authorities that a raid was contemplated by a band of men in California and that an emissary was sent among us to feel the ground. Finding, however, that his coming was heralded and that he was watched, he made himself 'scarce,' and has not been seen since.... This is the whole story." Editorial, *Daily British Colonist*, 25 February 1868.

Further precautions and preparations were made, nonetheless, including putting the naval ships on a readiness basis. "Precautionary," *Daily British Colonist*, 9 March 1868.

14. "H.M.S. Sparrowhawk...," *Daily British Colonist*, 20 March 1868; "The Sparrowhawk...," *Daily British Colonist*, 21 March 1868.

Steamed out of Esquimalt at 7.45 AM, on rounding Sea Bird Point on Discovery Island, found the Hawaiian barque *Rosalie* on shore on the S.W. side, loaded with lumber, and close round the point on the Eastern side saw the Hawaiian ship *Fanny* (late *Vortigern*) on shore with 1300 tons of Coals on board. Communicated with both of them, and found that they did not require our assistance, as they were much damaged and filling with water. The sails were not yet furled in either vessel, but the crew of the *Fanny* were unbending their's, the men of the *Rosalie* had taken shelter on the rocks as she was on the Weather side, and likely to break up. The *Rosalie* was from Moody's Mills in Burrard Inlet bound for Australia, and the *Fanny* from Nanaimo bound for San Francisco, and were both in tow of the *Isabel* yesterday evening, but on coming on to blow were obliged to be cast off, and put under sail. The first vessel got on shore about Midnight, and the other at 2 AM. Before leaving the wrecks, the *Isabel* steamed in from Cadboro Bay to their assistance, we then proceeded on our passage. Arrived off the Government House at New Westminster at 5.10 PM, where we moored.

An Official dinner was given by the Governor in the Evening to the members of the Legislative Council.

March 21st. Attended Governor Seymour at the opening of the Legislative Council at 1 PM.[15]

March 27th. The stern wheeler *Onward*, Captain Irving, returned from her first trip to Yale this afternoon, bringing down $100.000 in gold dust. The ice had sufficiently broken up, to allow her to get up without much trouble.

March 28th. Left New Westminster at 7 AM with Walker and Mr. and Mrs. Dendney. Fired 8 shots from the 20 Pounder for Short Practice, at the Zen rock.

Anchored at Esquimalt at 3.40 PM.[16]

Return of spring

AFTER THE COLD WINTER WE HAD EXPERIENCED, THE warm spring set in much earlier than usual, and the flowers were much in advance of the last two years. Picked my first Nosegay on the 29th March near Belmont, consisting of the Ribes and White Lilies. Killed 4 snakes on the 31st March.[17]

Puget Sound tour

APRIL 15TH. AS ADMIRAL HASTINGS WAS anxious to see the principal towns and saw mills in Puget Sound, he embarked this morning with Commander Liddell, Lieut. Brooke, Staff Comr. Carr, Mr. Drew Launcey & Stock, and we steamed out

15. The *Sparrowhawk* was "Dressed" for the occasion. Entry for 21 March 1868, Master's logbook, Adm. 53/9257.

Important matters dominated deliberations of the legislative council, particularly whether the newly united colony should seek entrance to the newly formed Dominion of Canada or come under the American Constitution; whether New Westminster or Victoria should be the seat of government of British Columbia; and the somewhat strained relations between council and governor. *Dictionary of Canadian Biography*, "Seymour," 714–715.

16. "HMS Sparrowhawk…," *Daily British Colonist*, 26 March 1868.

17. A naval regatta was held at Esquimalt, 2 April 1868. The *Sparrowhawk's* gig, dinghy, and copper punt won their races. "The Squadron Regatta," *Daily British Colonist*, 4 April 1868.

ESQUIMALT harbour, with the Fisguard and Race light-houses. Sept. 27, 1867.

(original watercolor size: 10 x 7.5 in./21.5 x 19 cm)

Old H.B. Co's Fort at Nanaimo, now used as a Prison. May 4, 1866.

(original watercolor size: 14 x 9.13 in./35.5 x 17.5 cm)

The Sparrowhawk's boat establishment at Esquimalt. June 29, 1867.

(original watercolor size: 9.88 x 6.38 in./25 x 16 cm)

Dog tombs at Gold stream, 12 miles from Victoria. May 9, 1868.

(original watercolor size: 9.88 x 6.75 in./25 x 17 cm)

The English Camp on the island of San Juan. May 12, 1868.

(original watercolor size: 14 x 9.88 in./35.5 x 25 cm)

Vancouver Island. Victoria, from Rock Bay. July 2, 1867.

(original watercolor size: 14 x 9.5 in./35.5 x 24 cm)

of Esquimalt at 11 AM, with a fair wind from the S.W which enabled us to make all plain sail.[18]

Stopped off Port Townshend at 3.5 PM for a short time to allow Brooke & a few others land to see the Collector of Customs. Captain Beck, the Sailing Master of the U.S. Surveying schooner *Fauntleroy* came on board, and lent me a published account of the U.S. Survey of these waters, with Charts of the principal harbours. Arrived at Port Gamble at 5.50 PM, where we found 7 large vessels loading alongside the Pier. Landed with the Admiral and others to see the Saw Mills being the largest of the 10 in the Sound. There were 150 men employed about the Mills, and 150 in the woods cutting & bringing the lumber down, and were able to saw 100.000 feet in 24 hours.

Most of it was cut with circular saws, and there was only one gang saw which had attached to it at the time 8 different saws. The principal Mills in the Sound were Utsalad[d]y, Port Discovery, Port Ludlow, Port Gamble, Seabeck, Port Madison, Port Blakely, Port Orchard, Seattle, and Olympia. We saw at Port Gamble men of every nationality, that had been attracted here by high wages, and amongst them saw two of our Deserters Francis Elliott[19] (A.B & Seaman Gunner 1st A.) who had run shortly after our arrival from England, and Henry Way (Boy) that had left at San Francisco. To shew there was no Government authority to appeal to, and that mob law rules the place, a seaman belonging to a Scotch vessel *[blank]* of Leith, had deserted a few days previously breaking his engagement, and had come down to the Pier under the stern of the vessel & began to abuse the Captain. The latter not liking this landed with a Revolver & had the man seized, brought on board and handcuffed, and appealed to the Admiral for protection in case these lawless came down to rescue him. This could not be done, as by the Extradition treaty directly a man puts his foot on American soil he is *free*. Half an hour after we had left the vessel, 60 or 70 men came down to the vessel, and a delegate of the party went on board to tell the Captain in plain words that he had better release the man. Understanding what this meant, the man was liberated, and he bounded on shore amidst the cheers of the mob.

April 16th. On Dolphin & Comrie landing this morning to see the Saw Mills, a Boy of the name of Harvey deserted from the Dingy and of course was not seen again.

Left Port Gamble at 7.15 AM, and steamed down the Sound passing close in to Seattle and Steilacoom, and anchored about 2 miles off Olympia in 16 feet at 5.5 PM. I landed with Liddell, Brooke, Launcey & the Pilot Mr. D. Wallace, and called on the Governor Moore. After we had returned on board in the Gig, Stone and Phillpots (Ordn[ance]) deserted in her, and managed to get to the shore about ¼ mile distant before the Dingy could catch her. 3 shots were fired at them by Dolphin with a Revolver but was prevented by the Admiral from firing again.

---

18. Departure for the week's tour of Puget Sound had been scheduled for the previous day. "Visit," *Daily British Colonist*, 14 April 1868. High wind forced the postponement. "H.M.S. Sparrowhawk…," *Daily British Colonist*, 15 April 1868; "The Sparrowhawk…," *Daily British Colonist*, 16 April 1868.

19. When the *Sparrowhawk* first arrived at Esquimalt, his name was published as Beynon Elliott. "Arrival of H.M.S. Sparrowhawk," *Daily British Colonist*, 30 October 1865.

A party of Officers landed in the First watch to see if they could capture the men on their entering the town, and the Governor was requested to have them delivered there with a reward of $30 each, but we never heard of them again.

April 17th. After breakfast landed with the Admiral and suite, and called on the Governor Moore where we met the principal inhabitants of Olympia. Before leaving we all had a drink, and then started off for Dumwater [Tumwater], 1½ mile distant where there was a very picturesque cascade, a grist and saw mill which were both driven by water power, and then went on to the Prairie land situated ½ mile further on the road to Portland. General McKinney, the Indian Overseer, lent the Admiral a one horse Buggy, in which I took a seat. The Tumwater is a small river that runs up 25 miles above Olympia, and keeps about the same Volume throughout the year. Olympia is the Capital of Washington Territory and is a small town containing about 600 inhabitants. Very badly situated at the head of Budd Inlet, as vessels drawing more than 6 feet of water cannot approach within 1½ mile of it. A little land has been cleared in the vicinity for farming purposes, but nothing of very great extent. There is only one Street that contains shops, and this is connected with the Piers (Main Street).

April 18th. Left Olympia at 4.20 AM, but shortly after the sun had risen a dense fog came on which obliged us to anchor for more than 2 hours, this did not entirely clear away till nearly 11, when we saw Mount Rainier very clearly, its Peak having an elevation of 14000 feet.

Steaming today with 3 Boilers that sent the ship on at times 10.5 knots. Anchored in Griffin Bay at 6.40 PM.[20] Went on shore immediately with the Admiral, Brooke and Liddell, and on landing met Dr. Semple who had brought an Ambulance waggon down to drive us up to the American Camp, about a mile off. On arriving there called on Major and Mrs. Allen and after a short visit of about 10 minutes drove back again. The Camp is situated on the slope of an open prairie ground, fenced in in the form of a square, the Officers quarters forming one side of it.

April 19th. Left Griffin Bay at 7.10 AM, and steamed along the East side of San Juan to Roche Harbour where we anchored at 9.0. After breakfast I landed with the Admiral and Carr at the Marines Camp, where the Admiral read the morning service. After a slight lunch at the Delacombe's returned on board. Left Roche Harb. at 2. PM, and arrived at Esquimalt at 4. after a short passage of *[blank]*. The Admiral and suite then left the ship after having been on board 4½ days.[21]

The American survey of Puget Sound has been going on for the last 12 years, and they have not yet published a Chart of these inland waters, the only plan given in the Admiralty Charts was roughly done by Commodore Wilkes in 1841, and this cannot be depended upon. A few of the principal harbours have been sketched in [by] the U.S. Coast Survey, but they are not for general use. By our track up and down it seems there are but few dangers in the main channels, but as these few are but imperfectly known a Pilot has to be taken, the Government charges for whom are $8 a foot each way.

---

20. San Juan Island. Porcher's log, 300.

21. "Return of H.M.S. Sparrowhawk with Admiral Hastings," summarizes the tour. *Daily British Colonist*, 20 April 1868.

April 15th	From Esquimalt to Port Gamble	55	miles	
16th	Port Gamble to Olympia	77		
18th	Olympia to Griffin Bay	105		
19th	Griffin Bay to Roche Harb. & Esquimalt	40		
		277	**miles**	

Distances to Puget Sound, San Juan, and return

~

Deadman's Island visit

May 6th. Visited Deadman's Island with Farrant,[22] that is situated near the entrance to Esquimalt harbour, and was formerly used for a Naval Cemetery.[23] Counted 29 graves there, the men having principally belonged to the *Ganges*, *Topaze*, *Satellite*, and *Brisk* from 1859 to 1861, the only Officer being Mr. Macauley, Chief Engineer of the *Brisk*, that had an Iron headstone with the letters raised in relief, and an Iron railing. They were in good preservation, only one wooden head stone having fallen from decay, and this was propped up against a tree. Some goats were grazing about, but few people ever land on this deserted spot now.

~

San Juan errand

May 7th. As the *Forward* was hauled up on Laing's Ways to have her bottom repaired, we were obliged to go to San Juan in her place this day, and gave a passage to Mr. Wakeman, and Nicholson Midshipman. Steamed out of Esquimalt at 8.15 am, and anchored off the entrance to the Mosquito channel in 2½ hours, the distance being 19 miles. Landed at the Camp, where we sent some Provisions, and Mr. Colling paid the Marines, and embarked a prisoner and 5 Witnesses to await a Court Martial. Found Colonel Grey U.S.A. and Mr. Slater here on a visit. During the time we were on shore, a marine of the name of Davis was drowned in front of the Camp by a canoe capsizing. Left again at 4.45 pm where we arrived in 2½ hours.

~

Gold Stream picnic

May 9th. Accompanied the Admiral and Mrs. Hastings to a picnic at Gold Stream. The party consisted of Mr. & Mrs. Perry, Dawkins, Brooke, Dent & Fisher, and started shortly after 11, in 2 carriages, a cart with the provisions, and I had a horse from Bowman. The distance from the Admiral's house is about 8 miles, and 10' from Victoria, the road passing by Colwood Farm and Langford Lake, the carriage road ending at Ash's house that overlooks the Gold stream & close to the Leading Peaks, and only 1½ mile from the Saanich Arm. The scenery is very good the whole way, the road being cut through thick woods, over open prairie grounds, and lakes at short distances, making a pleasing variety in the drive. Ash's house is situated about half way between Victoria and Leech river and a good halting place for weary travellers. It is about 300 feet above the stream, the descent being by a rather steep trail, that leads you to a rustic bridge over the stream, and then takes you on to the

22. Nathaniel Farrant had replaced John Dearden as Chief Engineer of the *Sparrowhawk*, 21 April 1866. *Navy List* (January 1867): 217.

23. Admiral Hastings had been directed to purchase ground at Esquimalt for a naval cemetery. "Admiral Hastings received…," *Daily British Colonist*, 6 May 1868.

Saanich Arm and Leech river. Gold stream is a good sized mountain torrent, completely shut in by the steep hills on all sides with good sized pools here and there that afforded capital fishing, and enabled us to catch a dozen small trout, during the time we were there. Saw several small shafts that had been sunk near the banks, but the quantity of the gold found was so small, that the place was given up in favor of Leech river. A miner that we met here shewed us about $150 worth of gold dust, that had lately been collected at the latter place, and told us that there were 15 men at present working there. There was no cultivated ground here owing to the coldness, the only object of interest being the burial place of 2 dogs with the following inscriptions on wooden head boards: In memory of my dog Lum. Died Dec. 7th 1867, & on the other Billy Dec. 9th 1865.

The country was full of flowers, the largest white blossoms of the Dogwood being very conspicuous, sun flowers, hyacinths, vetches, &c.

Routine activities

May 11th. After taking on board some Provisions, left Esquimalt at 3.0 pm, exercised firing shot & shell at Kellett's Bluff, and anchored in Roche Harbr. at 6.pm.[24] Exercised at Night quarters.

May 12th. Exercised firing shot and shell at marks on Henry Island. Landed with Boys and Moreshead at the Lime Kiln, and then went on to the Camp where we spent the day, and I put in Delacombe's & Beardon's houses in my sketch of the Camp. Delacombe & Hamburg came on board in the Evening for a passage to Victoria.

May 13th. Left Roche Harbour at 4.30 am with a light breeze, but before arriving at Trial Island it came on to blow very hard from the S.W. which nearly stopped our way, stopped near the *Zealous* at 9 am which we found at anchor in Royal Roads, then proceeded into Esquimalt where we anchored at 9.30, to embark Perry, Brooke and Denny. As soon as they were on board, steamed back to the *Zealous* where we anchored near her at 0.45 pm. Attended at a Court Martial to try a Marine belonging to the detachment at San Juan for firing at a Corporal & knocking a Private down, which was finished by 4.30 pm. We then steamed in to Esquimalt where we anchored at 5.30.[25]

Move to Victoria

May 14th. Left Esquimalt at 3.20 am, stopped off the Mosquito channel at 5.35 to land Captain Delacombe, Inman, Hamburg and 7 Marines, then steamed round to Roche Harb. to meet the Boat, when we proceeded for New Westminster where we anchored off the Camp at 1.45 pm. Crossed the Bar of the Fraser at High water, & only carried 17 feet in places.

---

24. The Victoria press had reported New Westminster as the destination. "The Zealous...," *Daily British Colonist*, 12 May 1868.

25. The newspaper's report varied somewhat from Porcher's record here. "HM Ship Sparrowhawk...," *Daily British Colonist*, 14 May 1868.

May 18th.[26] As Victoria was to be proclaimed the Capital[27] on the Queen's Birthday, the Governor as well as the Officials had been making preparations for leaving New Westminster for some time past, and at Noon the Governor, Mrs. Seymour, Lowndes & the servants embarked without any ceremony or anybody coming down to see them off. Steamed away from the Camp at 0.15 PM, and on passing New Westminster, not a Flag was hoisted as was usual on ordinary occasions, and hardly a soul was to be seen. Arrived at Cadboro Bay in little less than 6 hours where the Governor & party disembarked and we then proceeded on to Esquimalt where we anchored at 8.15.[28]

26. "H.M.S. Sparrowhawk...," *Daily British Colonist*, 18 May 1868.

27. When the island and mainland colonies were united in 1866, Victoria and New Westminster both sought designation as the capital of the new colony. In years of economic decline, both were keenly aware of the stimulus and prestige that could accrue from being designated as the capital. Victoria was the largest city and commercial center of the colony. The protective Esquimalt naval base was in proximity. New Westminster was the gateway to the interior of the mainland. A shift in the preference of the London government, indecision of the governor, and political maneuvering in the legislative council gave Victoria the prize. Ormsby, *British Columbia*, 220–226; *Dictionary of Canadian Biography*, "Seymour," 713–715.

28. The Governor's party "drove to Government House, where it was met by the Volunteers, under Capt. Pearse, presenting arms, the band playing the national anthem. The Sparrowhawk drawing too much water for the bar at the entrance of the harbor, when at low tide, prevented the vessel steaming into town." "Arrival of the Governor and Mrs[.] Seymour," *Daily British Colonist*, 19 May 1868.

The Sparrowhawk participated in the 25 May 1868 celebration of Queen Victoria's birthday. "The Mechanics' Institute Excursion," *Daily British Colonist*, 26 May 1868.

Chapter Eight

Three Final Cruises

28 May–1 August 1868

[The last two months of duty for Edmund Porcher as commander of H.M.S. *Sparrowhawk* were some of the busiest for his Esquimalt-based tour of duty. For two weeks in late May and early June, he carried the admiral on an inspection trip to locations on the Queen Charlotte Islands and the mainland as far north as the southern tip of Alaska. A mid-July assignment to investigate murder cases involving Indians also became a mission to rescue the officers and crew of the U.S.S. *Suwanee*, wrecked off the northern tip of Vancouver Island. The police aspect of his charge was not completed because of the *Suwanee* emergency, so Porcher again headed northward on 17 July for his last Esquimalt station cruise. This two week cruise into the northern reaches of the British Columbia coast included dispensing justice in Indian-related matters, inspecting a military installation, conducting business with a trading post, and visiting a coal mining operation.]

Northern inspection cruise

May 28th. As the Admiral wished to see the Northern parts of the colony, ["along the east coast of Vancouver Island and the mainland of British Columbia,"][1] and the fine weather having set in, he came on board this morning with Lieut. Brooke, Wag, Capt. Williams R.M.A., Rev. Thos. R. Hamilton, Mr. Drew, and Lord Richd. Cecil.[2] Steamed out of Esquimalt at 11.30 AM, and anchored at Nanaimo at 7, having made the distance of 76 miles in 7½ [hours], or at the rate of 10 knots.

["The day was fine and the scenery in winding through the mazes of islands in the archipelago between Vancouver and the Mainland appeared very picturesque, the rocky promontories of the land about Victoria and Esquimalt being exchanged in passing up the gulf for the softer and more undulating scenery of the Islets their precipitous sandstone cliffs adding to the richness and variety of the colouring. On the northern end of Salt Spring Island considerable agricultural settlements exist, possessing excellent grazing land, while from its quarries a superior kind of sandstone, weathering and becoming hard from exposure, is procured. On San Juan Island also there are some good farms and a limestone of a very superior quality, now becoming an article of considerable export.

"The run through Active Pass was rather exciting, the tide being in our favor carried us through as if borne on the surface of a mountain torrent. The cliffs on each side of the Pass, which is about ⅓ of a mile broad, rise in some places to the height of about 500 feet and are composed of a recent sandstone, in many places decomposed and detached, leading to the formation of picturesque dells and hollows, and occasionally so fretted by atmospheric influences as to resemble the portal of some old Norman keep. A few clearings exist in the curving bays, the white cottages of the settlers nestling among the trees, adding to the picturesqueness of the scenery.

"At the northern end of the channel, which is about 3 miles in length, on Gonzalo Island, an immense boulder of Syinitic [*sic*] Granite was observed, transported no doubt, at some former period by glacial action from the Cascade range, indeed, you see everywhere indications in the grooving of the rocks and in the yellowish and varied colored clay of the cliffs, with their sand and shingle terraces traces of the northern drift the result of the universal ice action, nowhere so well marked as on this coast.

"From time to time a glimpse was obtained of the fertile valley of Cowichan, the characteristic divide in the central ridge of the Island marking the line of the Cowichan river and the entrance to the lake. The river is said to be about 40 miles in length, although perhaps in a straight line not more than 26 and covered with a forest of magnificent spars; its breadth being about 40 feet and navigable to within 4 miles of the lake. The lake is about 22 miles long and 1 mile wide. Silver veins have

---

1. "Cruise of H.M.S. Sparrowhawk," *Daily British Colonist*, 23 June 1868. See also, chapter 6, note 3, above.

2. It was reported that the cruise was to "proceed round the Island…on an official inspection." "The Sparrowhawk…," *Daily British Colonist*, 28 May 1868. See also "The Sparrowhawk…," *Daily British Colonist*, 29 May 1868.

The Victoria press anticipated this cruise for several weeks. "We understand Admiral Hastings…," *Daily British Colonist*, 4 May 1868.

been discovered on its shores and coal is said to crop out on the banks of the river. This lake, however, like most central portions of the Island has never yet been thoroughly explored."][3]

May 29th. On the *Emily Harris*, and a sloop hauling off from the Coal Wharf, we steamed alongside of it at 9.35 AM, and took in 109 tons of Coals. Owing to so many vessels having lately gone to Nanaimo, there was no surplus stock above ground, and vessels had to depend on the quantity taken out of the pit daily, which generally amounted to 150 tons, the Miners receiving $1¼ for each ton sent up, and had now to supply their own oil and powder for blasting.

["One of the vessels, the *Hamley*, wanted 'stiffenning,' viz. about 20 tons, to prevent the pos[s]ibility of her turning over, and the *Emily Harris* required about 30 tons for the use of the Active;.... The slip or fracture in the coal seam of this mine still continues to dip vertically, and unless the borings at Chase river prove more successful than hitherto, the production of coal at least as far as the present seam is concerned must soon cease or resort be had to the old working on Newcastle Island.

"This is much to be regretted, as an immense amount of capital has here been spent upon wharfs and tramways that will be entirely thrown away. No doubt a good deal of this was superfluous, as also the building of an hotel, miners houses, &c., but the harbor is an exceedingly good and capacious one, protected as it is by Newcastle and Douglas (Protection) Island, the soundings allowing ships of large tonnage to go alongside the pier and coal from the shoot; indeed, at the present time, the demand for this coal is greater than ever, being a good gas coal, and in point of quality not having its equal on the Pacific Coast, and more especially as Bellingham Bay has ceased to be wrought and the Mount Diabola mines are almost exhausted.

"The day of our stay at Nanaimo was occupied by our party variously, according to taste, the majority going out fishing up the Nanaimo river, while a small majority, accompanied by Rev. P. Jenns, went to Fossil Point, Departure Bay, and Newcastle Island, on a geological voyage of discovery.

"The old workings on Newcastle Island occur in Exit Channel, close to the beach, near the north end of the Island, and consists of two seams, a few yards only apart, the upper called the Douglas, and the lower the Newcastle; the first being about 6 feet thick, the other about 3; both dipping at about 20 deg., and have for their roof a course conglomerate and a floor of sandstone; the roof has, however, tumbled down in some places, and the gallery being filled with water, it was impossible to venture far with the workings. We believe coal was first discovered and worked here in 1850.

"After considerable difficulty and having very much overshot our mark we discovered the fossil beach, and were rewarded by a fair collection, consisting of specimens of Pectoris, Cardia, plagiostoms, &c. The sandstone here nests on traps which has in some places flowed over it, leaving prominent nodules projecting from and marking out the previous fluid condition of the trap in a most characteristic manner."][4]

---

3. "Cruise of H.M.S. Sparrowhawk," *Daily British Colonist*, 23 June 1868.

4. Ibid.

Hauled off from the Wharf at 5.0 PM, and steamed out of Nanaimo at 5.35. On leaving had 60 Tons of Coals on the Upper deck, which brought the ship down to 11 Ft. 8 in, and 12 ft. 9 in. aft being a good trim for steaming, as we went 8.5 knots easily with 2 boilers going only 70 revolutions. Kept under weigh all night and passed Cape Mudge as daylight was appearing.

May 30th. Steaming about 7½ knots during the night. Passed thro' the Seymour Narrows at 3.35 AM, a strong ebb tide rushing thro' it, causing very strong tide ripples, and making the ship difficult to steer.

["[T]he tide here is often exceedingly strong, running like a mill stream 7 or 8 knots an hour, the tidal junction of the waters separating Vancouver Island and the Mainland, meeting, forms here a race, the channel not being more than 900 yards in breadth, the flood tide of the North Pacific flowing in the one direction S.E., through Queen Charlotte Sound, and N.W. through the Gulf of Georgia on the other.

"During the forenoon we steamed along Johntone Straits and Broughton Straits through a succession of sheltered channels, surrounded by scenery of the wildest grandeur, the Straits being pierced in every direction by numerous canals, forming a succession of fiords extending far inland, enclosing numerous landlocked harbors, which when commerce becomes more extended will be more highly valued than at present.

"Our course lay through an archipelago studded with Islands of all sizes and shapes, their shores being sometimes low and undulating, at others steep and mountainous, having in the back ground, on the Mainland side, a succession of serrated mountain ranges capped with perpetual snow, while on the Island side appeared a succession of more rounder metamorphic mountains, with here and there bosses streaked and polished, assuming the characteristic form of "Roches Moutaunees," the result of ice action, while now and again a panoramic view was obtained of the Cascade range, which looked with its numerous irregular peaks like the confused waves of a rough sea, the snow-capped mountains, forming a magnificent back-ground for the dark green belt of forest below.

"After passing Comox, between Cape Mudge and the Mouth of the Nimkish river the coast is densely wooded and mountainous, some of the ranges rising to 5000 feet, and with the exception of patches of delta land at the mouths of such large rivers as the Campbell and Salmon rivers, which are said to have valleys well suited for agricultural settlement, no other good agricultural land exists. The Campbell, on a former visit, was ascended in one of the ship's boats, over 1 mile, and appeared to have some good land on its banks fitted for agriculture, which it is to be hoped some enterprising persons may take advantage of."][5]

Stopped off the Huts built near the Coal seam at Sooquash, 8 miles to the Eastward of Fort Rupert, where Mr. Chas. Wallace came on board in a canoe, and told us he was sending a scout down to Alert Bay with 30 tons of Coals for the H.B.C. steamer *Otter* that afternoon. From the mouth of the Nim[p]kish river up to Beaver harbour there is a deep fringe of alluvial soil resting on a sandstone formation which here

5. Ibid.

crops out and extends horizontally a short distance beyond Fort Rupert. Coal has been worked at intervals all along this ledge, cropping out in many places close to the surface, and apparently continuous with the measures at Koskeemo on the opposite coast 7' distant.

["Indeed we believe it was here the coal was first discovered in rather an amusing way. The story goes, that shortly after the establishment of Fort Rupert, the chief trader in charge told the Indians that he would show them a superior fuel to wood, and which was used by the white men, and had been brought a distance of a six months' voyage across the sea. The blacksmith's forge was set up and the Indians assembled, when it was found that coal was no novelty to them, the chief pointing to a short distance from the Fort where he said there was *hyiu*. From this time it was partially worked, digging it up with hatchets and what rude implements they were in possession of."][6]

In 1846 HMS. *Cormorant* procured 62 tons here at the expense of about a dollar a ton in presents to the chiefs. From 1849 up to the discovery of coal at Nanaimo in 1850, coal was brought here to some extent by regular miners, but since that the place has been abandoned until the last month when Mr. C. W. Wallace has again opened the seam in a different place which seems to promise well, having already with 6 men got out about 60 tons. The thickness of the vein varies from 18 inches to 2 feet and runs in a N.W direction, dipping at about 20 deg. is apparently free from faults, and is expected to improve on going deeper.

["Some of the men engaged here report that 8 miles up the Nimkish, a lake exists about 20 miles long and from 3 to 4 wide, at the end of which is a large valley, and rolling country of fine prairie land, the origin of several rivers and extending close to the agricultural settlement at Comox; no doubt the watershed of the Campbell, Salmon, Adams rivers, &c."][7]

Anchored off Fort Rupert at 3.0 PM, having run the distance from Nanaimo in 21½ hours. Landed with the Admiral to see Captain and Mrs. Monat, and walked round the Fort. ["Fort Rupert is now in charge of Captain Monat, and is built after the usual typical form, square stockaded around, inside which, are the employees houses, a bastion in each corner and gallery running around and a well cultivated garden outside.

"The Indian village is built in a semicircle round the bay at the north end of the fort, consisting of about sixty lodges. Very few of the natives were in the village; all, with the exception of the old people, having gone up to Shawiti, at the head of Jervis Inlet, collecting their great fish harvest of the eulachon, where upwards of 2000 Indians from all parts of the coast were assembled. The tribe occupying the village are the Qua Quas, a few years ago numbering about 1400, but now reduced by disease and whisky to about 120, and were at this rate dying off rapidly, the women ceasing to be fertile and the men becoming a prey to galloping consumption, the result of their impaired vitality. On walking round the village there was to be observed the

6. Ibid.

7. Ibid.

old shot holes made by H.M.S. *Clio* two years ago, and we were constantly appealed to whether King George (who, by the way, 'never dies' here) was *hyas sullocks*; and on being informed that the amiable monarch's *tumtum* was *hyas closh* were greatly relieved.

"The natives here are like many in civilized life, living on their past reputation; at one time they were very wealthy and gave away a large amount of property, which is now returning to them at the various potlaches of the other tribes. In fact it is the old rule that whatever you may give away you expect a fair equivalent for."][8]

We then crossed over the Shell Island to see 3 additional tombs that had been erected there lately, amongst them Joe the Indian Interpreter that accompanied us to Quatsino Sound in February 1867, and from the exposure on that occasion, he never recovered, and died shortly afterward.

["[O]ver one was placed a canoe with a figure representing the principal chief who had died lately, what the object is thus placing canoes, guns, kettles, etc., over the graves is somewhat difficult to understand, some say it is to assist the departed in Hades, others again with a greater show of reason believe that as we well know it is a great breach of Indian etiquette even to mention the name of a deceased person, and that his belongings are so placed that nothing can remind the survivor of his previous existence, be that as it may, this chief had been a long time ailing and his 'tillieums' had been devoted in their attentions. But one day he conceived the idea of sending for his relatives and dividing his property, after which he was starved and maltreated to death, showing the phases of Indian nature and that strong resemblance to civilized life, and within forty-three minutes he was afterwards doubled up in a box (before *rigor mortis* set in) and placed in the cemetery. The winter here was not particularly severe, the spirit thermometer descending to within 5 deg. of zero."][9]

Hauled the seine on the Western side of the bay, and caught several flat and other small fish. ["After spending a pleasant evening with Capt. Monat, we left early next morning for Bella Bella."][10]

May 31st. Left Fort Rupert at 4.30 AM, and steamed through the Goletas channel, and Shadwell Passage.

["Between Beaver harbour and the commencement of Charlotte Sound, an extensive group of islands exist, low and undulating, the formation being that of a recent sandstone interspersed here and there by dark bands of shale indicative of the existence of coal. The channel between the island and mainland is a sheltered one and admirably adapted for steamers, the only portion at all hazardous being the northern exit, Newiti Bar, over which the soundings are not more than 1½ to 3 fathoms, from here across Queen Charlotte Sound a distance of about 20 miles open to the ocean swell of the North Pacific is the only portion at all exposed in the passage to the northern portion of our possessions, the rest being sheltered navigation; perhaps the most wonderful that can be seen in any part of the world; indeed we believe few countries possess such an extensive seaboard in proportion to the coast

---

8. "Cruise of H.M.S. Sparrowhawk," *Daily British Colonist*, 23 June 1868.

9. Ibid.

10. Ibid.

line; a series of channels and arms of the sea that may be pursued without interruption or exposure to the oceanic swell."][11]

On crossing Queen Charlotte's Sound it came on a thick Fog which forced us to go easy at the rate 4' when near Egg Island, but it suddenly cleared up at 0.15 PM, when within 5 miles of Cape Calvert.

["The passage through Fitzhugh Sound was bounded on either side by a succession of mountains of varying height from one to three thousand feet clothed from base to summit with pines which here began to assume somewhat of a stunted aspect, large tracts up the sides of the hills appearing blasted as if swept by a devastating hurricane, in other places broad avenues were cleared away by snow slides, the trunks lying prostrate in every direction. Numerous islands were passed, our course winding through a succession of narrow crooked passages and canals of varying width, at times so narrow as almost brushing the foliage of the pines on either side."][12]

Anchored at Bella Bella at 7.30 PM in 13 fathoms. Here we found the Indians had abandoned the small island on which they previously lived, and taken up their residence on the opposite shore. Went on shore with Mr. Moss and saw his house, and the Ranch surrounding it. Many of the Indians were ["away at the Naas River fishing, the few that remained being"][13] down with measles which had been fatal here: their treatment being during the heat of the fever to plunge into the sea & remain for hours.

June 1st. Left Bella Bella at 4.30 AM. The *Beaver* had lately resurveyed Dall Patch, a small shoal half way between Kyn*[illeg.]* Harbour and Regatta Rock, on which they found only 6 feet at Low water, 8 fathoms being the least water down in the chart, this obliges ships to keep close to Defeat Point where it is steep close to. Passed through Milbank Sound[14] without any swell, thro' Klemptor Passage a very narrow pass,[15] and anchored in Lowe Inlet at 7.30 PM, where we found the *Beaver* at anchor, having been here the last 10 days surveying it.

["At Bella Bella we were warned of the existence of a rock lately discovered in Seaforth Channel at the entrance to Milbank Sound, on which one of the steamers going to Sitka had lately struck upon, but which we managed to avoid.

"Our course during the day lay through a succession of sheltered channels enclosed by precipices and lofty mountains terminating in fantastic shaped peaks and pinnacles or rock towering up into the skies, their summits clothed with a glittering mantle of perpetual snow, numerous cascades thundered down the precipitous sides of cliffs upwards of three thousand feet in height, their origin looking in the distance like silvery threads, while from the numerous lateral valleys rushed a succession of mountain torrents. The shores jutted out in frequent promontories opening into harbours and large sheets of water, looking like lakes, above which towered in

---

11."Cruise of H.M.S. Sparrowhawk," *Daily British Colonist*, 2 July 1868. See also, chapter 6, note 3, above.

12. "Cruise of H.M.S. Sparrowhawk," *Daily British Colonist*, 2 July 1868.

13. Ibid.

14. Ibid. By way of Seaforth Channel.

15. Ibid. And through Finlayson Channel into Grenville Channel.

indescribable beauty and majesty, brilliant snow-clad peaks in strong relief against the blue sky.

"But beautiful as these calm blue waters were, lying placid as lakes, with every variety of point and bay, the quiet and stillness undisturbed except by the plunge of a frightened seal or the flight of a flock of ducks or northern divers soon becomes monotonous, even the emerald green pines assume a somber character, and one longed for the sight of a canoe, a log cabin or cultivated land, and even the appearance of an Indian cemetery, with its coffins placed high up in the trees, and the usual display of tattered blankets and flags was hailed with satisfaction as a variety, silence and shade profound so brooded over the scene."][16]

This is a safe and snug harbour about 1½ mile in length by ½ mile broad, walled in on each [side] by granite hills covered with pines rising in some places to 2000 feet, and at the very end of the Inlet a river falls about 10 feet over a granite ledge; beyond this appeared another cascade, on the other side of which the river widens into a lake.

Metlakatla–Fort Simpson country

June 2nd. Left Low Inlet at 4.30 am, and steamed through Grenville Channel and Chatham Sound against a N.Wy. breeze. ["On passing up the Greenville [*sic*] channel the scenery partook much of the same character as that already described, snow-covered mountains of massive grandeur towering up on every side, cleft by deep dells and ravines, down which torrents raved with foam and thunder, leaping from cliff and summit, rendering the atmosphere moist with their spray, like the falling of a dense Scotch mist. The lateral valleys appeared to extend from east to west, containing bowl shaped hollows marking the position of mountain lakes; everywhere the rocks showed indications of glacial actions, being extensively grooved and striated, while from time to time the bright blue glint of ice on some of the more distant heights showed that this influence was still active."][17]

When near Whale rock about 15' from Metlakatlah, it came on a fog which thickened as we advanced, and were close upon the rocks off Cridge Island before we saw them, this obliged us to stand off a short distance to the S.W. and anchored at 1.0 pm in 17¼ fathoms.

At 5.30 pm, the H.B.C. steamer *Otter* towing the American barque *Oakland* suddenly appeared in the fog, and anchored near us. Capt. Lewis came on board, and told us they were from Tongas[s], bound to the Southward. At 7.0 pm the fog cleared away, and we steamed into the Metlakatlah harbr. where we anchored at 7.45.[18] Mr. Duncan came on board. Very little signs of life were to be seen the whole way up thro' these Interior channels, nearly the only Indians we saw were in Grenville Channel this morning in 2 Canoes going to the Southward under full sail, one with two Spreet sails on a single mast, and the other with two masts.

---

16. "Cruise of H.M.S. Sparrowhawk," *Daily British Colonist*, 2 July 1868.

17. Ibid.

18. "Arrival of the H.B. Co's Steamer Otter from the North," *Daily British Colonist*, 8 June 1868.

June 3rd. On landing at Metlakatlah we found some marks of progress since our last visit a year ago, a commodious market place has been built and the saw mill is in progress & expected to be finished during the summer, but the soap manufacture from the Oolichan grease has not as yet turned out a success. Admiral Hastings had a gathering of the Indians at the Mission house, and addressed them saying how gratified he was to see the progress they had made in the arts of civilized life, and assured them of the Governor's sympathy and protection, ["who would not fail to protect the mission from any molestation. The question as to what had best be done with the three slaves who had escaped and taken refuge at the Mission was brought forward by Mr. Duncan. The Admiral in reply stated that slavery did not now exist under British rule and that although he would not consider justifiable to take slaves out by force from the tribe they were among, yet if they escaped to the Mission or on board ship he would consider himself justified in protecting them."][19]

And was answered by Paul Legaic ["in Tshmsean, which was translated by Mr. Duncan, he expressed how gratified they all were by this visit, being like children crawling before they were able to walk, the assurance that they would be protected made their hearts glad and knowing that they would be looked after would prevent them from revenging their own injuries.

"The Admiral then adjourned to Mr. Duncan's house, where the school children were assembled, amounting to about fifty, including fifteen girls, boarders in the house. A class was examined in English reading, copy books were looked at, and a few songs in English and Tshmpsean were very sweetly sung by the children, whose progress was very gratifying. The Mission Indians dress in English clothing and address you with 'how do you do, sir,' 'thank you, sir;' but go into their houses and you find that they have thrown aside that clothing for a blanket, and that their knowledge of the English language is that of a parrot, and confined to a few set phrases; in fact it is merely the gloss of civilization and saturated with specific disease, as the adults here are in common with all the Indians round the coast the hope of future years must rest with the rising generation."][20]

The numbers now belonging to the Mission are 374, of whom 87 are children, and perhaps about 100 more who are living here with their friends as visitors.[21] Landed an anchor, 2 months provisions, and 12 tons of Coals for the *Beaver*.

Left Metlakatlah at 4.30 PM, and anchored at Fort Simpson at 7.15 in 10 fathoms. Landed at the Fort and saw Mr. Cunningham who is now in charge of the Post, Mr. Mauson in charge of the Trade up the Stickeen [Stikine River], and is at present living here with his family, until a new house has been constructed further inland out of the American territory, and Mr. H. Hawkins.

A sloop of the name of the *Ocean Queen* had been selling Whiskey to the Indians at Fort Simpson this morning, but had left in the Forenoon for the [Inner?] channel to the South, where she had been going on with her illicit trade. Sent the Whale

19. "Cruise of H.M.S. Sparrowhawk," *Daily British Colonist*, 2 July 1868.

20. Ibid.

21. Ibid. These visitors "have not yet professed Christianity."

[boat] away in search of her in charge of Lt. Townshend,[22] but after going 6' was obliged to give it up, having heard from a canoe that she had gone to sea.

June 4th. Landed this morning with the Admiral & Staff, and saw the Chief Sebapien of the Kinthralta's in Ogden channel, about the 2 slaves that had lately made their escape to Metlakatlah. Also inquired into some murders that had lately taken place up the Naas river, where 2 of the principal Chiefs of this Fort had been killed in a drunken brawl, which their people had revenged in the usual manner by killing 5 of the first Naas tribe they had come across, consisting of 3 Mission Indians & 2 of their friends.

["The[ir] village was thinly peopled, most of the tribe being up the Nass fishing, those left behind either suffering from measles or recovering from an attack; those visible were in very deep mourning, displaying their grief by short cropped hair and blackened faces....

"At the end of the village we observed rather a characteristic memorial of a chief who had lately died; on the top of a pole about 30 feet high was placed his effigy as large as life, bearing under his right arm his crest engraved on a copper plate 6 feet by 3, the top of the pole being draped with black cloth, while at the foot was carved a life like representation of a bear carrying in its mouth another copper plate. Such armorial distinctions strongly reminding one of the similar practice in May Fair in regard to escutcheons. All the houses are decorated with the crests of the residents, the carvings of the different totems representing birds and wild animals having in many cases a very artistic finish, but numerous as they are they are all reducible to four, the eagle, raven, bear and wolf, the others being related to those."][23]

Left Fort Simpson at 0.10 PM for the Kincaulith mission at the entrance of the Naas river,[24] having an Indian Pilot on board of the name of Henry who had been in the *Forward* and anchored off Mr. Tomlinson's settlement at 4.10 PM, but his services were not much required.

["[P]assing the extremity of the Chympsean Peninsula named by Vancouver Point Maleskyne and entering Observatory Inlet, one of those numerous canals that Vancouver tried through which to find the long sought north-west passage. This inlet runs in a north-easterly direction and is about 1½ miles in breadth, having at its entrance on the south side Point Maleskyne and on the north Point makes the extremity of the Prince of Wales Island, the southern extremity of which by the treaty of 1825 is the beginning of the Russian (now American) Possessions, while from the entrance to the Portland Canal diverging at Point Ramsden in a north-west direction and 21 miles above Point Maleskyne begins the boundary line of the 10 marine league coast strip. Above this about 21 miles is Salmon Cove the seat of

---

22. Reginald C. Townshend had replaced Matthew J. Harrison as a Lieutenant on the *Sparrowhawk*, 1 February 1868. *Navy List* (April 1868): 217.

23. "Cruise of H.M.S. Sparrowhawk," *Daily British Colonist*, 2 July 1868.

24. Here and as in a few other instances Porcher's initial erroneous spellings of place names are corrected in later usage probably reflecting his subsequent learning of their proper form. Kincaulith and Naas a few pages later are correctly rendered as Kincolith and Nass.

the mission and a short distance beyond which the Inlet terminates and the Nass River discharges itself."][25]

Landed with the Admiral & Staff, and paid a visit to Mr. Tomlinson and his bride who had only arrived from Victoria a fortnight ago. The settlement at present consists of 5 houses & 40 inhabitants and small gardens had been commenced in front of the houses.[26]

["Mr. Tomlinson, the Missionary, who has here taken up his residence, we hope will meet with success; he intends building a church, and hopes ultimately to attract the natives from the villages, distant about 14 miles, up the river. A tribe numbering about 1000 and speaking a language, a dialect of the Tsimpsean, which seems to extend inland as far as the McKenzie River, while all along the coast the chiefs of tribes speaking a totally different language, all more or less acquire it, looking on it somewhat in the same light as a Court language."][27]

A Log church capable of containing of 200 was in course of erection, and as Mr. Tomlinson is a medical man afterwards contemplates the erection of a Hospital which might be attended with the best results.

["[T]he contact of the whites having degenerated the Indians, both morally and physically,…we owe it to ordinary philanthropy to endeavor to mitigate those ills that this has produced, and now such an attention to these physical ills, combined with regard for their social, mental and moral improvement, will undoubtedly be attended by the best results. An institution supplying properly prepared food well ventilated rooms, and good nursing, will be the greatest possible advantage."][28]

Took a short walk to the banks of the King Cole river, where there are several stages erected near it for drying fish during the proper season.

["The water at Salmon Cove appeared much discolored and contained a large amount of sediment, the density according to the hydrometer being 1006 and the temperature 48°. The discoloration was noticed by Vancouver, as also the strength of the undertow; but he failed—as in the case of the Columbia and Fraser—to discover the river."][29]

The situation of the Mission is on a patch of delta land, immediately behind it is protected from the Northerly winds by stunted and scraggy pines, and at the back again there are snow-clad mountains rising to the height of 3 or 4000 feet: a scene of the most perfect desolation.

June 5th. Left the Naas river at Noon and anchored off Devastation Island, Metlakatlah at 6.40 PM, having the ebb tide in our favour the greater part of the day. Found the *Beaver* here, having arrived yesterday. Sent a seining party away, which returned with a fair show of fish. One Salmon weighing 22 lbs.

---

25. "Cruise of H.M.S. Sparrowhawk," *Daily British Colonist*, 2 July 1868.

26. Ibid. The settlement was "situated on the same spot that Vancouver placed his observatory on his visit here in July, 1793."

27. Ibid.

28. Ibid.

29. Ibid.

Return to Esquimalt

June 6th. Left Metlakatlah at 4.40 am, with misty weather, which partly cleared away by the time we arrived in Ogden Channel. ["The passage through Ogden Channel was between a succession of low and broken islets, the prevailing vegetation being yellow cypress *(cupressus nookensis),* the numerous passages between the islands, forming a network of irregular sheltered water communication, deep and narrow but abounding in anchorages, through which channels and in which harbors the Great Eastern might pass and anchor securely. At the exit to Ogden channel are a succession of heads and islands named after the officers of the *Sparrowhawk*, such as Dolphin and Gibson Islands, Comrie Head, etc., and who had on this occasion the pleasure of seeing for the first time their namesakes. Between this and the entrance to Skidegate channel, Queen Charlotte Island, is a distance of 40 miles."][30]

When clear of the land set the Jib and Gaff Foresail to a N.W. breeze which set the ship on with the steam 9 and 9.8 knots. ["The soundings are very shallow, varying from 8 to 13 fathoms; while over the Skidegate Bar, the entrance to Cowquitz harbor, the depth is not more in some places than from 8 to 10 feet, after passing which the channel is deep and broad and the harbor a safe and capacious one."][31]

Entered Skidegate Harbr. without any trouble, and anchored at Cowgitz at 6.40 pm in 9 fathoms. Mr. King in charge of the works came on board.

["On approaching the land about Skidegate appears low lying and gradually slopes towards the central mountainous ridge of the island, which runs in a N.N.W. and S.S.E. direction. At the entrance of the harbor numerous masses of a coarse conglomerate were observed while about 50 yards distant from the beach the land appears slightly elevated, assuming a terrace-like aspect, which on subsequent examination was found to be a raised beach, in which were imbedded numerous recent shells."][32]

June 7th. There had been no addition to the buildings we had seen before, and consisted of a dwelling house, a store, and some other sheds, and occupied now by a superintendent and two miners, the Indians had cleared out immediately after our first visit. Went up to examine the Coal mine, situated about 2 miles from the landing place, ascending by a steep and difficult trail. The entrance to this new seam is 600 feet above the sea level, and some trouble in making a road as the forest consists of the largest hemlock, ["we have ever seen, many of the trees we should think averaging 40 feet in circumference, while interspersed were"][33] good sized cedar and menzies spruce ["with a thick underbrush of sallal and Pannax Horrida. Several detached boulders of sandstone were passed and about 50 yards below the mine a sandstone reef cropped out."][34]

The workings are carried on on the side of a gulch, and a tunnel had been run in about 210 feet, about 50 feet below where the coal originally was found cropping

30. "Cruise of H.M.S. Sparrowhawk," *Daily British Colonist*, 2 July 1868. See Introduction, note 15, above.

31. Ibid.

32. Ibid.

33. Ibid.

34. Ibid.

out. About 120 feet of slate was tunnelled thro' when sandstone was come upon, 46 feet further the coal bed was struck dipping ENE to an angle of 80 degrees, the breadth of the seam being 6 feet, but divided into 2 parts by the intrusion of a slate. ["The walls consist of slate on the one side, and sandstone on the other—the sandstone, in all probability, forming the roof, and the slate the floor; but as the strata here have been tilted up and fractured—the coal lying in synclinal trough—it is difficult to say what the normal relation of the measures are."][35]

The tunnel is about 6 feet in breadth, and 8 feet in height, and at present they are working that portion of the seam which is free from slate and 3½ feet thick. About 60 tons of coal had been got out, having all the appearance of anthracite coal of good quality, ["having a good lustre irredescent compact and hard, breaking with a conchoidal fracture and behaving under the blowpipe in a similar manner as compared with Welsh anthracite, burning with very little flame,"][36] and if it continues in the same state a tramway will have to be made to the settlement.

["The slate wall, or more properly speaking the black shale, contains numerous fossils, a collection which was made *in situ*, including several Bivalves resembling arcas (?) some joints of an encrinite, or orthocerite and several impressions of Dicotyledonous leaves. The future prospects of the mine, we think, are very promising; of course everyone knows that anthracite is debituminized ordinary coal and that this occurs where uplifting or metamorphic action has taken place, such as in the vicinity of trap dikes.

"Here we think that both elevation and the intrusion of trap dikes have had to do with this change, as the top of Mount Seymour close to, it is said, to consist of Feldspathic Trap, and we have seen at least one trap dike in a neighboring ravine. Of course faults are likely under such circumstances to be met with and it is not impossible that as the centre of disturbance is receded from, the bitumen will increase.

"Of this island, second only in importance to Vancouver, being 160 miles long and 60 miles in varying breadth, we are almost as ignorant to-day as regards its physical geography, harbors, resources, people, etc. as at the period of its discovery by La Perouse in 1786. Indeed we believe it is laid down on the charts about 9 miles too much to the westward. The shallow roundings between it and the mainland, the absence of certain animals such as deer, raccoons, etc. so common on the continent suggest peculiar geological questions relative to its age. Lakes of considerable extent are said to exist in the interior, and numerous open pra[i]ries, gold has been found and copper and other minerals are known to exist. The Hydahs who inhabit the island are said in all to number about 5000, they live principally by fishing, halibut of enormous size being caught here, one of which brought alongside during our stay weighed 96 pounds; dogfish are also numerous, the natives preparing large quantities of the oil."][37]

Gave a passage to the 2 Miners that had been working here, having finished their 2 months engagement, and left Mr. Thos. King alone here.

---

35. Ibid.

36. Ibid.

37. Ibid.

June 8th. Left Cowgitz at 4.30 AM, and cleared the channel to the Northward of the Bar rocks by 7.10 AM, when we shaped a course for the Goletas channel. Very little wind the whole day, but were enabled to set the Fore and Aft sails to a light S. Ey. wind.

June 9th. Crossed the Nahwitti Bar at 9.20 AM in 7½ fms, and stopped off Fort Rupert for a quarter of an hour, to land the 2 slaves we had brought down from Metlakatlah, and to communicate with Captain Monat. Stopped for a few minutes off the new Coaling station, and Mr. Chas. Wallace came on board for a passage to Victoria. Drizzling showers the whole day. Anchored in Knox Bay at 9.40 PM in 25 fathoms, close in to the shore.

June 10th. Left Knox Bay at 3.15 AM, passed the Seymour Narrows in smooth water, and anchored at Esquimalt at 9.30 PM, having run today 170 miles.[38]

On our arrival we had only 8½ tons of Coals remaining, having burnt on our cruize 159 tons in running 1245 miles, or at 7.8 knots to the ton of Coals.

Distances run, northern cruise

May 28th	From	Esquimalt to Nanaimo	76 miles
29th, 30th		Nanaimo to Fort Rupert	180
31st		Fort Rupert to Bella Bella	100
June 1st		Bella Bella to Low Inlet	120
2nd		Low Inlet to Metlakatlah	60
3rd		Metlakatlah to Fort Simpson	22
4th		Fort Simpson to Salmon Cove, Naas river	27
5th		Salmon Cove to Metlakatlah	45
6th		Metlakatlah to Skidegate	120
8th, 9th		Skidegate to Knox Bay	325
10th		Knox Bay to Esquimalt	170
			1245 miles

Sparrowhawk *recommissioning*

July 1st. A mail arrived from England today, bringing the news that the *Sparrowhawk* was to be paid off at Esquimalt, and re-commissioned the following day by Commander Mist.[39] Dined at the Government House, and during the dinner the Governor received a Telegram from the Duke of Argyle dated from Willis's rooms at 8 PM, during a dinner given to Mr. Cyrus Field, and was received at 9 PM.

---

38. For a brief itinerary of the cruise, see "Return of H.M.S. Sparrowhawk," *Daily British Colonist*, 12 June 1868. Admiral Hastings complimented Porcher on his performance on the cruise. "I have much pleasure in conveying to you the expression of my satisfaction at the able manner in which you directed the Navigation of your ship under circumstances of difficulty presented by the intricate nature of the inland waters through which we passed, and to thank you for the satisfactory manner in which you conducted the different duties connected with our cruise." George F. Hastings to Porcher, 12 June 1868, Porcher manuscripts, Beinecke Rare Book Manuscript Library.

39. This was also reported in the Victoria press. "HMS Sparrowhawk," *Daily British Colonist*, 2 July 1868.

The Saw Mills at Nanaimo. May 29, 1866.

(original watercolor size: 14 x 10 in./35.5 x 25.5 cm)

The 4th Lake or Pike's, 7 miles from Victoria. June 19, 1868.

(original watercolor size: 14 x 10 in./35.5 x 25.5 x 25 cm)

The Nahritti village on Hope Island, ½ mile from the rocks where the U.S. Steamer Suwanee was lost on July 9, 1868.

(original watercolor size: 13.88 x 9.88 in./35 x 25 cm)

Waterfall near Carter's Bay, about 120 feet in height. July 21, 1868.

(original watercolor size: 14 x 10 in./35.5 x 25.5 x 25 cm)

The Missionary station of Kincolith, at the mouth of the Nass river. July 26, 1868.

(original watercolor size: 9.88 x 6.5 in./25 x 16 cm)

The deserted village of the Cheslakees, at the mouth of the Nimpkish river. July 30, 1868.

(original watercolor size: 13.88 x 9.25 in./35 x 23.5 cm)

The Karmutsen Lake, 12 miles long, with the Nimpkish river flowing out of it. July 30, 1868.

(original watercolor size: 9.88 x 7.13 in./25 x 18 cm)

The difference of longitude between the 2 places being 8¼ hours, gave 9 hours as the real time the message had taken coming.[40]

~

Indian troubles and rescue mission

July 9th.[41] As several murders had lately been committed on the Northern coast, and it was thought desirable to ascertain the real facts of the case, before any thing could be done by the Civil authorities, the Admiral ordered us up again in that direction to make the necessary enquiries, and the presence of a man of war occasionally in these waters was considered useful in keeping the Indians in due order.[42] We accordingly left Esquimalt at 11.40 AM for Nanaimo where we lashed alongside the Coal Wharf at 7.30 PM, having run the distance of 76 miles in 7 hours 50 min. at the rate of 9¾' an hour.

July 10th. Took in 77½ tons of Coals, which made the quantity we had on board up to 165 tons, of which 60 were on deck, her trim being 10.8 in. Ford., and 12 Feet 3 in. Aft.

Cast off from the Coal Wharf at 4 PM, and steamed out of the harbour at 4.45 PM, keeping under weigh all night.

July 11th. Passed thorough the Seymour Narrows at 4 AM. At 6 AM, met a Canoe off Pender Island, 16 miles to the North of Seymour Narrows, in which we found Captain Cooper (Harbour Master) and Lieut. Com. Wildes U.S.N. taking the intelligence down to Victoria, that the U.S.S. *Suwanee* on her passage from Nanaimo to Sitka, had been wrecked in the Shadwell Passage, about 180 yards to the Westward of Centre Island, on the 9th July at 6 AM, having Captain Cooper on board as Pilot, and steaming at the time 8 knots.

These two gentlemen left the vessel for Fort Rupert at 11.30 AM. the same day, after she had broken in two, in one of the ship's boats in order to hire a canoe to take them down to Esquimalt for assistance, and succeeded in obtaining one from the H.B. Fort for $10, engaged 6 Indians at $15 each, and if they reached their destination in less than 4 days a dollar in addition, besides having to pay for the food for the whole party, making in all to about $150. The *Suwanee's* Complement was 139 men,

---

40. Although his first transatlantic submarine telegraph cable broke down after only three weeks of service in 1858, Cyrus Field persistently promoted a replacement which was successfully laid in 1866. In the difficult days of Anglo-American relations following the American Civil War, the Duke of Argyll—with Field and others—had cooperated to overcome post-war tensions. Meanwhile, British Columbia had been brought into the telegraphic network of the United States with the extension of a line northward from Seattle. *Dictionary of American Biography*, s.v. "Field, Cyrus West," by P. B. McDonald; Akrigg and Akrigg, *British Columbia Chronicle*, 323–324.

41. On 7 July, an athletic sports event pitted personnel from the squadron then in Esquimalt. *Sparrowhawk* men took honors in several events: J. Sparks in the "flat race for seamen, 220 yards"; R. Graham in the "walking contest of half a mile"; J. Plunkett in the "flat race of half a mile"; J. Prentice in the "flat race of 220 yards for boys under 18"; M. Sullivan in throwing the cricket ball. J. Morris, ship's steward, was an umpire, and Lt. Townshend served as a steward for the occasion. "Naval Athletic Sports," *Daily British Colonist*, 8 July 1868.

42. "Naval Matters," *Daily British Colonist*, 9 July 1868; "For the North," *Daily British Colonist*, 10 July 1868.

and carried 10 Guns, of which 4 were 9 inch, 2, 100 Pr. Rifled (weighing 9 and 10.000 lbs each) and 4 smaller one's. She was one of the iron double enders built during the late war for river service, of 1030 Tons, and only drew 8. feet 6 inches aft and 7.0 feet Forward.

Stopped for a few minutes off Alert Bay to allow a canoe to come alongside with a letter from Mr. Fouchet,[43] dated 19th June, to say that some Indian murders had taken place not far from there, and if something was not done, some retaliation would take place. Stopped off Looquash to see Mr. C. W. Wallace, who came alongside in a canoe, and told us that his Scow was loaded [with] 30 tons of Coals, and a lighter with 15 in readiness for H.B.C. steamer *Otter*.

Anchored in Shadwell Passage in 10 fathoms at 5.40 PM, close to the wreck of the *Suwanee*, her bow and stern were then under water, but her Paddle wheels and Wheel houses well up, as she had grounded on a rock amidships, which at spring Tides was 4 feet out of the water. The Fore part had broken entirely off before the Paddle boxes, and was separated 20 feet.

July 12th. Returned Commander Richd. L. Law's visit at his encampment on shore, and in the afternoon pulled round with him, Comrie, and Blenkinsop[44] to the Nahwitti village about ½ mile distant. It was their principal settlement, and consisted of 10 lodges containing about 150 inhabitants, some of them were ornamented in front by painted designs, and a few figures on posts, that gave it rather a pleasant appearance. Most of the women had conical heads, like those at Koskeemo. During the last two days, the Indians had made good use of their time, and plundered the wreck properly, as they had laid their hands on everything they could take away, Roller handspike, Metal bolts, rope, canvas, books, bottled fruits, boots, preserved meats, &c (Ragout of Turkey one of the Indians was eating said was *hyas closh* and offered me some, and afterwards a cigar.)

July 14th. Having offered the services of the *Sparrowhawk* to Comr. Law, and his not caring much about saving the heavy Guns, machinery, or any thing else in the vessel, made up his mind to leave with the greater part of the crew, and embarked this afternoon with 11 Officers and 93 men (in all 105) with all their personal luggage, leaving behind 4 Officers and 30 men to look after the stores that had been landed. Steamed out of Shadwell Passage at 4.15 PM for Fort Rupert where we anchored at 6.50 PM.

July 15th. Left Fort Rupert at 3.30 AM, passed the Seymour narrows at 1 PM at nearly slack water, and kept under weigh all night in the Gulf of Georgia.

July 16th. Passed thro' the Active Pass at 4 AM, and anchored in Esquimalt at 7.55 AM. Found the U.S.S. *Pensecola [Pensacola]* here bearing the flag of Rear Admiral

---

43. While Fouchet is clearly an accurate transcription of Porcher's script here and in a later reference (entry for 30 July 1868, below), he probably referred to Leon Fouquet O.M.I. In 1863, Father Fouquet, an Oblate of Mary Immaculate missionary, had founded Saint Mary's Mission on the Fraser River. Suttles, "Central Coast Salish," 471; Ormsby, *British Columbia*, 204.

44. Blenkinsop (Blinkinsop) served as an interpreter. "Naval Matters," *Daily British Colonist*, 9 July 1868.

Thatcher, to which vessel we transferred the Officers & crew of the *Suwanee*.[45] Called on board & gave Admiral Thatcher a sketch of the late wreck.[46]

Distances to Shadwell Passage and return

July 9th	From	Esquimalt to Nanaimo	76 miles
10th, 11th		Nanaimo to Shadwell Passage	200
14th		Shadwell Passage to Fort Rupert	25
15th, 16th		Fort Rupert to Esquimalt	245
			546 miles

Last northern cruise

July 17th. As the last cruize terminated in a different way than we expected when we left on the 9th inst, we started again this morning on our Northern trip and left Esquimalt at 4.30 AM., and arrived at Nanaimo in 9 hours. On a sloop hauling off from the Coal Wharf, we steamed alongside, and took in 42 tons of Coals, which made the quantity we had on board up to 142 Tons, of which 40 were on deck, and her trim was 11.1½ Ford. and 12 Feet 3 in Aft.

July 18th. Cast off from the Coal Wharf, and steamed out of Nanaimo at 4.45 AM; on passing Cape Mudge fund that the Flood tide was running in strong against us, and forced us to anchor on the Western shore of Discovery Passage opposite the Eucletaw village at 1.45 PM, in 12 fathoms. The tide was running 3 ½ knots when we anchored, being out of the strength of the tide. Being slack water at 3.30 PM, we weighed and proceeded through the Seymour Narrows, and anchored in Blenkinsop Bay 38 miles beyond it at 8.30 PM in 9 fathoms. Ran today 122 miles.

July 19th. Left Blenkinsop Bay at 4.30 AM, stopped off Wallace's Coal Wharf to allow a boat to come off, and anchored off Fort Rupert at 10.30 AM, where we remained during the rest of the day. The distance run being 57 miles.

In the afternoon landed with Blenkisop at the Fort, and saw Captain Monat who shewed us over the garden, in which were growing Potatoes, Cabbages, Turnips, Peas, Onions, Lettuces, Radishes, Tomatoes, Rhubarb, Gooseberries, Currants, Strawberries, Apples, 2 Cherry trees, and 1 Cucumber.

---

45. The accident occurred in Shadwell Passage between two islands off the northern tip of Vancouver Island. "Loss of the U.S. Steamer Suwanee," *Daily British Colonist*, 15 July 1868.

See also "The Wreck of the Suwanee," *Daily British Colonist*, 17 July 1868; "Further News of the Late Wreck," v 18 July 1868; "The New World and the Grappler," *Daily British Colonist*, 21 July 1868; "Complimentary," *Daily British Colonist*, 12 August 1868; "U.S.S. 'Suwanee'—1868," Rogers, *Shipwrecks of British Columbia*, 170–173. Rogers also noted the accident as #387 on the endmap "Shipwreck Chart No. 2," and as #2 on "Shipwreck Chart No. 3." The latter erroneously indicates 9 June 1868 as the date of the incident.

46. R. L. Law, commander of the *Suwanee* conveyed his gratitude to Porcher through Admiral Thatcher aboard the *Pensacola*. Porcher was also complimented, through channels, by President Andrew Johnson. Law to H. K. Thatcher, 23 July 1868, endorsed by Thatcher to Porcher, n.d.; W. G. [Romaine?] to Porcher, 29 September 1868, Porcher manuscripts, Beinecke Rare Book and Manuscript Library.

The H.B.C. steamer arrived here at 5 PM, bringing down the 4 Officers, 30 men, and Stores from the wreck of the U.S.S. *Suwanee*. The *Otter* had left this for the wreck on Thursday the 16th, as Mr. C. W. Wallace had made an agreement with the Commanding Officer to take the Stores down they had saved for $19 a ton, and then handing them over to the *Otter* who agreed to take them for $10, thereby pocketing $9 for each ton himself.

July 20th. Left Fort Rupert at 3.40 AM, on steaming through the Shadwell Passage it came on a thick Fog, which obliged us to anchor at 6.30 AM in 8 fathoms, close to the wreck of the *Suwanee*. Being at the time low water Spring tides, I went on board the wreck, and found the rocks alongside were 4 feet out of the water, the crew of the *Otter* had cut the mainmast away to get the wire rigging off, the 6 large Guns were still on deck, and the vessel remained in her original position. The Engine room was then nearly clear of water, and the Indians were hard at work, hooking up the remainder of the light stores from the bottom of the hold, and we had no difficulty in getting a few hundred weight of brass from the engines and guns.

The Fog partly cleared away by 2.50 PM, when we weighed and steamed across Queen Charlotte's Sound, and anchored at Safety Cove at 7.30 PM, in 16½ fathoms.

July 21st. Left Safety cove at 4.30 AM, when off Namu Harbour it came on a dense Fog that lasted an hour, & forced us to go very easy, on passing Port McLoughlin 2 Deer crossed our bows within 50 yards of us, as soon as we observed them we stopped and fired on them, and sent the Dingy in chase, but they landed in time to get into the woods. Stopped off Bella Bella, and found that Mr. Moss had left for Bella Coola 8 days before, & was expected back in 4 days, I therefore left a message for him and proceeded. Anchored in Carter's Bay at 5.5 PM in 17½ fathoms. Walked up to the waterfall about a mile from the ship, which was the finest thing of the kind I had seen in the country, being 120 feet in height, and a large body of water coming down. The walking up by the banks of the river was very tedious, up and down hill, over and under trees, and every conceivable obstacle, the right bank being the best. Sent a seining party away that brought on board about 3 dozen trout, and 22 crabs.

July 22nd. Left Carter's Bay at 4 AM, exercised at General Quarters firing at the trees near Holmes's Bay, and anchored in the Inner harbour at Metlakatlah at 7.30 PM in 8 fathoms. Drizzling rain nearly the whole day.

July 23rd. Spent the day at Metlakatlah, looking over the settlement, and pulled up to the Saw Mill with Duncan and Blenkinsop. It is being built at the end of an inlet, about a mile from the settlement, and will be driven by water power, as there is a stream immediately at the back of it, which will afford a good supply nearly the whole year round. It will probably be finished in 2 months time.

Fort Simpson area duties

JULY 24TH. LEFT METLAKATLAH AT 7.30 AM, and anchored at Fort Simpson at 10.40 AM, in 11 fathoms. Found the *Beaver* here. Examined an Indian with Pender, Blenkinsop, and Cunningham for firing his gun 4 times at a canoe that was leaving for the Nass river, and nearly hitting one of the *Beaver's* boats. Sentenced him to place 10 Blankets in the Fort, as a security for his good conduct for the next six months. Tried a very good Indian dish called Lebore, made from berries mashed up, and mixed with sugar.

July 25th. Left Fort Simpson at 7.30 AM for Tongass with Pender, Dr. Chismore U.S.A., Mrs. Hunt and family belonging to the Indian tribe there, and anchored off this newly made settlement at 9.30 AM in 20 fathoms. This Military Post was commenced 4 months ago, in the best situation on the most Southern part of the American territory, and where there will be a Custom house. The island on which it is placed is about a mile long and densely wooded with an Indian ranch on the S.W side. At the time of our visit there were 100 men stationed there, that were busily employed constructing log and lumber houses, 20.000 bricks had just been landed to build the chimney's &c. As there had been constant rain, every thing looked very miserable, and the ground covered with mud.

Captain Pearse in charge of the detachment had completed his house on a rising ground, and was living in it with his wife and 6 children. Our visit was principally to inform them of the loss of the *Suwanee*, which vessel was bringing them up money and supplies. Steamed back to Fort Simpson at 11.0 AM against a strong S.E wind with drizzling rain, where we arrived at 2.30 PM, the distance being 16 miles. Pender then went on board the *Beaver* & we proceeded on to the Nass river, where we anchored at 6 PM in 12 fathoms, near the Kincolith mission.

July 26th. Landed at the mission with Blenkinsop and Comrie. The framework of 3 new houses had been commenced by 20 new settlers from the village up the river, the number belonging to the mission being now about 60. Owing to the murders that had taken place in April last, at the drunken feast up the river, there was no business going on between this tribe and the Indians at Fort Simpson, as neither side considered themselves safe.[47] As Mr. and Mrs. Tomlinson had not tasted any meat since our visit here 7 weeks ago, we made them a present of 66 lbs of Fresh beef, half a sheep 24 lbs, a Bag of biscuit 65 lbs, and a few pieces of Pork.

July 27th. Mr. Tomlinson sent his letters on board at 3.30 AM, and we left the Nass river at 4.30 AM, and anchored at Metlakatlah near the *Beaver* off Devestation Island at 10.30. I had a meeting with Nav. Lieut. Pender, Duncan, and Blenkinsop about what had better be done concerning the disturbances at the Nass, and we all came to the conclusion that it would be useless speaking to either side unless it could be carried out, and that Mr. Duncan had better write the whole particulars to the Governor, which he did.[48] Finished up our accounts with the *Beaver*, took Mr. Duncan's letters and 8 boxes of Furs, and then left Metlakatlah for the last time at

47. "[T]he river had been under blockade by Chimsean Indians in consequence of having had two of their chiefs killed by the Naas Indians at a whisky feast up the river. The Chimpseans had come up to be avenged, but were disarmed by Mr. Tomlinson, the Missionary, and were compelled to leave for Fort Simpson. Shortly after this the Naas natives came down in a large body to attack the others. This state of things is most disastrous to the mission—no communication can take place with Fort Simpson, and *vice versa*. Mr. Tomlinson professes to be in danger of his life." "Cruise of the Sparrowhawk—The Late Indian Outrages," *Daily British Colonist*, 3 August 1868.

48. "At the Metlakahtla mission a massacre had been heard of at Ackwillgate about 100 miles up the Skeena river, wherein three Indians of the mission had been shot, one fatally, one seriously and the other slightly." Ibid.

1.30 PM, and anchored in Lowe's Inlet at 9.25 PM in 18 fathoms. Drizzling rain the greater part of the afternoon.

Return to Esquimalt

July 28th. Left Lowe's Inlet at 4.30 AM, and anchored at Bella Bella at 6.45 PM. Drizzling rain and thick weather the greater part of the day, but cleared up shortly before we entered Milbank Sound. Mr. Moss had not picked up any more particulars connected with the late murders in the vicinity of Safety Cove. The names of the Indians that had committed the deed were We-la-koh, his Son, and Coot-such, all belonging to Rivers Inlet. The late Jack Knight had been a notorious Whisky-seller, and never kept faith with the Indians, which might well account for his losing his life, his companion was a runaway Apprentice from the *Marmara*. Mr. Moss had heard from the Indians exactly the same story of the *Thornton*, as Mr. Blenkinsop had obtained from the Nahritti [Nahwitti] Indians on our former trip.

July 29th. Left Bella Bella at 4.25 AM, exercised at general quarters firing shot & shell at the trees off Safety cove, and arrived in the Shadwell Passage at 2.15 PM, where we stopped for ¾ hour near the wreck of the *Suwanee* & *The New World* was at anchor near the wreck and had been here for the last 8 days, & was expected to remain 3 or 4 days longer.

The crew had recovered 5 of the large guns valued at $11000 each, and were on board the *New World*, one had gone overboard and they were trying to raise it. This vessel had been chartered to come up here at $500 a day. The Commanding Officer Lieut. Comr. Woods U.S.N. came on board, and after receiving their letters proceeded, and anchored off the Coal mine at Sooquash at 7.15 PM. Went on shore with Blenkinsop and Comrie.

Seven men were employed here at $35 a month, with their board, &c. They were now digging about 30 yards from the beach, and had to clear away 10 or 12 feet of the soil before coming on the coal. There was 4 or 5 feet of black vegetable soil below the surface, underlying which there was stiff white clay until you come to the seam which is 2 feet thick. The coal was visible on the beach, and extended as far back as they had tried. The Hudson Bay Company had taken out 6000 tons in 1849, having commenced on the beach, and worked inland about 300 yards. A fine day.

July 30th. Took in 10½ tons of the coal, and was tested on our way down. Mr. Farrant's (the Chief Engineer) reported that it was superior to the Nanaimo Coal in as much that it made but little ash and smoke compared to it, was entirely free from sulphur, made rather more clinker, very little deposit of soot was found in the tubes, whereas they were very foul after steaming with the Nanaimo coal for the same length of time. The consumption was also in favour of the Sooquash coal,[49] and in steamers making long voyages, it must be a very considerable saving on account of it making so little soot.

---

49. Suquash was situated about eight miles southeast of Fort Rupert on the coast of Vancouver Island, to the west of Malcolm Island. It was near an ancient Indian sealing place. Gough, *Gunboat Frontier*, 33.

After 8 hours trial, on both occasions using 13 lbs of Steam, Vacuum at 25 inches, 70 Revolutions, 10.75 mean pressure, 278 Horse power, the consumption of the Nanaimo Coals was 1680 lbs against 1568 of the Sooquash, and 30 percent of smoke, ash & clinker, against 20 per cent of the latter, the Nanaimo gave out very dense black smoke, against light brown of the other. Left Sooquash at 5.40 AM, and anchored in Alert Bay at 7.30 AM in 7½ fathoms. The same letter was brought on board by the Indians from M. Fouchet (Roman Catholic missionary) that I had seen before on the 11th inst. Left the ship at 9 AM with Dolphin and Blenkinsop in a canoe for the Cheslakees village at the entrance of the Nimpkish river where we landed, and I made a sketch of the old village on the Upper part of the hill, and we then proceeded up the river in a better Canoe manned by 4 young Indians, the distance being 8 miles, up a succession of rapids, and in order to make the Canoe as light as possible, we were obliged to get out and walk in several places. Arrived at the Karmutsen Lake in 4½ hours & remained on the shores of it for an hour, whilst I was making a sketch of it.

It was 12½ miles long, by 3 in brea[d]th, high mountains rising from it, in some parts to a height of 5000 feet. The Nimpkish river was very picturesque, and fishing villages were built along the banks, it was very shallow at this time of year, which made it very exciting in coming down, shooting the different rapids. Went in the canoe today about 20 miles. Sent a seining party at the entrance of the river where they caught 90 trout.

July 31st. Left Alert Bay at 4.30 AM, passed the Seymour Narrows at 0.45 PM with a strong tide in our favour, which sent the ship on over the ground 15 miles an hour, and from here to Cape Mudge a distance of 10 miles at the rate of 12½'.

Anchored in Nanoose Harbour at 9.25 PM in 16 fathoms.

Exercised at Night Quarters.

August 1st. Left Nanoose Harbour at 4.40 AM, and arrived at Nanaimo at 6.20, where we found 2 large Merchant ships and the Grappler alongside the Coaling Pier, and on sending Lieut. Dolphin on shore to see the Manager Mr. Nicholl was informed that we could not have any Coal today, we therefore proceeded at 7 AM for Esquimalt where we arrived in 9 hours.[50]

---

50. A sloop master complained that the mission of the *Sparrowhawk* had fallen short of all that it should have accomplished. "The Late Indian Outrages," *Daily British Colonist*, 5 August 1868.

Distances run, last northern cruise

July 17th	From Esquimalt to Nanaimo	76 miles
18th	Nanaimo to Blenkinsop Bay	122
19th	Blenkinsop Bay to Fort Rupert	57
20th	Fort Rupert to Safety Cove	63
21st	Safety Cove to Carter's Bay	92
22nd	Carter's Bay to Metlakatlah	128
24th	Metlakatlah to Fort Simpson	22
25th	Fort Simpson to Tongas[s] & back	33
	Fort Simpson to Kincolith mission	27
27th	Kincolith mission to Metlakatlah	45
	Metlakatlah to Lowe's Inlet	60
28th	Lowe's Inlet to Bella Bella	120
29th	Bella Bella to Sooquash	107
30th	Sooquash to Alert Bay	12
31st	Alert Bay to Nanoose Harb.	148
August 1st	Nanoose Harb. to Nanaimo & Esquimalt	90
		1202 miles

Chapter Nine

Return to England

1 August–14 October 1868

[After Porcher's successor recommissioned H.M.S. *Sparrowhawk* and attendant details were taken care of, Porcher spent several days making social calls. He resided at the homes of the governor and bishop in his last days at Esquimalt. This gives a measure of the man, and to the extent that he had become a part of colonial life during his nearly three years' posting. He departed Esquimalt by steamer on the last day of August. With stops at San Francisco and Acapulco, he arrived at Panama nineteen days later. Crossing the Isthmus by rail, Porcher booked passage for England. With only a refueling stop at St. Thomas, Porcher debarked at Southampton on 14 October to await a new assignment.]

Preparations and farewells

On arriving at Esquimalt we found that Comr. H. W. Mist had arrived to recommission the vessel, and we commenced to make preparations to pay the vessel off.[1] We were inspected by Admiral Hastings on the 12th inst. and paid off by Captain Dawkins on the 17th August.[2] The same afternoon 15 of the men exchanged with the same number on board the *Scout*, and the remainder of the Ship's Company went on 4 days leave. Only 31 men volunteered to rejoin the vessel, most of whom were boys (8) that had lately joined, and some continuous service men that had nearly completed their 10 years. Lieut. Dolphin, Townshend and Mr. Clift and Campbell[3] (Engineers) left the ship the same day to await a passage to England, the other Officers had to remain in the ship until their successors arrived from England.[4]

Packed up the goods I did not immediately want in a wooden case, and sent it on board the *Scout* that was going to leave for England in the first week of September, and the remainder that I was going to take with me overland consisted of a Portmanteau, Tin case, Black leather bag, and Hat case.

Drove up to the Government House where I remained with the Governor and Mrs. Seymour until the 20th inst., and then paid a visit to the Bishop and Mrs. Hills, where I was hospitably received, and remained at their house until I left the Colony. Paid farewell visits, or left P.P.C. cards on Mr. and Mrs. Crease (Attorney General), Mr. & Mrs. Wood (Solicitor General), Mr.& Mrs. Joseph Trutch (Surveyor General), Mr. Pemberton (Stipendiary Magistrate), Mr. & Mrs. W.A.G. Young (Colonial Secretary), Mr. & Mrs. Josh. Needham (Chief Justice), Mr. & Mrs. Elliott (Sheriff). Sir James Douglas (ex Governor), Mr. Cameron (ex Chief Justice), Mr. & Mrs. Garashe (Wells Fargo), Mr. and Mrs. Alston (Registrar General), Mr. & Mrs. Watson (Bank of British Columbia), Rev. and Mrs. Hagman, Rev. and Mrs. J*[illeg.]*, Rev. and Mrs. Reece, Rev. and Mrs. Gribbell, Rev. and Mrs. Owen, Mr. and Mrs. Rhodes, Mr. & Mrs. Macdonald, Mr. & Mrs. Pearse, Mr. & Mrs. Jackson, Mr. & Mrs. Franklyn, Mr. & Mrs. Drake, Mr. & Mrs. Charles Wallace, Mr. and Mrs. McKenzie, Dr. & Mrs. Tolmie (H.B.C.), Mr. & Mrs. Thompson, Mrs. Roscoe, Capt.

---

1. By 8 August Porcher was posting a notice under "New Advertisements" of his departure from the colony and asked for "all accounts due by him be sent in before the 15th inst." *Daily British Colonist*, 8 August 1868, and thereafter to 17 August.

2. Henry W. Mist had arrived 19 July 1868. "The Sparrowhawk," ibid., 20 July 1868. The *Sparrowhawk* was recommissioned under command of Mist, effective 18 August 1868. *Navy List* (October 1868): 218; (January 1869): 218. For some of the details concerning the recommission process, see entries for 12, 14, 17 August 1868, Master's logbook, Adm. 53/9257. The subsequent commissioned history of the *Sparrowhawk* may be traced in the three Master's logbooks, 18 August 1868–5 October 1872, Adm. 53/10023, Adm. 53/10024, Adm. 53/10025; and appropriate issues of *Navy List*. The *Daily British Colonist* maintained a reliable and reasonably detailed running account of its activities.

3. John Clift and James Campbell. "Arrival of H.M.S. Sparrowhawk," *Daily British Colonist*, 30 October 1865.

4. Those who had two years' service on the *Sparrowhawk* were eligible to return to England. "HMS Sparrowhawk," *Daily British Colonist*, 2 July 1868. A farewell editorial stated that H.M.S. *Sparrowhawk* under Porcher's command had been "more identified with the Colony than perhaps many others…constantly employed visiting the different settlements it has been generally on Colonial Service, carrying mails, visiting the Indian missions." "The Sparrowhawk," *Daily British Colonist*, 18 August 1868.

The CATHEDRAL at VICTORIA, destroyed by fire in 1869. August 29, 1868.

(original watercolor size: 9.88 x 6.5 in./25 x 16.5 cm)

CENTRAL AMERICA. The Railway Station at PANAMA. Sept. 21, 1868.

(original watercolor size: 14 x 9 in./35.5 x 23 cm)

The Statue of Tomas Herrera, in the Plaza at Panama. Sept. 22, 1868.

(original watercolor size: 6.88 x 8.5 in./17.5 x 21.5 cm)

West Indies. The Harbour of St. Thomas, the scene of the severe hurricane, and tidal wave in October 1867. Sketched September 28th 1868.

(original watercolor size: 14 x 9.5 in./35.5 x 24 cm)

Stamp, Misses Nagle, Mr. Finlayson, and at Esquimalt Colonel & Mrs. Foster, Mr. & Mrs. Perry (Secretary), Mr. & Mrs. Wakeman, Mr. & Mrs. Spack, Mr. & Mrs. Dobbie, &c.

Esquimalt to Panama

August 31st. Left the Bishop and Mrs. Hills at 2 pm, after having been there 11 days, and drove down to Esquimalt, and paid a farewell visit to the Admiral & Mrs. Hastings at Maple bank, called on board the *Zealous* and *Scout*, and finally left Esquimalt in the *John L. Stephens*[5] at 5.30 pm. I was accompanied by Lieut. Dolphin, and Townshend,[6] and Mr. Clift & Campbell (Engineers) as we steamed past the ships, the band of the *Zealous* played "Auld Lang Syne," and were cheered by the men of the *Sparrowhawk* and *Scout*. The *John L. Stephens*, Captain Metzger, 1836 tons, was named after one of the first discoverers in Central America, was 270 feet long, and the finest vessel that ran between San Francisco and Victoria, and had on board 200 Passengers, many of whom had come from Portland.

The weather was so foggy after leaving Esquimalt, that we could not see the Race rocks, or the light at Cape Flattery, but at times during the night heard the surf breaking on the Vancouver Island shore, and sounded in 30 fathoms. This Fog continued for two days, and then lifted sufficiently to see the land near the Umpqua River & the remarkable rocks off Cape Blanco.

September 4th. Foggy during the night when passing Point Reyes, which forced us to stop continually. Lashed alongside the Holladay and Brenham Wharf at 8.30 am, having made a quick passage in 3 days and 15 hours. Put up at the Occidental Hotel where we breakfasted, and then called on Mr. Bowker, the English Consul, and went with him to the Offices of the Pacific Mail Steam ship Company, where we took 3 outside Cabins for our party of 5 in the *Golden City* on the Upper Deck. Left cards on Mr. Walker, of Faulkner Bell & Co., and Captain Harrison, (Mare Island Pilot) and met Prendergast, Turner, Borthwick, and Pilot Wallace. Went over the Industrial Exhibition with Bowker, which was a temporary building in one of the squares, and contained the principal California products, the best being the woollen manufactures particularly the Blankets, a few pieces of machinery in motion, including the quartz crushing mill, some first class Photographs such as the large views of the Yo Semite valley, some inferior paintings, fruit, &c. I then took a drive with Bowker to the new Stone Dock which is in course of construction higher up the Bay, and about 7 miles off on the mission road. It has been excavated out of the solid rock, is 320 feet in length, and capable of taking in the largest vessels, the only part not completed being the entrance, which was giving some trouble, as the Copper dam was not watertight, and letting in a large quantity of water which required powerful pumps, to keep the water clear, and allow the men to work.

---

5. An American steamer. Porcher log, 304–305.

6. "Leaving," *Daily British Colonist*, 31 August 1868; "The steamers JL Stephens and Pacific...," *Daily British Colonist*, 1 September 1868.

Near this is a small floating Dock 230 feet in length, but only capable of taking in vessels drawing 13 feet of water. This has been purchased by the company that is building the stone dock, so as to have the docking of all vessels in their own hands.

September 5th. After calling on Bowker, drove down to the Wharf with Capt. Harrison, embarked on board the *Golden City*, and left San Francisco punctually at 11 AM.

The *Golden City* Captain Farmsworth, was the largest vessel on the line, being 3590 tons, 350 feet in length, and was very roomy, having a clear hurricane deck over all with a few cabins amidships. She could carry 271 First Class Passengers, 195 2nd Class, 388 Steerage, & 196 Deck, in all 1174 [*sic*]. She had only one Engine, the cylinder being 105 inches [in diameter],[7] and the length of stroke 12 feet.

The Fares from San Francisco to New York by these steamers were 1st Class $110 for outside Cabins, and $60 inside, 2nd Class $41, and 3rd Class $30, being so low on account of an Opposition line, out of which the Company had to pay $25 for all Passengers passing across the Isthmus of Panama.

Among the Passengers were several of the Officers of the U.S. Navy, three of whom we had known before in the *Suwanee*, Lieut. Comr. Wood and Clark *(Suwanee)* Lieut. Com. Cook & wife, L. Wilson *(Saramac),* Dr. Wheeler, W. N. Watnough, Coleman *(Onward),* & Mr. Holland Engineer *(Suwanee).* (8). There was also an agreeable man in a Roman Catholic Bishop Looten, who had been recently appointed to the diocese of Idaho, having been for the last 9 years in charge of an Orphan school near San Francisco. He had been stationed between 1852-7 at Victoria, and spent a great portion of that time in visiting the Indians in the vicinity and the Gulf of Georgia, and spoke Chinook fluently. He knew Sir James Douglas well during the time he was stationed there, as well as Dr. Helmcken whose Photograph he had, and to whom he corresponded occasionally. He was a native of Bruges, and born in 1827, and finished his education at Paris.

We had fine weather the whole way to Panama, so that with plenty of companions we enjoyed ourselves as well as could be expected in a Passenger vessel. Our principal amusements were reading, and in the Afternoons and Evenings in playing cards with the American Officers, such as Poker, Euchre, and California Jack all good games in their way, but the former was generally preferred. There were 3 Congregational Preachers on board, that performed the service on Sundays, and had prayers every evening at 8 o'clock in the Ladies Saloon. On the 11th inst. a Second Class Passenger died of general debility, age 67, and was buried in the afternoon. As some of the Company's vessels had been destroyed by fire, every precaution was taken against it, by keeping the vessel close in to the land, and exercising the crew occasionally at fire quarters, the ship being well supplied with pumps most of which were worked by steam, and had a Fire Raft which I had not seen before. It was pumped up with air in 7½ minutes, and was capable of holding 50 men. It was made of india rubber cased in canvas, in 3 separate air tight cases, so that in case one part was torn, the others would hold good, and enabled to pull as fast as a boat.

7. Porcher's log, 305.

September 12th. Arrived at Acapulco at 5.30 PM, which was a very good spot, but being completely landlocked, and surrounded by high land, there is little circulation of air and consequently the weather is very oppressive, and considered one of the hottest places on the Mexican Coast, and unhealthy. After obtaining pratique I went on shore in a canoe with Lieut. Comr. Wood, and walked through this miserable town after dark, which was faintly lighted with a few oil lamps. A strong Fort is built at the end of the town near the entrance, which was lately held by the French Troops. As the place is liable to frequent earthquakes, the houses are built low on the ground floor, with verandahs to protect the inhabitants from the sun and rain. Called on the American Consul *[illeg.]* a man of rather bad character, and on Dr. Billings the American Health Officer, no English Consul having been stationed here for the last 10 years. A Tidal wave had occurred here a few weeks before, and the water had washed up into the middle of the town. After taking in a supply of coals and provisions, and leaving a small quantity of merchandise, we left Acapulco at 10.15 PM.

Crossing the Isthmus

SEPTEMBER 19TH. ARRIVED OFF THE P.M.S.S. Company's stores at Panama at 2.30 AM. The Luggage was landed before daylight, as it can only be done when the water is above half tide. As it was low water during the forenoon, we were obliged to remain on board, and finally left the *Golden City* with all the Passengers at 2 PM, in a large Steam Tender and landed at the Railway Terminus. The Passengers that were going by the New York steamer, left immediately by the train for Colon. Our party walked into the town, and put up at the Grand Hotel, where we were comfortable enough during our stay. Called on Mr. Henderson, the English Consul, where I met Commander Bridges of the *Chanticleer*.

We remained at Panama 3 days, which was quite sufficient time to see the place. The town was formerly well fortified but is now like every thing else in the country going to decay.

The sea wall was strongly built, but in consequence of its being continually exposed to a heavy surf when the water is high, several breaches have been made in the wall, and will in due course of time all come down, as it is never repaired.

The stone used for building the town is porphyry, and is obtained in the vicinity. The population is now about 9000.

One of the best walks in the evening when the sun has lost most of its power is to the Cemetery, situated a short distance outside the town. There is no Protestant church or Clergyman at Panama, although there are many English and American residents that belong to the Episcopal faith.

September 22nd. Took leave of the Consul, and booked our luggage at the Railway station, my 4 articles, Portmanteau, Tin case, Bag, and Hat case, weighed 150 lbs, for which I had to pay $2.50 for 50 lbs excess of what is allowed.

The charge for Luggage above 100 lbs consists of 3 cents a lb. in the California steamers, 5 cents crossing the isthmus, and 2 cents in the New York steamers, making in all 10 cents for every pound. Left Panama by the 2.30 PM train, and arrived at

Colon in 3¼ hours, when we embarked on board the Royal Mail Steam Packet Company's ship *Seine*, and steamed away at 6.30 PM for Southampton. The whole country crossing the isthmus 47 miles in length, was densely wooded, and there were but few cleared places.

Panama to Southampton

THE *Seine* WAS COMMANDED BY J. M. GILLIES, and was a very comfortable vessel of 3440 tons, being 350 feet in length, and 42 feet beams, and capable of carrying 417 After Cabin Passengers, 165 Fore[war]d. Total 582, and had 9 Boats hoisted up above the Paddle boxes. The Fares from Panama to Southampton was [*sic*] £49, and in the Cabins on the lower deck forward £38.10. The price of Wines we found to be very different to the American steamers, on board the *Golden City* Champagne was $3, Sherry $2½, Ale 75 cents, Ale Pints 50¢ &c.

On board the *Seine* they were Champagne 6/. Sherry 4/. Brandy 5/. Ale 1/. Ale Pints 6d. &c.

September 27th. Arrived at St. Thomas at 11 AM, having taken 4¾ days from Colon, steaming against a strong N.E trade wind. Lashed alongside the Coal Hulk *[illeg.]* which was moored off Water Island, where the Mail steamers generally remain, being better protected from the wind, than opposite the town of St. Thomas's.

Remained here two days, during which we filled up with Coals and took in 2 Million of Dollars.

September 28th. Spent the day on shore, but the heat was so great that it was but little amusement moving about in the sun. I landed close to the vessel, and walked up to the Town about 1½ mile distant, and through the Fort that was built near the landing place. Remained during the middle of the day at the Commercial Hotel, where I made a sketch of the Harbour from the balcony, having in the foreground some Tamarind Trees and a Spruce Pine.

The damages occasioned by the hurricane & tidal wave in October 1867, were still very visible in every part of the harbour, the steamer *Columbia* & several other vessels were sunk in the middle of the harbour, and were being raised by a Scotchman of the name Murphy, other ships were washed up high and dry on the beach, and so much damaged that it would not be worth the expense in getting them off, and fragments of the different wrecks were washed up in every part of the shores. The Cocoa nuts & other trees also suffered as most of the branches were blown away, and many of the houses still remained unoccupied. As so much damage is occasioned by these hurricanes, and many lives are continually lost by yellow fever, that the American Government have given up the idea of buying the island from the Danish Government for the present, as there are other more desirable locations.

The R.M.S.P. Cos. ship *Seine* arrived from Jamaica, and the *Tamar* from the Windward Islands, bringing us mails & Passengers. Amongst them were Captain and Mrs. Coventry 15th Reg. Dr. and Mrs. Hyde, Captain Russell & 28 men of the 16th Reg. Lt. Col. Arbuthnot R. Artillery, Major Miller, late 54th, Mr. Vivero of Guayaquil, Mr. Baird Stipendiary Magistrate of Demarara, Mr. Field of Colon, Lieut. Wray 84th Reg., Mr. Alexander & Scott of Trinidad, &c.

Left St. Thomas's at 10.15 AM of the 29th September, and after a fair passage of 16 days arrived in England. The *Seine* was one of the most easy vessels I was ever in, which made up for her not having the same speed as some of the other vessels.

October 14th. Arrived at Plymouth at 2.45 AM, where we remained 3 hours to land the Mails & a few of the Passengers, and then proceeded on to Southampton where we arrived at 5 PM, having raced and beaten the P and O Cos. steamer *Ceylon* on the greater part of the day. Landed at the Custom House with our baggage, and when it was passed, took it to the Railway station, and left for London at 7.20 PM with Mr. Alexander & Scott (of Trinidad), arriving in London at 10.15, after having been absent upwards of 3½ years.

Distances, Vancouver Island to England

From	Esquimalt to San Francisco	770	miles
	San Francisco to Panama	3280	
	Crossing the isthmus of Panama	47	
	Colon to St. Thomas	1040	
	St. Thomas to Southampton	3622	
		Total 8759	

Expenses, Vancouver Island to England

From	Esquimalt to San Francisco	$40	
	California State Tax on landing	5	
	San Francisco to Panama	52	
	Crossing the isthmus of Panama	25	
	Excess of luggage 50 lbs for crossing	2½ =	
		124½	or £25. 8. 4
	Colon to Southampton		49. 0. 0
	Travelling expences allowed by the Admiralty		9.15. 3
	Other expences not allowed		1.11.10
			£85.15. 5

Bibliography

The principal complementary documentation for Edmund Porcher's journal is in three Master's Logbooks of H.M.S. *Sparrowhawk* (Adm. 53/9255, 53/9256, 53/9257), in the Public Record Office, Kew, England. Except to make reference to a few relevant details not recorded by Porcher, they are not cited herein. They are frequently valuable to check on unusual place or person names or to corroborate what appear to be questionable items in Porcher's account.

The chronicle of the ship's post-Porcher years, 18 August 1868–5 October 1872, is also contained in three Master's Logbooks (Adm. 53/10023, 53/10024, 53/10025).

Other than for his own journal, and the Master's Logbooks, the most comprehensive and substantive record of Porcher's tour of duty is found in the *Daily British Colonist* (after 25 June 1866, *Daily British Colonist and Victoria Chronicle*). From one-sentence notes to detailed accounts, sometimes including reprinting portions of participant journals, this newspaper gave excellent coverage of Royal Navy activities and frequently of the ships' commanders.

Some minor details are in Colonial Correspondence (File 355) and in the Clippings File Folder (Porcher Island), in the Provincial Archives of British Columbia, Victoria. P. W. Brock's "Dossier: H.M.S. Sparrowhawk, 1856–1872," in the Maritime Museum of British Columbia, Victoria, provides some technical data, including some Porcher has not noted.

The Navy List, listed below, is an indispensable reference for tracing Royal Navy vessels and their officer personnel complements. Roger Flynn Sarty, "Silent Sentry: A Military and Political History of Canadian Coast Defence, 1860–1945" (Ph.D. thesis, University of Toronto, 1982) gives a general overview with a slightly different emphasis. Together, the several publications of Barry M. Gough, listed below, afford the most comprehensive account of the presence of the Royal Navy in the waters of the Pacific Northwest.

Robert G. Albion, *Naval & Maritime History: An Annotated Bibliography* 4th ed. (Newton Abbot, Devon, England: David & Charles, 1973) and *Canada Gazetteer Atlas* (n.p.: Macmillan of Canada in cooperation with Energy, Mines and Resources Canada and the Canadian Government Publishing Centre, Supply and Services Canada, 1980) are helpful reference tools. The specific publications used in the preparation of this volume are listed here as well as in the notes.

Akrigg, G.P.V., and Akrigg, Helen B. *British Columbia Chronicle, 1847–1871: Gold & Colonists*. Vancouver: Discovery Press, 1977.

Barratt, Glynn. *Russian Shadows on the British Northwest Coast of North America, 1810–1890: A Study of Rejection of Defence Responsibilities*. Vancouver: University of British Columbia Press, 1983.

Bemis, Samuel Flagg. *A Diplomatic History of the United States*. 4th ed. New York: Henry Holt and Company, 1955.

Blackman, Margaret B. "Haida: Traditional Culture." In William C. Sturtevant, ed. *Handbook of North American Indians*. Vol. 7: *Northwest Coast*. Edited by Wayne Suttles. Washington: Smithsonian Institution, 1990. 240–260.

Bolt, Clarence. *Thomas Crosby and the Tsimshian: Small Shoes for Feet Too Large*. Vancouver: University of British Columbia Press, 1992.

Clayton, Daniel. "Geographies of the Lower Skeena." *BC Studies* 94 (Summer 1992): 29–58.

Codere, Helen. "Kwakiutl: Traditional Culture." In William C. Sturtevant, ed. *Handbook of North American Indians*. Vol. 7: *Northwest Coast*. Edited by Wayne Suttles. Washington: Smithsonian Institution, 1990. 359–377.

Colledge, James Joseph. *Ships of the Royal Navy: An Historical Index*. 2 vols. Newton Abbot, Devon: David & Charles Publishers, 1969–1970.

Collier, Simon. "Chile from Independence to the War of the Pacific." In Leslie Bethell, ed. *The Cambridge History of Latin America*. Vol. 3: *From Independence to c. 1870*. Cambridge: Cambridge University Press, 1985. 583–613.

Columbia Mission. *Seventh Annual Report of the Columbia Mission [of the Church of England], for the Year 1865*. London: Rivingtons, 1866.

———. *Tenth Annual Report of the Columbia Mission [of the Church of England], for the Year 1868*. London: Rivingtons, 1869.

Davis, Nathan. *Carthage and Her Remains: Being an Account of the Excavations and Researches on the Site of the Phoenician Metropolis in Africa, and Other Adjacent Places. Conducted under the Auspices of Her Majesty's Government*. London: Richard Bentley, 1861.

"Deaths." *Gentleman's Magazine and Historical Review*, January 1858, p. 113.

Dictionary of American Biography. S.v. "Field, Cyrus West," by P. B. McDonald.

Dictionary of Canadian Biography.

vol. 4. S.v. "Cook, James," by Glyndwr Williams;
vol. 4. S.v. "Hearne, Samuel," by Clarence Stuart Mackinnon;
vol. 4. S.v. "Vancouver, George," by W. Kaye Lamb;
vol. 9. S.v. "Brew, Chartres," by Margaret A. Ormsby;
vol. 9. S.v. "Seymour, Frederick," by Margaret A. Ormsby;
vol. 10. S.v. "Cameron, David," by William R. Sampson;
vol. 10. S.v. "Douglas, Sir James," by Margaret A. Ormsby;

vol. 11. S.v. "Kennedy, Sir Arthur Edward," by Robert L. Smith;
vol. 11. S.v. "Moody, Richard Clement," by Margaret A. Ormsby;
vol. 11. S.v. "Tolmie, William Fraser," by W. Kaye Lamb;
vol. 12. S.v. "Begbie, Sir Matthew Baillie," by David Ricardo Williams;
vol. 12. S.v. "Finlayson, Roderick," by Eleanor Stardom;
vol. 12. S.v. "Hills, George," by Jean Friesen;
vol. 13. S.v. "Trutch, Sir Joseph William," by Robin Fisher.

Ditchfield, Peter Hampson, and Page, William. *The Victoria History of Berkshire*. 4 vols. London: Archibald Constable and Company, 1906–1924.

Doig, Ivan. "The Tribe That Learned the Gospel of Capitalism." *American West* 11 (March 1974): 42–47.

Douglas, W. A. B. "The Seaward Flank: Defending the Indefensible." *Journal of the West* 32 (October 1993): 19–29.

Dunn, John A., and Booth, Arnold. "Tsimshian of Metlakatla, Alaska." In William C. Sturtevant, ed. *Handbook of North American Indians*. Vol. 7: *Northwest Coast*. Edited by Wayne Suttles. Washington: Smithsonian Institution, 1990. 294–297.

Fisher, Robin. *Contact and Conflict: Indian-European Relations in British Columbia, 1774–1890*. 2d ed. Vancouver: University of British Columbia Press, 1992.

Gibson, James R. "The Maritime Trade of the North Pacific Coast." In William C. Sturtevant, ed. *Handbook of North American Indians*. Vol. 4: *History of Indian-White Relations*. Edited by Wilcomb E. Washburn. Washington: Smithsonian Institution, 1988. 375–390.

———. *Otter Skins, Boston Ships, and China Goods: The Maritime Fur Trade of the Northwest Coast, 1785–1841*. Seattle: University of Washington Press, 1992.

Glover, William. "The Politics of Nation Building and the Defense of British Columbia, 1871–1939." *Journal of the West* 32 (October 1993): 31–37.

Gough, Barry M. *Distant Dominion: Britain and the Northwest Coast of North America, 1579–1809*. Vancouver: University of British Columbia Press, 1980.

———. *Gunboat Frontier: British Maritime Authority and Northwest Coast Indians, 1846–1890*. Vancouver: University of British Columbia Press, 1984.

———. *The Northwest Coast: British Navigation, Trade, and Discoveries to 1812*. Vancouver: University of British Columbia Press, 1992.

———. "Official Uses of Violence against Northwest Coast Indians in Colonial British Columbia." In *Pacific Northwest Themes: Historical Essays in Honor of Keith A. Murray*, 43–69. Edited by James W. Scott. Bellingham: Center for Pacific Northwest Studies, Western Washington University, 1978.

———. "The Records of the Royal Navy's Pacific Station." *Journal of Pacific History* 4 (1969): 146–153.

———. *The Royal Navy and the Northwest Coast of North America, 1810–1914: A Study of British Maritime Ascendancy*. Vancouver: University of British Columbia Press, 1971.

———. "Sea Power and Canada: The Long View of History." *Canadian Defence Quarterly* 20 (Winter 1990): 41–49.

———. "Sea Power and the History of Western Canada." *Journal of Canadian Studies* 8 (May 1973): 50–59.

———. "Send a Gunboat! Checking Slavery and Controlling Liquor Traffic among Coast Indians of British Columbia in the 1860s." *Pacific Northwest Quarterly* 69 (October 1978): 159–168.

———. "'Turbulent Frontiers' and British Expansion: Governor James Douglas, the Royal Navy, and the British Columbia Gold Rushes." *Pacific Historical Review* 41 (February 1972): 15–32.

Graebner, Norman A. "Maritime Factors in the Oregon Compromise." *Pacific Historical Review* 20 (November 1951): 331–345.

Hacking, Norman R. "Steamboating on the Fraser in the 'Sixties." *British Columbia Historical Quarterly* 10 (January 1946): 1–41.

Hajda, Yvonne. "Southwestern Coast Salish." In William C. Sturtevant, ed. *Handbook of North American Indians.* Vol. 7: *Northwest Coast.* Edited by Wayne Suttles. Washington: Smithsonian Institution, 1990. 503–517.

Halpin, Marjorie M. "Duncan, William." In William C. Sturtevant, ed. *Handbook of North American Indians.* Vol. 4: *History of Indian-White Relations.* Edited by Wilcomb E. Washburn. Washington: Smithsonian Institution, 1988. 641.

Halpin, Marjorie M., and Seguin, Margaret. "Tsimshian Peoples: Southern Tsimshian, Coast Tsimshian, Nishga, and Gitksan." In William C. Sturtevant, ed. *Handbook of North American Indians.* Vol. 7: *Northwest Coast.* Edited by Wayne Suttles. Washington: Smithsonian Institution, 1990. 267–284.

Hamilton, William B. *The Macmillan Book of Canadian Place Names.* Toronto: Macmillan of Canada, 1978.

Hancock, Anson Uriel. *A History of Chile.* New York: AMS Press, 1971.

Harper, J. Russel. *Early Painters and Engravers in Canada.* Toronto: University of Toronto Press, 1970.

Hills, George. "1865 and 1866. Notes and Incidents of Mission Work. Extracts from the Bishop's Journal." Columbia Mission. *Eighth Annual Report of the Columbia Mission [of the Church of England], for the Year 1866.* London: Rivingtons, 1867.

———. "1866 and 1867. Notes and Incidents of Mission Work. Extracts from the Bishop's Journal." Columbia Mission. *Ninth Annual Report of the Columbia Mission [of the Church of England], for the Year 1867.* London: Rivingtons, 1868.

Howay, F. W. "Early Settlement on Burrard Inlet." *British Columbia Historical Quarterly* 1 (April 1937): 101–114.

Jenkins, Brian. *Fenians and Anglo-American Relations during Reconstruction.* Ithaca: Cornell University Press, 1969.

Jones, Wilbur D., and Vinson, J. Chal. "British Preparedness and the Oregon Settlement." *Pacific Historical Review* 22 (November 1953): 353–364.

Judd, Gerrit P., IV. *Members of Parliament, 1734–1832*. New Haven: Yale University Press, 1955.

Jukes, Joseph Beete. *Narrative of the Surveying Voyage of H.M.S. Fly, Commanded by Captain F. P. Blackwood, R.N., in Torres Strait, New Guinea, and Other Islands of the Eastern Archipelago, During the Years 1842–1846: Together with an Excursion into the Interior of the Eastern Part of Java*. 2 vols. London: T. & W. Boone, 1847.

Kennedy, Dorothy I. D., and Bouchard, Randall T. "Northern Coast Salish." In William C. Sturtevant, ed. *Handbook of North American Indians*. Vol. 7: *Northwest Coast*. Edited by Wayne Suttles. Washington: Smithsonian Institution, 1990. 441–452.

Kerr, J. B. *Biographical Dictionary of Well-Known British Columbians, with a Historical Sketch*. Vancouver: Kerr & Begg, 1890.

Kinkade, M. Dale. "History of Research in Linguistics." In William C. Sturtevant, ed. *Handbook of North American Indians*. Vol. 7: *Northwest Coast*. Edited by Wayne Suttles. Washington: Smithsonian Institution, 1990. 98–106.

Kuykendall, Ralph S. *The Hawaiian Kingdom*. 3 vols. Honolulu: University of Hawaii Press, 1947–1967.

Lamb, W. Kaye. "Correspondence Relating to the Establishment of a Naval Base at Esquimalt, 1851–57." *British Columbia Historical Quarterly* 6 (October 1942): 277–296.

Laughton, J. K. "The Study of Naval History." *Journal of the Royal United Services Institution* 40, part 2 (1896): 795–820.

Long, John W., Jr. "The Origin and Development of the San Juan Island Water Boundary Controversy." *Pacific Northwest Quarterly* 43 (July 1952): 187–213.

Longstaff, Frederick V. *Esquimalt Naval Base: A History of Its Work and Its Defences*. Victoria: Victoria Book & Stationery Co., 1941.

Loo, Tina. *Making Law, Order, and Authority in British Columbia, 1821–1871*. Toronto: University of Toronto Press, 1994.

Middleton, Lynn. *Place Names of the Pacific Northwest Coast*. Seattle: Superior Publishing Company, 1969.

The Navy List. London: John Murray, 1815– . Until 1870 issued quarterly as *The Navy List*. After 1870 issued quarterly as *The Navy List. Containing the Officers on the Active and Retired Lists of the Royal Navy, General Regulations, Etc. Etc. Etc.*; and monthly as *The Monthly Navy List. Containing the Officers on the Active List of the Royal Navy*.

Nunn, Frederick M. *The Military in Chilean History: Essays on Civil-Military Relations, 1810–1973*. Albuquerque: University of New Mexico Press, 1976.

O'Byrne, William R. *A Naval Biographical Dictionary: Comprising the Life and Services of Every Living Officer in Her Majesty's Navy, From the Rank of Admiral of the Fleet to That of Lieutenant, Inclusive. Compiled from Family and Authentic Documents*. London: John Murray, 1849.

Ormsby, Margaret A. *British Columbia: A History.* Toronto: The Macmillans in Canada, 1958.

Peake, Frank A. *The Anglican Church in British Columbia*. Vancouver: Mitchell Press, 1959.

Pettit, Sydney G. "'Dear Sir Matthew': A Glimpse of Judge Begbie." *British Columbia Historical Quarterly* 11 (January 1947): 1–14.

Preston, Antony, and Major, John. *Send a Gunboat! A Study of the Gunboat and Its Role in British Policy, 1854–1904*. London: Longmans, Green and Co., 1967.

Reece, W. S. "Cowitchen. European and Indian Mission." Columbia Mission. *Ninth Annual Report of the Columbia Mission [of the Church of England], for the Year 1867.* London: Rivingtons, 1868.

Register of Graduates and Former Cadets of the United States Military Academy. Cullum Memorial Edition. West Point, N.Y.: West Point Alumni Foundation, 1970.

Reid, Robie L. "The Chinook Jargon and British Columbia," *British Columbia Historical Quarterly* 6 (January 1942): 1–11.

Rogers, Fred. *Shipwrecks of British Columbia*. Vancouver: J. J. Douglas, 1973.

Ronda, James P. *Astoria & Empire*. Lincoln: University of Nebraska Press, 1990.

Sarty, Roger. "'There will be trouble in the North Pacific': The Defence of British Columbia in the Early Twentieth Century." *BC Studies* 61 (Spring 1984): 3–29.

Scheina, Robert L. *Latin America: A Naval History, 1810–1987*. Annapolis, Maryland: Naval Institute Press, 1987.

Schurman, D. M. "Esquimalt: Defence Problem, 1865–1887." *British Columbia Historical Quarterly* 19 (January–April 1955): 57–69.

Seaburg, William R., and Miller, Jay. "Tillamook." In William C. Sturtevant, ed. *Handbook of North American Indians*. Vol. 7: *Northwest Coast*. Edited by Wayne Suttles. Washington: Smithsonian Institution, 1990. 560–567.

Senior, Hereward. *The Fenians and Canada*. Toronto: Macmillan of Canada, 1978.

Shaw, George C. *The Chinook Jargon and How to Use It: A Complete and Exhaustive Lexicon of the Oldest Trade Language of the American Continent*. Seattle: Rainier Printing Company, 1909.

Silverstein, Michael. "Chinookans of the Lower Columbia." In William C. Sturtevant, ed. *Handbook of North American Indians*. Vol. 7: *Northwest Coast*. Edited by Wayne Suttles. Washington: Smithsonian Institution, 1990. 533–546.

Smith, Robert L. "The Kennedy Interlude, 1864–66." *BC Studies* no. 47 (Autumn 1980): 66–78.

Smith, Robert Murdoch, and Porcher, Edmund A. *History of the Recent Discoveries at Cyrene, Made during an Expedition to the Cyrenaica in 1860–61, under the Auspices of Her Majesty's Government*. London: Day & Son, 1864.

Suttles, Wayne. "Central Coast Salish." In William C. Sturtevant, ed. *Handbook of North American Indians*. Vol. 7: *Northwest Coast*. Edited by Wayne Suttles. Washington: Smithsonian Institution, 1990. 453–475.

Swanton, John R. *The Indian Tribes of North America*. Bureau of American Ethnology, Bulletin 145. Washington: Government Printing Office, 1952.

Talbott, Robert D. "The Chilean Boundary in the Strait of Magellan." *Hispanic American Historical Review* 47 (November 1967): 519–531.

Thompson, Laurence C., and Kinkade, M. Dale. "Languages." In William C. Sturtevant, ed. *Handbook of North American Indians*. Vol. 7: *Northwest Coast*. Edited by Wayne Suttles. Washington: Smithsonian Institution, 1990. 30–51.

Thorne, R. G. *The History of Parliament: The House of Commons, 1790–1820*. 5 vols. London: Published for the History of Parliament Trust by Secker & Warburg, 1986.

Tompkins, Stuart R. "After Bering: Mapping the North Pacific." *British Columbia Historical Quarterly* 19 (January–April 1955): 1–55.

Tovell, Freeman M. "The Other Side of the Coin: The Viceroy, Bodega y Quadra, Vancouver, and the Nootka Crisis." *BC Studies* 93 (Spring 1992): 3–29.

Trutch, Joseph W. *Report and Journal by the Hon. the Chief Commissioner of Lands and Works, of the Proceedings in Connection with the Visit of His Excellency the Late Governor Seymour to the North-west Coast, in Her Majesty's Ship Sparrowhawk*. Victoria: Government Printing Office, 1869.

Walbran, John R. *British Columbia Coast Names, 1592–1906, to Which Are Added a Few Names in Adjacent United States Territory, Their Origin and History, with Map and Illustrations*. Ottawa: Government Printing Bureau, 1909.

Werlich, David P. *Peru: A Short History*. Carbondale and Edwardsville: Southern Illinois University Press, 1978.

Who Was Who, 1897–1916. London: A. & C. Black, 1920.

Yamauchi, Edwin. "The Archaeology of Biblical Africa: Cyrene in Libya." *Archaeology in the Biblical World* 2 (Fall 1992): 6–18.

Index

A

Acton, Captain, 29, 33
Alaska. *See* Russian America
Alexander, Mr., 154, 155
Allen, Major and Mrs., 122
Alston, Mr. and Mrs., 103, 103n41, 150
Arbuthnot, Lieutenant Colonel, 154
Ash, Mr., 123

B

Bailey, Mr., 79
Baird, Mr. (Stipendiary Magistrate), 154
Ball, Mr., 61
Ball, Mr. H. M. (Gold Commissioner), 107
Barclay, Lieutenant, 62, 67
Barnard, Mr., 86, 105
Bazalgette, Captain, 46, 68, 70, 80, 81
Beardon, Mr., 124
Beck, Captain, 121
Begbie, Judge Matthew Baillie, 85, 85n36, 87
Bevis, Mr., 89
Billings, Dr., 153
Birch, Arthur Nonus, 48, 48n27, 49, 61, 85
Birch, Mr., 61, 84, 85
Bisell, Mr., 49
Black, Dr., 105
Blenkinsop, Mr. (interpreter), 142, 144, 145, 146, 147
Bond, Mr. (Master), 43
Borthwick, Mr., 151
Boucht, Captain, 80
Bowker, Mr. (Consul), 43, 119, 151, 152
Bowman, Mr., 123
Boys, Alfred (Paymaster), 60, 60n2
Bradbury, Commander G. H., 26
Brennan, Mr., 69, 103
Brett, Commander, 14
Brew, Mr. (Stipendiary Magistrate), 69
Bridges, Commander, 153
Brooke, Lieutenant, 120, 121, 122, 123, 124, 128
Brooks, G. W., 43
Brown, Dr., 68
Brown, Mr. (coal mine manager), 55
Brunner, Alfred (fiddler), 46-48, 67
Bryden, Mr., 45
Buckley, Rev. A., 67
Burke, Mr. (Consul), 62
Burton, Dr. (Staff Surgeon), 103, 114
Bushby, Mr., 105, 112, 116

C

Caldbeck, Captain T. B., 21
Callao, Peru, 32-33
Calvert, Mr. (Gunner), 88, 104
Cameron, Chief Justice David, 150
Campbell, James (engineer), 150, 151
Campbell, Lord George, 116
Carlton, Charles, 75, 76

Carr, Staff Commander, 103, 104, 114, 120, 122
Cartage, John, 76
Cave, Rev., 84
Cecil, Lord Richd., 128
Cheslakee Indians, 147
Chismore, Dr., 145
Christie, Mr., 81, 114
Church of St. Paul, 69
Chympsean Indians, 51n35, 52, 53
  village, 96-97, 137, 145n47, 145n48
  See also Metlakatla Indian mission
Clark, Mr., 152
Claudet, Mr., 105
Claylick, Euclataw Chief, 41, 42
Clayson, Edward (Gunner's Mate), 46-48, 67
Clift, John (Engineer), 150, 151
coal mining, 45, 55, 64-65, 66, 80, 129, 131, 138-139, 146
Coleman, Mr., 152
Colling, Mr. 123
Colon, Lieutenant, 29
Compton, Mr., 50, 56
Comrie, Surgeon Peter, 16, 17, 21, 30, 33, 40, 41, 42, 52, 55, 56, 67, 103, 121, 138, 142, 145, 146
Cook, Lieutenant Commander and Mrs., 152
Cooper, Captain (Harbor Master), 60, 88, 90, 112, 141
Cooper, Lieutenant, 46
Coot-such (Indian), 146
Cornwall, Mr. and Mrs. Henry, 106, 110
Coutts, Burdett, 49
Coventry, Captain and Mrs., 154
Cowichan Bay, 41
Cransford, Mr., 67
Crawford, Captain, 15
Crease, H. P. P. and Mrs. (Attorney-General), 150
Crewe, Mr. (Engineer), 104
Cunningham, Mr., 135, 144

D

Dally, Mr. 67, 68, 105
Davis, Mr., 123
Dawkins, Captain, 103, 104, 114, 116, 123, 150
Dawson, Mr. (Leading Stoker), 80
Dean, Mr. (storekeeper), 20
Dearden, John, 45, 49n31
Delacombe, Captain and Mrs., 119, 122, 124
Dendney, Mr. and Mrs., 120
Denman, Admiral Joseph, 37, 60, 67, 69
Denny, Mr., 124
Dent, Mr., 123
deserters, 46-47, 121-122
Dobbie, Mr. and Mrs., 151
Dolphin, Lieutenant, 47, 47n26, 60, 70, 78, 81, 121, 138, 147, 150, 151
Domeyko, Don Ignacio (geologist/surveyor), 22
Donald, Mr., 67
Doolan, Rev. Robt. R. A., 52, 54
Douglas, Commander, 32
Douglas, Sir James (Governor), 68, 68n18, 150
Drake, Mr. and Mrs., 150
Drew, Mr. (Assistant Paymaster), 103, 120, 128
drownings, 80-81, 123
Duncan, William, 49, 51, 51n35, 52, 53, 54, 93-96, 134, 135, 144, 145
Dundas, Rev., 29

E

Elliott, Beynon. *See* Elliott, Francis
Elliott, Francis (Benyon Elliott), 121
Elliott, Mr. and Mrs. (sheriff), 150
Emma, Dowager Queen, 35, 35n9
English Camp, Royal Marines, 46
Erskine, Mr. (Consul), 15
Esquimalt naval base, 3-4, 118, 118n9
Etheridge, Mr. 85
Euclataw Indians, 40-41, 40n3, 42, 42n9

F

Falkland Islands, 19-20
Stanley, 19
Farmsworth, Captain 152
Farrant, Nathaniel (Chief Engineer), 49n31, 123, 123n22, 146
Fell, Mr., 82
Fenian alerts, 60-61, 60n1, 119, 119n13
Ferrale, Patrick (Sergeant), 75, 75n12
Field, Cyrus, 140, 141n40
Field, Mr., 154
Finlayson, Chief Factor Roderick, 67, 67n20, 151
Fisher, Mr., 123
Fleming, Captain, 61
Foley, Mr., 116
Fort Rupert, British Columbia, 50
Fort Simpson, British Columbia, 53, 96
Foster, Colonel and Mrs., 78, 114, 151
Fouchet, Mr. *See* Fouquet, Father Leon
Fouquet, Father Leon, 142, 142n43, 147
Fox, Commander, 62
Franklin, Lieutenant Commander 67, 68
Franklyn, Mr. and Mrs., 150

G

Gamble, Mr., 29
Garashe, Mr. and Mrs. (Wells Fargo), 150
Garland, Mr., 29
Garratt, Mr., 49
Gillies, Commander J. M., 154
Gillson, Archdeacon, 67
gold mining, 108-109
Goring, Mr., 112
Green, William L. (Consul), 35, 35n36
Grey, Captain, 68
Grey, Colonel, 123
Gribbell, Rev. and Mrs., 150
Guilford, Lord, 43

H

Hagman, Rev. and Mrs., 84, 150
Haida Indians, 55, 56, 56n44, 139
Hale, Mr. (Chief Constable), 105
Halleck, General Henry W., 44, 44n14, 62, 83
Hamburg, Mr., 124
Hamilton, Rev. Thos. R., 103, 114, 128
Hanham, Commander T. B., 36
Harkey, Mr., 121
Harper, Mr., 109
Harris, Mr., 81, 103
Harrison, Captain 62, 63, 151, 152
Harrison, Lieutenant Matthew J., 76, 76n13
Hart, Mr., 78
Harvey, Commodore T., 32, 33
Hastings, Rear Admiral George F. and Mrs., 103, 104, 114, 115, 120, 122, 123, 134, 150, 151
Haviland, Miss, 29
Hawbury, Dr., 46
Hawkins, Mr. H., 135
Hawkins, Philip I., 40
Hayman, Rev. W., 116
Hearne, Mr., 104
Henderson, Mr. (Consul), 153
Henry (Indian pilot), 136
Hetherington, Mr. (Engineer), 104
Hichbone, Philip (constructor), 62
Hills, Bishop George and Mrs., 42, 42n8, 49, 52, 55, 56, 69, 85, 87, 103, 150, 151
Hoffmeister, Captain, 119
Holland, Mr. (Engineer), 152
Holmes, Mr., 47
Hone, Mr., 105
Honolulu, Hawai'i, 35-36
Horn, Mr., 96
Horton, Mr. 106
Hunt, Mr. (Consul), 16

Hunt, Mr. and Mrs. (trader), 90
Hydah Indians. *See* Haida Indians
Hyde, Dr. and Mrs., 154

I

Indians, 86, 87, 88, 106, 110, 134
  council with, 69
  fishing, 85
  mission school, 81, 86
  murder trials, 52-53, 96
  policing of, 40-41, 42n9, 96
  village, 73, 73n5, 91, 131
  village destroyed, 50, 50n34
  See also under tribal designations
Inman, Mr., 124
Irving, Captain, 85, 120

J

Jackson, Mr. and Mrs., 150
James, Captain, 68
Jenns, Rev. P., 129
Jermingham, Sublieutenant, 19

K

Kamehameha V, King, 35, 35n9
Kelly, John (Stoker), 78, 80
Kennedy, Governor Arthur Edward, 40, 40n2, 48-49, 67, 68
Ketson, Mr., 90, 93, 99
Kinahan, Lieutenant, 88
King, Thos., 138
Kingscote, Mr., 61
Kishon (Indian). *See* Kitbrone
Kinthralta Indians, 136
Klaskino Indians, 76, 76n14
Kitbrone, 52, 52n36
Knight, Jack (whisky trader), 146
Kriember, Mr., 117
Kwakiutl Indians, 72n2

L

Launcey, Mr., 120, 121
Law, Commander Richd. L., 142
Leary, Humphrey, 76
Legaic, Chief Paul, 97, 135
Lekwiltok Indians. *See* Euclataw Indians
Lemascheffsky, Captain 80
Liddell, Commander, 120, 121, 122
Lighte, Henry, 22
Lima, Peru, 33-34
  churches, 33
  library museum, 33
  vultures as scavengers, 33
Lindfors, Captain, 80
Loncanaje, Antonio (whisky trader), 51
Looten, Bishop, 152
Lorenzo, Mr. (whisky trader), 51
Lorraine, Lieutenant Sir Lambton, 43, 44
Lowndes, Mr., 125
Lumber camp, 60-61

M

Macauley (Chief Engineer), 123
MacClinton (Colonel Surgeon), 19
Macdonald, Mr. and Mrs., 150
Maclean, Lieutenant, 103
Madeira, 15
Magellan, Strait of, 20-23, 26-28
  Port Famine, 22
  Port Tamar, 23
  Puerto Bueno, 26
  San Felipe, abandoned, 22
  Sandy Point settlement, 20-22
Manson, Mr., 96
Mason, Charles (Consul), 62, 82
Maunsell, D. C., 50, 61, 69, 84, 85, 104, 112
Mauson, Mr. (H.B.C. agent), 52, 135
McDougal, Captain David, 62, 63
McDowell, General I., 44
McKay, Mr. and Mrs., 87, 105, 110
McKenzie, Mr. and Mrs., 150
McKinlay, Mr., 109
McKinney, General, 122
Meiggs, Mr., 30-31
Meksutoff, Governor Prince, 99, 100, 101

Metlakatla Indian mission, 51n35, 52, 54, 92-96, 135
Metzger, Captain, 151
Millan, John, 118n8
Miller, Major, 154
Mist, Commander Henry W., 140, 150
Monat, Captain and Mrs., 67, 73, 131, 132, 140, 143
Moody, Richard Clement, 48, 48n29
Moore, Governor, 121, 122
Moore, Lieutenant, 68
Moore, Mr., 41
[Morenby?], Miss, 105
Moreshead, Mr., 124
Moriat, Mrs., 90
Moss, Mr. (Indian Agent), 51, 133, 144
Moss, Mr. (pilot), 104, 146
Murphy, Charles, 119

N

Nagle, the Misses, 151
Nahwitti Indians, 142
Naylor, Mr., 116
Needham, Chief Justice Joseph and Mrs., 67, 67n19, 85, 88, 150
Needham, Miss, 48, 87, 88
Neeshnewah (Indian chief), 52
Nelson, Mr., 105
Nelson, Uriah, 116
Nestor, Mr. and Mrs., 67
New Archangel, Alaska, 99-101
New Westminster, British Columbia, 48-49
  Government House, 48
Nicholl, Mr., 66, 147
Nicholson, Midshipman, 123
Nott, Mr. (trader), 82, 103

O

Ogden, Mr. (Chief Factor), 109
Oldfield, Captain, 70, 77, 84, 103
O'Reilly, Captain and Mrs., 79, 86
Owen, Rev. and Mrs., 150

P

Packer, Captain, 62
Parejia, Admiral, 32
Parry, Rev. W. W., 103
Patrick, Dr. and Mrs., 67
Pearse, Captain, 145
Pearse, George (whisky trader), 51
Pearse, Surveyor General, 69, 84
Pearse, Mr. and Mrs., 88, 150
Pemberton, Mr. (Stipendiary Magistrate), 78, 150
Pender, Lieutenant, 144, 145
Pender, Mr., 49, 50, 55, 92
Perry, H. and Mrs. (Secretary), 103, 123, 124, 151
Philipps, Mr., 79
Phillpots, Mr. (ordnance), 121
Pinch, Mr. (Leading Stoker), 80
Pipio, Mr. (geologist, surveyor), 22
Pooley, Mr., 116
Porcher, Edmund Augustus
  artistic talents, 5, 8, 11n21
  biography, 4-6, 10n2
  Esquimalt assignment, 7
  evaluation of, 104n47, 140n38, 143n46, 150n4
  public lecture, 77n16
  return to England, 7-8
  voyage to Esquimalt, 6-7
Prendergast, Mr., 36, 151
Price, Captain, 67, 116
prisoners, 44-45

Q

Qua Qua Indians, 131-132
Quatsino Indians, 73-74, 73n6, 74n7, 74n8

R

Rathmusen, Captain W., 26
Reece, Rev. W. S. and Mrs., 81, 103, 150
Rhodes, Mr. and Mrs., 144, 150

Rio de Janeiro, Brazil, 15-18
botanical gardens, 17
docks and shipyards, 16
hospitals, 16-17
nearby village, 18
sewerage system, 16
Tijuca Forest, 17-18
Robinson, Captain, 76
Robinson, Mr., 114
Rogers, Mr. (lumber superintendent), 61
Roll, Lieutenant Cooper, 69, 85
Roscoe, Mrs., 150
Rothwell, Mr., 81
Rouse, Mr. (Consul), 29
Royal Navy,
Pacific role, 1-4
Russell, Captain, 154
Russian America, 98-101

S

Sacquenan, Mr., 47
San Francisco, California, 43-44, 63-64, 151-152
Sanders, Mrs., 105
Sanford, Captain, 62
Santiago, Chile, 29-31
cathedral, 30
museum, 30
Schythe, Governor Don G., 21, 22
Scott, Captain, 62
Scott, Captain F., 14
Scott, Mr., 154, 155
Seaweed, Joe, 73, 81
Sebapien, Chief, 136
Semple, Dr., 122
Severance, Mr., 36
Seymour, Rear Admiral Sir Michael, 14
Seymour, Governor Frederick and Mrs., 68, 68n23, 69, 70, 82, 84, 85, 90, 93, 99, 104, 112, 120, 125, 150
Sharp, Mr., 67
ship's names
Active (mail steamer), 65
Alert, 56, 60
Alexandra (HBC stern wheeler), 92
Alexandra (Russian steamer), 80
Amelia (river steamer), 62
Amethyst (American), 79
Apurimac (Peruvian ironclad frigate), 32
Ariel, 29
Beaver (surveying steamer), 49, 50, 55, 56, 88, 104, 133, 135, 137, 144, 145
Berenguela (Spanish warship), 32
Blanca (Spanish warship), 32
Brisk, 123
Calypso (H.M.S.), 22
Ceylon (steamer), 155
Chanticleer, 153
Chilaco (Peruvian wooden paddle), 32
Cleopatra (sailing frigate), 15
Clio (H.M.S.), 37, 40, 44, 47, 69, 92
destroys Indian village, 50, 50n34
Colorado, 26
Columbia (steamer), 154
Constantine (Russian), 80
Cormorant (H.M.S.), 131
Cyane (US storeship), 62
Devastation (H.M.S.), 37
Diana, 78, 118
Eagle (sloop), 96
Egmont (storeship), 15-16
Eliza Anderson, 47
Emily Harris (sloop), 129
Enterprise, 48, 66, 67, 82, 107, 109
Ethiope (mail steamer), 15
Fanny (Hawaiian, formerly *Vortigern*), 120
Fauntleroy (US survey schooner), 121
Fideliter, 78
Forward (H.M.S.), 37, 42, 45, 60, 62, 80, 84, 88, 102, 104, 114, 119, 123
Ganges, 123
Gazelle (schooner), 76
Golden City, 151, 152, 153, 154
Goldstream (schooner), 51
Hamley, 129
Harrier (warship), 19

Independence (US receiving ship), 62
Isabel, 78, 120
James Town (US storeship), 62
John L. Stephens (American steamer), 151
Leagundi (Peruvian wooden screw gunboat), 32
Leander (H.M.S.), 32
Leviathan, 48, 49, 61, 69, 82, 88, 104
Lilloett (stern wheel river steamer), 61, 88, 105
Loa (Peruvian ironclad Merrimac class), 32
Malacca, 80, 88, 102, 104
Marmara, 146
Mauna Kea (Hawaiian barque)
  wrecked, 72, 76
  rescue of crew, 73, 75, 76
Megaera (storeship), 15
Monadnock (US warship Monitor class), 62, 63
Nereus (storeship), 29
New World, 146
Nicholas Biddle (merchant ship), 118
  grounded, 77-78
North Star (trading schooner), 50
Numancia (Spanish ironclad frigate and ram), 32, 33
Oakland (American barque), 134
Ocean Queen (sloop), 135
Onward (sternwheeler), 85, 86, 88, 105, 110, 120, 152
Ossipee (US), 119
Otter (HBC steamer) 42, 130, 134, 142, 144
Pallas (French frigate), 32
Parkingburgh (steamer), 26
Pensacola (US), 142
Petrel (HBC trading schooner), 55
Princess Royal (HBC), 88
Principe Umberto (Italian frigate), 29, 32
Reindeer, 118
Revolucion (Spanish warship), 32
Robert Cowan, 114
Rosalie (Hawaiian barque), 120
Saginaw (US), 67, 68
Saint John (English barque), 47
Saranac (US flagship), 62, 152
Satellite, 123
Scout, 65, 150, 151
Seine (steam packet), 154
Sheerwater (H.M.S.), 32
Sidon (H.M.S. steam frigate), 29
Sparrowhawk (H.M.S.), 1, 14, 37n11, 53n38, 138, 140
  damaged, 53-54
  dry dock repairs, 62-63
  history of, 6
St. Mary (US corvette), 32
Sutlej (H.M.S.), 28, 37, 40, 41, 43, 60, 65, 68, 69
Suwanee (US)
  wrecked, 141-142, 144, 145, 146, 152
Tamar, 154
Themis (yacht), 32
Thorndyke, 44
Thornton (sloop), 96, 146
Topaze, 123
Tribune (H.M.S.), 43, 68
Vanderbilt (US warship), 62
Vencedora (Spanish warship), 32
Victoria (Peruvian ironclad Monitor class), 32
Villa de Madris (Spanish flagship), 32
Vortigern. See *Fanny*
Zealous, 104, 117, 119, 124, 151
Shoudal, "Chieftainess," 97
Sitka, Alaska. *See* New Archangel, Alaska
Skinner, Mr., 41, 81, 103
Slater, Mr., 123
Spack, Mr. and Mrs., 151
Spanshott, Mr., 46
Spark, Mr. and Mrs., 114
Spratt, Mr., 117
Staley, Bishop Thomas Nettleship, 35, 35n9
Stamp, Captain, 60, 78, 151

Stapleton, Mr., 70, 81, 82
Stephens, Mr. (engineer), 51
Stock, Mr., 120
Stoehem, Mr. (surveyor), 79
Stone, Mr. (ordnance), 121
Sullivan, Commander, 67
Swinburne, Charles (merchant), 29
Synge, William W. F. (Commissioner and Consul General), 35

T

Thatcher, Rear Admiral, 62, 143
Thompson, Mr. and Mrs., 150
Tilling, Dr., 100
Titcombe, Mr. 68
Tlingit Indians, 99, 100-101
Tolmie, Dr. and Mrs. William Fraser (HBC), 66, 66n16, 67, 150
Tomlinson, Mr. (missionary), 137, 145
Townshend, Lieutenant Reginald C., 136, 136n22, 150, 151
Trutch, Mr. and Mrs. Joseph (Surveyor General), 85, 85n35, 86, 105, 112, 150
Tsimshian Indians. *See* Chympsean Indians
Turner, Mr., 151
Turner, Mr. (Engineer), 51

V

Valparaiso, Chile, 28-29, 31
  naval sick quarters, 31
Vereker, Mr., 67
Vivero, Mr., 154

W

Wag, Mr., 128
Wakeman, Mr. and Mrs., 123, 151
Walker, Mr., 116, 120, 151
Wallace, Mr. and Mrs. Charles W., 67, 130, 140, 142, 144, 150
Wallace, Mr. D. (pilot), 121, 151
Ward, Mr. and Mrs., 29
Watnough, Mr. W. N., 152
Watson, Mr. and Mrs. (banker), 150
Way, Henry, 121
We-la-koh and son (Indians), 146
Welcker, Colonel, 109
Weynton, Mr., 73
Wheeler, Dr., 152
whisky traders, 44-45, 44n16, 45n17, 51, 98, 135
Whitworth, Geo. F. (Customs Collector), 47
Wildes, Lieutenant Commander (US), 141
Wilkes, Mr. (coal mine fireman), 55
Wilkes, Commodore, 122
Williams, Captain R. M. A., 128
Wilson, Mr. L., 152
Wilson, Mr. (Customs Collector), 46, 47
Wing, Mr., 81, 82
Wood, Mr. and Mrs. (Solicitor General), 150
Woods, Lieutenant Commander (US), 146, 152, 153
Work, Miss, 67
Wray, Lieutenant, 154
Wright, Commander, 107
Wyllie, R. C., 36

Y

Young, Mr. W. A. G. (Colonial Secretary), 84, 119, 150
Yuculta Indians. *See* Euclataw Indians